A COLLECTOR'S
GUIDE TO RELICS
& MEMORABILIA

Jerry E. Patterson

A Collector's Guide to Relics & Memorabilia

Crown Publishers, Inc., New York

Inquiries should be addressed to Crown Publishers, Inc.,
419 Park Avenue South, New York, N.Y. 10016

Library of Congress Catalog Card Number: 74–80301

Printed in the United States of America.

Published simultaneously in Canada by General Publishing Company Limited.

Also by Jerry E. Patterson

Autographs: A Collector's Guide
Auction Antiques Annual 1970–71 (with Linda Rosenkrantz)

CONTENTS

ACKNOWLEDGMENTS

I have had much kind assistance in preparing this book, and I am grateful to the following persons and institutions for their interest and help and, in the case of illustrations, for permission to show relics in their possession. Any errors or omissions are of course entirely mine.

My brother Randolph Patterson has kept his eyes open for relics and has been particularly helpful with Napoleonic items; Albert K. Baragwanath, Senior Curator, Museum of the City of New York, has given me many leads; and my editor Mrs. Kathryn Pinney, who was enthusiastic about the project from its beginning, has been of the greatest help.

I am especially indebted to James F. Carr, who has kindly supplied many of the illustrations from the files of his forthcoming *Dictionary of Artists in North America.*

Also in the matter of illustrations, I am grateful to John Herbert, Christie's, London; Misses Liz Robbins and Peggy Shannon, Clark, Nelson, Ltd., New York; and Miss Joan Hartley of Sotheby Parke Bernet, Los Angeles, and of course to the auction houses themselves for permission to publish some of the interesting relics from their sales.

Most of the reading for this book was done at the New York Society Library. For more than two centuries New Yorkers have been thanking that institution for assistance, and I am pleased to add my gratitude to its staff. I have also benefited from the Frick Art Reference Library and, as every writer in New York

City must, from the incomparable resources of The New York Public Library.

I have also received help from the following:

Jane Austen Memorial Trust, Chawton, Hants.; Austrian Information Service, New York; Jack W. Herring, Armstrong Browning Library, Baylor University; Robert G. Newman, The Berkshire Athenaeum, Pittsfield, Mass.; Paul Brandt B.V., Amsterdam; Miss Kristine Haglund, Buffalo Bill Memorial Museum, Denver; H. G. Tibbutt and the Trustees of Bunyan Meeting, Bedford; Robert L. Coleman; Ralph Collier, Campbell Museum, Camden, N.J.; Miss Grace Hamblin, O.B.E., Chartwell, Kent; Miss Lorraine Seay, Henry Clay Memorial Foundation, Lexington, Ky.; Grover Cleveland Birthplace, Caldwell, N.J.; J. G. B. Swinley, Thomas Coram Foundation for Children, London; B. G. G. Wormald, Cromwell Museum, Huntingdon; William A. Stigler, Jefferson Davis Shrine, Biloxi, Miss.; Ned A. Bush, Sr., Eugene V. Debs Foundation, Terre Haute, Ind.; T. L. Paulsen, The Folger Coffee Co., Kansas City, Mo.; Howell J. Heaney, Free Library of Philadelphia; Miss Sue Ann Roderick, Barbara Fritchie Home, Frederick, Md.; German Information Center, New York; Mrs. Lois D. Childers, President Benjamin Harrison Home, Indianapolis; Watt P. Marchman, The Hayes Library, Fremont, Ohio; Helga Photo Studio Inc., New York; Mrs. Carolyn T. Gardner, The House of the Seven Gables Settlement Assoc., Salem, Mass.; Hamilton F. Kean, New York; Judith Landrigan and Edward J. Landrigan III, New York; Mark E. Neely, Jr., The Lincoln National Life Foundation, Fort Wayne, Ind.; William Cunningham, The David Livingstone Trust, Blantyre, Glasgow; Maj. Gen. Norman J. Anderson, MacArthur Memorial Foundation, Norfolk; Mrs. Sallie Tomb, George Marshall Research Foundation, Lexington, Va.; Peter Morse, Honolulu; Misses Charlotte La Rue, Mary Merrill, and Margaret Stearns, Museum of the City of New York; John F. Redding, National Baseball Library; William G. Tyrrell, New York State Parks and Recreation Dept.; Mrs. Pamela J. Wood, City of Nottingham Museum and Art Gallery; William H. O'Brien; Polish Museum of America, Chicago; Mrs. O. B. Quin, James K. Polk Memorial Auxiliary, Columbia, Tenn; Miss Dorothy June Williams, Riley Home, Greenfield, Ind.; K. L. Jeffrey, Milton's Cottage, Chalfont St. Giles, Bucks.; Les Jensen, The Museum of the Confederacy, Richmond; H. G. Dulaney, The

Sam Rayburn Library, Bonham, Texas; Mrs. Patricia Lowe, Will Rogers Memorial Commission, Claremore, Okla; Miss M. Campbell, Scottish Tourist Board, Edinburgh; Dr. Levi Fox, The Shakespeare Birthplace Trust, Stratford-upon-Avon; Miss Verna L. Pearthree, The Star-Spangled Banner House and Museum, Baltimore, Md.; Gervis Brady, The Stark County Historical Society, Canton, Ohio; Philip W. Stein; Mrs. Pat Halfpenny, City Museum and Art Gallery, Stoke-on-Trent; Mrs. Robert D. Nicholl, Mark Twain Memorial, Hartford, Conn; Angela Forenza, Van Cleef & Arpels, Inc., New York; Walt Whitman Home, Camden, N.J.; Mrs. L. Delehanty, Webster Birthplace, Franklin, N.H.; Miss Merrilee Gwerder, Wells Fargo Bank History Room, San Francisco; Sydney Cole, Wesley's Chapel, London; Raymond F. Pisney, Woodrow Wilson Birthplace Foundation, Staunton, Va.

INTRODUCTION

Collectors have recently paid large amounts of money to take possession of historical objects as diverse as Frederick the Great's flute (sold at auction for $13,000), the red shoes worn by Judy Garland in *The Wizard of Oz* ($15,000), George Washington's waistcoat ($700), and Adolf Hitler's 230-horsepower Mercedes-Benz automobile ($153,000). Other collectors have acquired a ring of Lord Byron's for $1,200, a lock of Napoleon's hair for $175, and one of Sir Winston Churchill's hats for $312. All of these items are relics of noted men and women, and it is emotional feelings about these people that were responsible for the high prices. Interest in the lives of famous people—loved, admired, or even hated —is so great and so widely felt that objects associated with them, even of slight or no intrinsic value in themselves, can be sold for substantial sums solely with the assurance that they were formerly in the possession of one of these notables. Relics are bought, sold, and displayed in private collections and museums today with as much enthusiasm as the relics of the saints were enshrined in earlier centuries of the Christian era. The collecting of physical remembrances must therefore be a deeply felt human need that crosses centuries and many civilizations.

Any dictionary gives many different definitions of *relic* and many uses within each definition. In this book the word *relic* refers primarily to objects that have specific known associations with notable persons. This is the basis of relic collecting. Objects deriving from famous places or events are secondary relics in the eyes of most collectors. Examples of these are also discussed here. The divisions overlap, however: the overcoat worn by President Abraham Lincoln to Ford's Theatre the night of his assassination is a relic of person, place, and event. Historic weapons—Napoleon's sword at the Battle of Waterloo—commonly have all three aspects of association.

Several other words are used to refer to these collected objects, including *memorabilia, memento,* and *souvenir.* These have a common definition as meaning "remembrance" or "recollection." Usage is ambiguous: the lovely French word *souvenir,* for example, has become debased by being used in America to describe roadside knickknacks sold to travelers. Newspapers in particular like to refer to almost anything older than yesterday as a "relic" whether or not it has any specific association. Here in this book, relic is the primary classification of the collected objects, generally referring to the most desirable and most expensive. The other words are used for more derivative objects. In catalogues and other literature, nonetheless, the collector will find all these words used synonymously.

Few true relics exist older than late medieval times, although greater antiquity is often claimed for religious relics, and assuredly few are available to collectors. The excavations of

These souvenirs of Israel are typical of the gifts exchanged today by heads of state and other visiting notables. The presentation of such appropriately inscribed items has changed little in centuries. All the items shown were presented to John V. Lindsay, Mayor of New York City, by visiting officials from Israel during his two terms of office, 1966–74, and are *left to right:* (1) medal showing ancient map of the Holy Land with a quotation from Leviticus 19:18, presented by Mayor Teddy Kollek of Jerusalem; (2) gold medal in a native olive wood box, from Zalman Shazar, President of Israel; (3) Hebrew Bible bound in silver inlaid with turquoise (six by three inches), given by Moshe Kol, Minister of Tourism; (4) gold medal (four inches in diameter) reproducing seal of the Crusader Kingdom of Jerusalem, presented by Prime Minister Levi Eshkol; (5) silver medal with lion shield, given by Prime Minister Golda Meir; (6) olive wood gavel, eleven inches long, from Teddy Kollek; (7) key to the city of Holon, Israel, six inches long, given by the mayor of Holon. Among other municipal souvenirs in the Lindsay collection is a coal *from* Newcastle, England. *Museum of the City of New York*

classical archaeologists, for example, seldom turn up any objects that can be definitely linked to historical persons. Today collectors are interested in relics that usually are no more than two centuries old. Beyond that, the history of most relics is likely to be doubtful.

During the last century or so since mass production methods became important, an enormous flow of commemorative objects has been produced. These are sometimes sold as "relics" of historic events, but they are of course not true relics because they are produced secondhand and have no specific history. There are a few exceptions that will be mentioned: when, for example, wood from an historic tree or building has been used to create a series of objects. Also mentioned are a few items such as the china used on historic American trains and equipment made for the Wells Fargo Company because, although mass-produced at the time, they have enough specific history to make them interesting to relic collectors. None of the commemorative items such as campaign buttons and other political Americana or the china, statuary, stamps, plaques, ingots, and so forth being issued today to mark current events is included.

Typically, a relic, apart from its history and perhaps a presentation case or mount, is indistinguishable from other objects of its kind—a ballpoint pen used for a presidential signature, for example, resembles any other ballpoint. The distinctive aspect of the relics trade is that objects otherwise of little intrinsic value or even none at all—such as hair—become valuable because of their associational history.

Only a few relics are recognizable at a glance as objects of historical or literary significance, and there is not always perfect agreement either as to exactly what an object is or who owned it, or where an historic event took place. Even Plymouth Rock has been doubted as the exact spot of the Pilgrim Fathers' landing. Faith in relics has to be supported by history.

The authenticity of nearly every relic rests upon the word of someone who is supposed to have firsthand knowledge of it and its association with the famous. Most relics have been annotated by perfectly sincere spectators, but faith still looms large in relic collecting, and it always will.

Provenance is the most important word in relic collecting. Provenance, sometimes spelled provenience, is the ancestry or descent of an object: its history, in other words. The simplest and most ancient form of provenance is verbal —"this sword was carried by my grandfather at Shiloh"—the story that in most people's experience accompanies family heirlooms; but provenance takes many more sophisticated forms: historical accounts or legal documents accompanying the relic, affidavits by persons acquainted at first hand with the history of the object, marks of previous ownership, printed references. Examples of the different kinds of provenance are given in this book. Its importance cannot be emphasized too much.

Most relics are by their nature unique, but in the collecting of relics certain types appear frequently and certain patterns recur in building collections. The description of many types of relics and many patterns in collecting in this book offers guidance to the collector in this unusual field. Many classes of relics are at present undercollected or just beginning to attract new collectors, and a number of these areas are pointed out in the following pages.

Prices are important to every collector and particularly so in a field where nearly every collectible is unique. Special emphasis has therefore been placed on prices in this book. *All prices mentioned are actual amounts recorded at auctions or by dealers. When a range of price is given, it is a composite of actual realizations.*

1

Antecedents

Before the sixteenth century, the word *relics* referred only to holy memorabilia. In the Western World they were the earthly remains of Jesus Christ and the saints of the Christian Church. The supreme relics were those of the Passion of Christ: the True Cross, the Holy Nails, the Holy Lance, the "Veronica" (handkerchief with which Christ's face was wiped on the way to Golgotha, leaving an impression of his features), the Holy Coat, and the Precious Blood are the most celebrated. Of these, the most venerated was the True Cross, discovered by the Roman Empress Helena in the fourth century and later divided into so many slivers that there were hundreds of places where a fragment could be seen and worshipped.

Saint Polycarp, burned at the stake about A.D. 155 because he was a member of the forbidden Christian cult, won by his martyrdom the distinction of being the first saint known to be honored with a regular annual feast. His charred bones were gathered up and preserved as relics, the first recorded instance of the veneration of such remains. Following Polycarp were literally thousands of holy men and women, mostly martyrs, who gradually became "saints." The term is used in the New Testament to refer to all full-fledged members of the Church of Christ, but early in the Christian era it came to identify persons especially admirable on account of their martyrdoms, and by the tenth century the process of "canonization" was developed. All over the Near Eastern and European world were shrines that preserved whole bodies of saints or their bones, hair, and fingernails. By the fourth or fifth century, the practice of making pilgrimages to holy places associated with the life of Christ or the saints was well established.

The cult of the saints with its shrines and relics posed some tricky questions for Christian theologians. The Eastern Orthodox Church, generally following the teachings of Saint John of Damascus, believed the earthly body of the saint had a kind of permanent grace. In Roman Catholic theory, devotees prayed *through* the saints to Heaven—the doctrine of "intercession"—not *to* the saint, and saintly relics were considered only as memorials. That distinction was difficult for the ordinary mind to make and was one usually disregarded by common folk. It was widely believed that where a relic of Christ or a saint was found, there the saint had his earthly habitation, and there, if venerated, he would see to it that God performed miracles or at least rendered some practical assistance to the visitor. The saints, although in Heaven, were not without mundane knowledge; they took a personal interest in the worshippers at their shrines and relics and to some granted special favors.

Assigning specific curative abilities to particular saints was a later refinement in the cult, but from the beginning some saints' relics were deemed more powerful and efficacious than others. Certain saints were widely regarded as especially powerful and had a more than local reputation. Others were suspected not only of

1

Physical remains of saints and other Christians were preserved in the early catacombs and later in such grisly sanctuaries as this "ossuary" in the Capuchin Church in Rome. *James F. Carr, New York*

inefficacy but of never having existed at all, owing their creation to pious fiction and the desire of some out-of-the-way spot to have a revenue-yielding shrine.

Along with these distinctions among the saints went the veneration of their remains and a connoisseurship in saintly relics. Relics were collected not only by the Church itself but by private persons, at least by royalty and the richer nobility.

The collecting of relics began about A.D. 313, when the Empress Helena (later a saint herself), mother of the convert Emperor Constantine, visited Jerusalem on a pilgrimage. There, she had the hill of Calvary excavated and found the relics of the Passion, the most important being the True Cross, as already mentioned. This landmark event is usually known by the infelicitous although quite prob-

able name "The Invention of the Cross." As the historian Sir Steven Runciman once pointed out, Saint Helena was not only the most exalted archaeologist ever to take the field but the most successful. The emperor ordered the Church of the Holy Sepulchre built on the site. It became and remains the chief sanctuary of Christendom and for Christians the most sacred place on earth.

The history of the Cross or the history of wood assumed to be the True Cross over nearly two millennia has been extraordinary. After its excavation, the major portion was placed in the Church of the Holy Sepulchre. There it remained except for a period in the seventh century when the Persians carried it away. When the Moslems captured Jerusalem in the year 638, they let it be—they, after all, respected Christ—but when the Crusaders captured the city in 1099, the Christian clergy fell out over ownership of this greatest of relics. The Eastern Christian priests, who had remained in charge of the Holy Sepulchre, decamped with the Cross and refused to surrender it until the "Latin" (i.e. Western) Patriarch put them to torture and forced them to reveal its hiding place. Strong emotions were aroused by this precious object.

The Holy Cross was captured from the Latin Kingdom of Jerusalem at the Battle of Hattin in 1187. Richard the Lion-Hearted tried to get it returned, but Saladin restored it to the Holy Sepulchre at Jerusalem; he refused to sell it to the wealthy Queen of Georgia in the Caucasus although she offered an enormous sum. At the end of the Fifth Crusade in 1221, an agreement was made between the Crusaders and the sultan by which the True Cross was to be given to them even though they were not getting the Holy City, but it had been misplaced and has yet to be found.

In the mid-fifth century the Empress Eudocia, born a pagan but a convert to the new religion, settled in Jerusalem with her imperial court. She too was interested in relics, and she started the fashion of collecting them by sending to the city of Constantinople the portrait of the Virgin Mary painted by Saint Luke, which for centuries was one of the chief relics of the Byzantine Empire.

The Byzantines were ardent relic collectors except during the period of "iconoclasm" in the eighth century, when hostility to images, religious pictures, the doctrine of the intercession of the saints, and the veneration of relics led to much destruction of icons and holy objects. Iconoclasm was an imperial policy, imposed from above: teams of men were despatched to various parts of the empire to destroy the suspect articles. But except for this interlude, which lasted about a century, Constantinople was the greatest storehouse in the world of Christian relics, far surpassing Rome or Jerusalem. The Byzantines considered as a landmark in their history the day in 627 when the Emperor Heraclius I restored the largest known fragment of the True Cross to Jerusalem, whence it had been removed by Persian infidels. The feast day commemorating this event, 14 September, was dedicated to "The Exaltation of the Cross."

In 943, the Byzantines besieged the city of Edessa in Asia Minor, which was held by the Moslems, but they were bought off by the Mos-

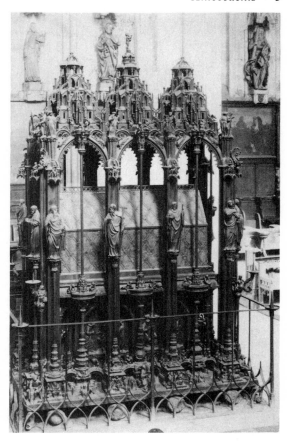

Medieval tombs were constructed as works of art and are large versions of the reliquaries used to house relics. This is the tomb of Saint Sebald in the church at Nuremberg, Germany, that bears his name, built in the thirteenth and fourteenth centuries. *James F. Carr, New York*

lem surrender of the famous *mandylion,* a miraculous picture of Christ. One historian has written that "the capture of this relic was regarded as equivalent to a territorial conquest." At Constantinople there was also the celebrated *keramidion,* which was a mud brick imprinted with Christ's features.

During the summer of the year 1098 when the army of the First Crusade was encamped in its thousands at Antioch in Syria, the Holy Lance that had pierced the side of Christ was dug up in the cathedral, where it had handily revealed itself to one of the Crusaders. The army was mostly overjoyed, although there was already a Holy Lance on view at Constantinople. The one found at Antioch was carried into battle against the Moslems. There was a certain skepticism regarding it, however; it is interesting to note that some Crusaders questioned, not the probability of finding a lance lost for a thousand years, but the authenticity of this particular one.

Mohammedanism, another great Near Eastern religion, developed like Christianity a cult of relics that persists today. Mohammed the Prophet insisted on his nondivinity, and Islam does not officially sanction the veneration of relics; that has not prevented his followers from piously preserving relics such as Mohammed's prayer mat, wine jar, the hilt of his sword, and more personal remains such as a tooth and hairs from his head and beard. His tomb and that of his daughter Fatima at Medina are visited by pious Moslems on their pilgrimage—the *hajj*—to Mecca, the Prophet's birthplace. At Mecca the holiest building in the Moslem world is the Kaaba, enclosing the most important Mohammedan relic, the Black Stone, which has a very ancient history of veneration, even predating Mohammed.

Devotion to relics developed also in many Eastern religions, most of them much more ancient that those of the Near East and Europe. Buddhism in particular places an emphasis on relics, and innumerable shrines flourish today, each with its relics—often of the Buddha himself. At Kandy in Ceylon, for example, an especially famous temple houses one of the Buddha's teeth. Through the centuries many relics have been found. In 1898, an urn was unearthed near his presumed birthplace north of Benares (he was born there about 563 B.C.) that purportedly contained some of the Buddha's remains. As recently as 1932, an English archaeologist directing a dig in the Madras Presidency in Southern India uncovered the ruins of a great stupa (shrine) that had been built to protect a fragment of the Buddha's bones. Better still, enclosed in a gold box that was in turn enclosed in a silver casket was the tiny bit of bone itself.

In the most distant bounds of Western Europe, relic collecting thrived almost from the time of the people's conversion to Christianity. The Anglo-Saxon King Athelstan, who reigned in England from 925 to 939, was one of the greatest royal collectors of his time in the relic line. Later generations of monarchs would accumulate paintings, manuscripts, and objects of rare and precious craftsmanship; Athelstan

yearned for holy relics. When ambassadors came from Hugh the Great, Duke of the Franks, to ask for Athelstan's sister in marriage to their master, they ingratiated themselves with the island monarch by presenting him with relics for his collection: the sword of the Roman Emperor Constantine in the pommel of which an iron nail was fixed, one of the four used in the Crucifixion of Christ, and a spear "said to be that with which the Roman centurion pierced Christ's side while He was on the Cross" (in other words, another Holy Lance). A small portion of the Crown of Thorns was also included but treated as a gift of lesser significance, since it was by no means to be regarded as unique: nearly every collection of relics contained its portion of the Crown and its fragment of the True Cross. Even as ardent as King Athelstan was for relics, he hardly rivaled his contemporary, King Henry I of Germany, who bartered an entire province, part of modern Switzerland, for still another Holy Lance.

The collection, preservation, and exhibition of relics was no placid area of medieval or even of later religious life. Prolonged, frequent, and often exceedingly bitter disputes arose over the authenticity and efficacy of various remains, usually between rival custodians at shrines depending on the extensive trade of tourists who visited relics. The medieval mind was not necessarily exercised about the problem of two or more bodies of a single saint being venerated at different shrines. Their existence probably meant only that the saint, whose powers were, after all, transcendent, had merely created other bodies to satisfy the ardor of his worshippers. Duplicate relics, so to speak, were certainly not uncommon. Gowns of the Virgin Mary were preserved in various cities—at Constantinople, Rome (*eight* churches displayed different garments), the Spanish Escorial, Avignon, Marseilles, Toulon, Brussels, and Novgorod in far Russia. Petticoats and girdles of the Virgin were numberless. Even relics that one would think inevitably unique were found in more than one place: *several* churches displayed heads of Saint John the Baptist.

Relics were multiplied by means that were simultaneously matter-of-fact and miraculous. Nails from the Crucifixion were increased by the simple process of using an "undoubted" nail or fragment to touch other nails, which then became equally holy. Saint Charles

Borromeo, the sixteenth century church reformer who, one is assured, had the reputation of cautiousness in anything to do with relics, created many new nails by rubbing his example against others, and presented them to friends, including King Philip II of Spain, as holy treasures.

There was—and is—not always perfect agreement as to just what a relic represented. In the Cathedral of San Lorenzo at Genoa, Italy, there has long been preserved an emerald dish perhaps brought back to that city by the Crusaders and said by its guardians to be the very vessel out of which Christ ate at the Last Supper. Nathaniel Hawthorne, who saw the dish in 1804, remarked sensibly that since the Last Supper was held in an inn, it seemed unlikely that the guests were served with emerald dishes. On the other hand, there have been those who claimed the dish was one of the gifts given by the Queen of Sheba to King Solomon on her famous visit. Or even the Holy Grail; a very ancient agate bowl in the Hapsburg treasure at Vienna also has the repute of being the Holy Grail, the cup used by Christ at the Last Supper, and in which Joseph of Arimathea caught the last drops of His blood at the Cross.

In medieval times relics were sometimes employed in ways that strike the modern mind as indecent if not downright blasphemous. A petticoat of the Virgin that had been given by the Emperor of Constantinople to Charlemagne and by one of Charlemagne's descendants to the Bishop of Chartres was carried as a battle flag by the warlike bishop in his campaign against the invading Normans in 908. According to sober historians of the time, the petticoat waving before the bishop's forces was responsible for repelling the Normans.

Naturally, relics as items of a value that transcended worldly things had to be housed properly and reverently. They were preserved in "reliquaries," caskets, boxes, and statuettes of various precious substances, often glass (then rare) or crystal—to permit viewing of the relic—and more or less elaborately decorated with gems or pieces of cut glass. All museums with collections of medieval art have examples of these reliquaries. Amazing numbers were created: in 1520, a German cathedral at Halle had 350 reliquaries in its inventory. An unusual vocabulary described certain types of reliquaries: a *marsupium,* for example, was a little bag (pouch) for carrying relics; a *monile,* a pendant in which a relic could be worn. A curiosity in the history of relic collecting is that with the passage of time the values, for most people, of relic and reliquary have been reversed. Now, medieval reliquaries are very highly prized for their gold, silver, and jewel value and their remarkable workmanship. At Aix-la-Chapelle (Aachen) in Germany, the ancient seat of the Carolingian empire, the bones of the Emperor Charlemagne are preserved in a stupendous reliquary called "The Golden Shrine of Charlemagne," which is six and one-half feet long and three and one-half feet high. Completed in 1215, four centuries after the emperor's death—the treasury took that long to accumulate the gold—the shrine is regarded as one of the greatest art treasures to have survived from the medieval world. No one is particularly interested anymore in the imperial bones it contains.

The casting of lots for Christ's garments at the foot of the Cross was the earliest commerce in relics. A European trade in holy objects developed very quickly. Relics were bought, sold, traded, and given as gifts like Duke Hugh's to King Athelstan. All in all, a good many relics changed hands. There were even dealers.

Trade in relics reached into very high places indeed. In the thirteenth century, the Latins who had conquered the empire of Byzantium found themselves almost totally without funds for defending it, whereupon they pawned Constantinople's most sacred relic, the Crown of Thorns (or at least a large portion of it), to the Republic of Venice. They were unable to redeem the pledge—indeed, their empire collapsed altogether in 1261—and they sold their interest in the Crown to Saint Louis, King of France, who redeemed it from the Venetians and took it to Paris, where it was lost during the French Revolution.

Even the Roman popes dealt in relics. Pope John XXIII (not the twentieth century one but an antipope, a former pirate, who reigned from 1410 to 1415) sold the head of Saint John the Baptist from Rome's Church of Saint Sylvester to the citizens of Florence for 50,000 ducats. The Council of Constance, which deposed John for sodomy and other crimes, canceled the sale, saying the deal was simony (that is, selling ecclesiastical property for profit), which of course it was. The head was returned to Rome, where it was destroyed during the sack of Rome by the imperial troops in 1527, not so great a loss as one might imagine, since at least eleven other heads of the Baptist could still be counted in various ecclesiastical treasuries of western Europe.

A certain amount of muddle ensued from all this movement of relics, particularly as the superstitious mind is not given to exactitude. Among the fabulous treasures of the Hapsburg dynasty was a relic described in the inventory of the Insignia of the Empire in 1246 as "the arm-bone of Saint Kunigund, wife of the Emperor Henry II." By 1350, this had become "the arm-bone of Saint Anne," and distinctly more important because Saint Anne was the mother of the Virgin Mary. So it is still described in the catalogue of Kunsthistorisches Museum in Vienna, where it is valued now for the gilded silver reliquary made in Prague in the fourteenth century.

The rules of the relic trade were rather peculiar. Throughout the medieval period the theft of holy relics was not considered a heinous crime. The power of the saints was such that theft was possible only if the saint himself wished to be moved, the thief being merely the passive instrument of the saint's intentions. In 828, for example, the Republic of Venice acquired by theft, pure and simple, the body of Saint Mark the Evangelist from the city of Alexandria, of which he had been first bishop. The saint became the patron of Venice and the very lodestone of its long-enduring greatness. His relics are still in the celebrated cathedral that bears his name in that city.

After "indulgences"—remission of punishment for sins—began to be granted by the Church for visiting shrines and relics, immense sums were raised by princes who owned the relics of popular saints. In the sixteenth century the Cardinal-Archbishop of Mainz printed a description of his collection of relics, available for the contemplation of the religious at the City of Halle, which included forty-two complete bodies of saints miraculously preserved, a piece of the manna with which the Children of Israel were fed during their years in the wilderness, and the basin in which Pontius Pilate washed his hands. The indulgence granted for visiting this powerful collection was not less than 39,245,120 years, 220 days. The Elector Frederick the Wise of Saxony (ruled from 1486 to 1525) during the same period accumulated at enormous expense precisely 5,005 holy relics. The visitation and contemplation of this collection could lessen

the devout pilgrim's stay in purgatory by 1,443 years. The pilgrim received a written indulgence to that effect from representatives of the Church. The elector kept his collection, which included such marvels as a drop of the Virgin Mary's milk, in the ducal church at Wittenberg in Saxony. It was to the door of that church that one of the elector's subjects, Martin Luther, nailed his ninety-five theses in 1517.

For more than a century after the declaration at Wittenberg set off the Protestant Reformation, there was much destruction of churches, their decorations and relics. Stained glass was smashed, silver vessels melted down, and relics and reliquaries broken up and scattered. Regularly organized teams roamed the countryside in northern Europe, wreaking havoc among the innumerable shrines and churches that had been built during the medieval period. In England the Civil War and Commonwealth period in the 1640s was an extremely busy period of iconoclasm. A curious English diary exists, kept in the years 1643/4 by one William Dowsing, who was a professional iconoclast. His official title was "Parliamentary visitor appointed under a warrant from the Earl of Manchester for demolishing the superstitious pictures and ornaments of churches, etc. within the county of Suffolk." Dowsing's diary records his services in destroying sacred pictures, organs (the stauncher Protestants opposed instrumental music in the churches), holy water "pots," covers for baptismal fonts (because they had images), and statuary (the prime target). A typical entry from Dowsing's diary:

> Clare. We brake down 1,000 Pictures superstitious; I brake down 200; three of God the Father and three of Christ and the Holy Lamb, and three of the Holy Ghost like a Dove with Wings; and the twelve Apostles were carved in Wood on the top of the Roof which we gave order to take down; and twenty cherubims to be taken down; and the Sun and Moon in the East Windows, by the King's Arms, to be taken down.

Since Dowsing was paid six shillings eightpence for each act of destruction, his odd profession must have provided quite a decent living.

The Protestant Reformation "secularized," so to speak, the collecting of relics, at least in much of northern Europe. Secular mementos began immediately to take their place: possessions of Martin Luther himself and other reformers were preserved and highly regarded. Many famous connoisseurs formed collections —often referred to as "cabinets"—of memorabilia. Nearly every great house or palace in Europe and England had some historical or literary relics. Since the Reformation, relics have generally been regarded as interesting objects reminiscent of a great man or woman and have not been venerated for their supernatural powers. There are other differences: the relics of the saints were presumed to be souvenirs of *good* people. Few people collected relics of sinners. After secularization, virtue mattered less; mere fame, or even notoriety, sufficed.

Objects that formerly received religious veneration—those that survived—were in but little demand in that part of Europe that became Protestant. In 1825 an alabaster box, said to be the very one mentioned by the Evangelist Mark that Mary Magdalen brought filled with ointment for anointing the body of Christ, was offered at a London auction. What a sensation had it been offered three centuries earlier! But in 1825 London, it sold for a mere half crown. Reliquaries, on the other hand, were widely preserved and collected because of their superb craftsmanship.

In Roman Catholic countries the veneration of religious relics, although unquestionably losing ground, has never ceased. The famous "Shroud of Turin," for example, still survives in that Italian city and is venerated by many Roman Catholics as the burial cloth of Jesus. The shroud is a piece of linen fourteen feet long, but only three feet wide, preserving on its surface the faint front and back impressions of a crucified man as if the shroud had been wrapped around him lengthwise as an Egyptian mummy was wrapped. Revered since the fourteenth century when it was discovered in a French church, the shroud was investigated in 1969 by various scholarly authorities using the most modern photographic techniques. The results of their inquiry have never been made public. There is a Holy Shroud Guild in the United States claiming five thousand members. When the shroud was shown on Italian television for the first time in 1973, Pope Paul VI reserved judgment on the question of the authenticity of the relic but recommended that television viewers abstain from alcoholic beverages while the shroud was on the screen.

Also in Italy, Neapolitans still keep an eye on the blood of San Gennaro (Saint Januarius) kept in two vials in their cathedral; it is supposed to liquefy and bubble on his feast day (19 September) and on two other annual occasions. If it does not liquefy or liquefies late, disaster is imminent. As recently as the cholera epidemic of 1973, thousands of Neapolitans crowded into the cathedral on 19 September and were overjoyed that the blood liquefied, which they took to mean that the epidemic was coming to an end.

The realistic eighteenth century did not much relish the collecting of memorabilia, but there were a few notable antiquarians, in England particularly, who continued to preserve "curios," as relics were then often called. Typical of the eighteenth century collector of relics was Horace Walpole, novelist (*The Castle of Otranto*) and tireless letter writer. At his "Gothic" house, Strawberry Hill, outside London, he displayed many treasures of historical interest. Lord Macaulay wrote: "In his villa every apartment is a museum; every piece of furniture is a curiosity; there is something strange in the form of the shovel; there is a long story belonging to the bell rope." Macaulay did not admire this collecting but he mentions some of the relics: "Queen Mary's comb, Wolsey's red hat, the pipe which [Admiral] Van Tromp smoked during his last sea fight, and the spur King William [III] struck into the flank of 'Sorrel' at the Battle of the Boyne." Also on view were the gloves of King James I, and the "speculum" of the sixteenth century occultist Dr. John Dee. This last item was a true curiosity and is still a highly prized object. Dee's contemporaries, who were afraid of him anyway (the Star Chamber tried him in 1555 for practicing sorcery against Queen Mary, but he was acquitted), thought the "speculum" was an enchanted mirror through which the astrologer spoke to the dead. When it came into the hands of Horace Walpole, he thought it a piece of highly polished coal and a work of art. At the sale of his possessions it brought twelve guineas (about $750 in modern terms) and then dropped out of sight for two generations. When it came to the British Museum in 1966 it excited considerable interest. Serious study revealed that it is in fact not coal but a piece of polished obsidian (volcanic glass), probably Aztec in origin and brought from Mexico by a Spaniard from whom Dr. Dee got it. (A "magician's bracelet" with three charms that had belonged to Dr. Dee sold at a Christie's auction in 1967 for $1,500.) Walpole followed all the auctions at which relics were offered for sale, much regretting, for example, that he was outbid for Oliver Cromwell's nightcap.

Auctions of books and paintings featured relics almost from the beginnings of public sales (or "vendues," as they were frequently called) in the seventeenth century, and by the nineteenth century auctions became the prime method for exchanging memorabilia, as they have remained. The English poet Samuel Rogers, who knew a lot about collecting—the auction sale of his possessions took twenty-one days in the year 1856—said, when asked what would become of his treasures: "The auctioneer will find out the fittest possessor hereafter. He who gives money for things values them." The London auction houses, especially Henry Stevens in Covent Garden, regularly sold historical and literary relics. Among the relics Stevens sold early in this century were:

- King Charles II's wig
- Alexander Pope's cane (brought £5, about $200 today)
- Sir Walter Scott's ink bottle
- Rope used to hang various notorious criminals
- Lord Palmerston's writing table
- The raincoat worn by Christian De Wet, the Boer leader, during the South African War (only six shillings)

An important modern religious memorial is this little private chapel of John Wesley's in his London house. Here the great leader of Methodism prayed and read his Bible each morning. The table, chair, and candlestick were all Wesley's. The chapel has become known as "The Power House of Methodism." *Wesley's House and Museum, London*

Even in the early American Republic there were auctions where a collector might find relics. A sale of "splendid and rare curiosities" held on 11 July 1842 at Harrington's Museum in Boston offered a piece of the keel of the explorer Capt. James Cook's ship the *Endeavour*, "an ancient spear made in the year 1686 supposed to have been used at the Battle of the Boyne," the bones of "the celebrated Indian Chief King Jacob," and a silver-mounted pistol taken from the Spanish Armada.

On both sides of the Atlantic the nineteenth century was a great age of relic collecting. It is no accident that throughout this book emphasis will be laid on the collecting of relics of nineteenth century notables. Indeed, many famous people of the era were relic collectors themselves. Sir Walter Scott's collection, for example, is discussed in chapter 7. In a time

when memorabilia are valued, relics can be quite consciously created, sometimes by people whom one would think above the manufacture of personalia. Johann Wolfgang von Goethe, for example, never the man to underestimate himself, was contacted late in his life by a writer who wanted to publish some letters Goethe and a young lady had exchanged during his student days in Strasbourg. Anxious that the letters *not* be published, Goethe wrote the young man denying permission but saying he quite understood that an author did not want to give up a project without recompense; therefore, he offered him

a silver cup, gilded on the inside, and used daily by me at table for drinking my wine.

This cup I am prepared to dedicate to you by having engraved on it the names of the recipient and the donor, together with the year of the event in question and the present year.

The author did not accept this shameless bribe, but even without the relic Goethe exerted other pressures and had his way—the letters were not published.

Relic collecting thrives today, and more relics than ever are being exhibited and seen by millions. There will be no shortage of relics so long as there is no shortage of newsworthy men and women. In 1970, "Beatle" Paul McCartney's shetland wool sweater was sold at an auction in New York for $95. At the same sale, a fur coat belonging to the rock singer Janis Joplin was sold and another singer's guitar, although the latter was described as

Relics of sporting accomplishments include some magnificent silver trophies. This is the "New Zealand Centennial Challenge Cup" for yachting, made in the 1880s. *James F. Carr, New York*

being in "uncertain condition." The briar pipe smoked by the baseball player Babe Ruth was sold at another auction for $170. And older relics are getting more valuable: in 1968, the American Trucking Association Foundation in Washington, D.C., paid $25,000 for a Brooks Brothers overcoat worn by Abraham Lincoln.

Memorabilia are constantly being created, and not on a diminishing scale. Witness the custom established by recent United States presidents of signing important state documents with several pens, which are then encased in presentation boxes and given away as souvenirs. Sometimes a dozen pens have been used to sign a single document, each pen making the merest stroke. Souvenir pens were distributed by the thousands during the terms of Presidents John F. Kennedy and Lyndon Johnson, but their proliferation was slowed by President Nixon. He tried signing documents with several pens, but his signature came out "so distorted that people didn't believe it was mine."

As many relics as ever are being preserved, and probably more are going into museums. Only a year after the death of Justice Hugo L. Black of the United States Supreme Court in 1971, his family presented to the Smithsonian Institution the copy of the Constitution that he carried in his vest pocket during his thirty-four years on the Supreme Court, along with his judicial robe, a pen that Franklin Roosevelt gave him at the signing of the Air Mail Act of 1934, and mementos of his funeral.

Ownership of objects, especially odd objects, by the famous makes many items attractive to the relic collector. The personal possessions of the controversial director of the Federal Bureau of Investigation, J. Edgar Hoover, were sold at auction after his death in 1972. They included some very unusual souvenirs, such as a whiskey decanter that played "For He's a Jolly Good Fellow" and a basket woven of Popsicle sticks. It seems safe to assume that such bizarre objects were sold for their value as relics of this prominent American figure.

One of the last acts of President Lyndon Johnson before his death in January 1973 was to send a used example of his famous Stetson hats to be sold as a presidential relic at a benefit auction at the Rochester, New York, City Art Center. He had thoughtfully signed it on the lining.

Even in the twentieth century the emotions aroused by some very ancient relics of state

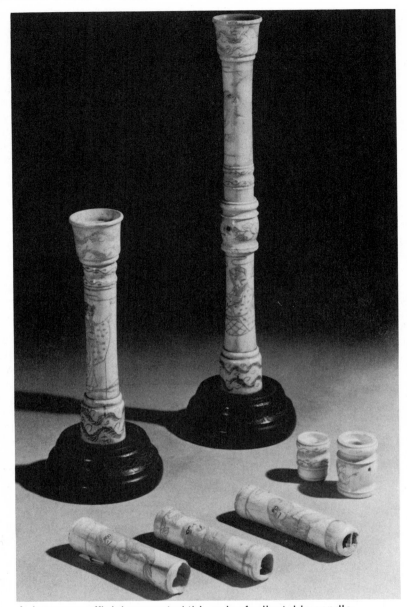

A Japanese official presented this pair of adjustable candlesticks to William Jennings Bryan on one of his round-the-world cruises. Carved of whalebone and decorated with Japanese motifs, they are mounted on decorated black wood bases. Such presentation items figure largely among the memorabilia of noted persons and are of great interest to the relic collector. *James F. Carr, New York*

have had political repercussions. In 1296, King Edward I of England defeated the kingdom of Scotland in battle and captured the "Stone of Scone," on which the kings of Scotland had been crowned since very ancient times. The stone, referred to then and now in Scotland as the Scottish Stone of Destiny, was traditionally thought to be that used by Jacob as a pillow at Bethel, as related in the twenty-eighth chapter of the Book of Genesis, taken by his descendants to Egypt, and from there to Ireland—difficulties of transport rarely stand in the way of myth—by the year 700 B.C., where "on Tara's Hill" in present County Meath it served as the "Lia Fail," the coronation stone of the early Irish kings. Legend does not say how it reached Scotland, nor when, but even in 1296, the stone certainly had a long history. Edward I took it to Westminster Abbey and placed it under the Coronation Chair (i.e. the throne). Some Scots have never become reconciled to its loss although it left their country nigh seven hundred years ago, and the crowns of England and Scotland were united in 1707 anyway. The Scots have repeatedly petitioned or demanded its return.

In 1924, there was a debate in the House of Commons in which—amidst the hilarity of the members—a Scottish parliamentarian traced the history of the Stone from Jacob and asked for it to be replaced at Scone. An English member rose to remind the House that Scotland still owed England a ransom never paid for the return of King James I of Scotland, captured by the English in 1406, and that the return of the Stone of Scone was dependent upon payment of that ransom. There the matter rested.

During both the First and Second World Wars, the Stone was taken from Westminster Abbey and hidden for the duration. On Christmas Eve 1950 a group of young "Scottish Nationalist" students at Glasgow University managed to steal the Stone, which is quite large and heavy, out of the Abbey and make off with it to Scotland to the delight of newspaper readers everywhere and the intense chagrin of the Dean and Chapter of Westminster. It was not recovered until the following April, when one of the thieves was traced because he had checked out of the Glasgow University Library every book it had on the Abbey. There were no prosecutions, and indeed one of the culprits published a memoir describing how he and his confederates made off with the relic.

The commerce in relics continues brisk. Auction houses all over the world, including the most internationally important, constantly sell relics of extraordinary variety. During a recent auction season the Hôtel Drouot, the state auction gallery in Paris, sold for $450 a baby's bottle from which an infant prince, son of Louis Philippe, King of the French, had taken nourishment in 1814. It was preserved in a green leather case lined with purple velvet. Christie's, the oldest English auction house,

sold for $200 an album of dried flowers saved by Queen Victoria from Prince Albert's funeral wreaths and from other royal graves. Parke-Bernet, the American auction house, sold a 1923 automobile that had been Rudolph Valentino's for $22,000 (in Los Angeles) and a pair of sugar tongs that had belonged to George Washington for $3,750 (in New York). At an auction in Edinburgh an ivory snuffbox in the form of a boar's head with Robert Burns association brought $500. And at one of the Metro-Goldwyn-Mayer movie memorabilia sales in Hollywood the trenchcoat worn by Clark Gable in the 1939 film *Comrade X* brought $1,250.

The actor Paul Newman riding the bicycle used in his motion picture *Butch Cassidy and the Sundance Kid*. The bicycle was sold at a 20th Century-Fox studio auction in 1971 for a record price of $3,100. *Sotheby Parke Bernet, Los Angeles*

Modern taste in preserving relics runs to complete preservation or restoration. At the Polish Museum of America, "The Paderewski Room" contains the furnishings of the suite in the Buckingham Hotel, New York, in which Ignace Jan Paderewski died in January 1941, a refugee from the Nazi conquest of Poland. The bed is the one in which he died. *Polish Museum of America, Chicago*

There are changing fashions in relics as in any collecting activity. Generally today there seems to be a preference for historical relics, taking "historical" in its widest meaning. A large market exists, for example, in the automobiles of famous people. Woodrow Wilson's 1919 Pierce-Arrow has lately been restored and put on display at Staunton, Virginia, the president's birthplace. The 1934 Ford automobile in which the notorious criminals Bonnie Parker and Clyde Barrow were killed was recently sold for $175,000, having earned, it was claimed, about $10,000,000 in fees for exhibition at county fairs, and the stripper Gypsy Rose Lee's 1956 Rolls-Royce Silver Cloud sedan sold in 1971 for $8,250.

There is interest, too, in theatrical and motion picture relics, the latter a recent field indeed, which is discussed at more length in chapter 8. A new era of relic collecting dawned in 1970/71, when the bicycle ridden by Paul Newman in the motion picture *Butch Cassidy and the Sundance Kid* sold for $3,100, and similar movie memorabilia are bringing extremely high prices. Interest is also strong in Nazi relics (so much so that they are being counterfeited); nearly anything relating to American presidents; guns and other weapons with provenance traceable to noted people; historic flags, and—always—in historic jewels.

Certain historical figures maintain a sort of permanent lead in relic collecting—the royal Stuarts, Marie Antoinette, Lord Nelson, Winston Churchill, Adolf Hitler, Abraham Lincoln, and Napoleon. The market for relics roughly classifiable as historical appears to be gaining at the expense of the literary market, but there are collecting perennials in the literary field too: any relic is nearly certain to sell well if it is connected with John Keats, Percy Shelley, Walt Whitman, Lord Byron, Charles Dickens, or Edgar Allan Poe. Every scrap of these authors has been collected for generations, and by now provenances (histories) of remarkable length and interest have been built up on their relics, as will often be shown. Outside this group of authors and a few others, literary relics are not quite so much in demand as they were in the nineteenth century, when collectors snapped up memorabilia of their favorite poets or novelists. At a time when relics of Judy Garland sell for more than those of Elizabeth Barrett Browning, the wise collector will take a new look at literary relics.

Twentieth century ease of travel has made it possible to see, compare, and study relics of many famous people, and contemporary methods of photography and other aids to research and establishing authenticity have reduced the element of faith in relic collecting. They have, however, in no way diminished the pleasure of seeking out and preserving souvenirs of noted people of the past.

The story of relic collecting is an extraordinary chapter in the history of taste, ancient and modern—there are apparently few limits to what may be sought, preserved, and treasured. In consequence, as will be shown, relics vary widely. In the presidential field alone, they range from the Masonic Bible used by George Washington at his first inauguration in 1789 and in this century by Presidents Harding and Eisenhower, which is now proudly displayed at Federal Hall, New York City, to a cigar half-smoked by President Ulysses S. Grant, which is exhibited at the Galena Historical Society in Galena, Illinois. One man's rubbish may be another man's relic.

A King James version New Testament, the "Jerusalem Red Letter" edition (the words of Christ are printed in red), is bound in boards made from the cedars of Lebanon mentioned in Psalm XCII—"The righteous shall flourish like the palm tree: he shall grow like a cedar in Lebanon." These volumes were popular mementos brought back from the Holy Land in the nineteenth and twentieth centuries and were often found in American Protestant households. Examples like this currently sell for about $50. *James F. Carr, New York*

2
Relics in All Their Variety

The fundamental relic is the actual body of a great man or woman. Since the martyrdom of Saint Polycarp, fragments of the corporeal being of celebrated people have been collected and revered. Countless bones, ashes, fingernails, and locks of hair have been accumulated: in many chapters of this book actual physical remains figure among the relics—especially in the case of noted people who have a special emotional hold on public attention: Lincoln, Napoleon, and Shelley are examples. This is the most basic relic collecting—the grisliest, too, and that in which the twentieth century is just as ardent as the past. In the sixteenth century people were already horrified at the Spanish Queen Juana "La Loca" ("The Mad"), who became mentally unstable after the death of her adored husband the Archduke Philip, called "The Handsome," at the age of twenty-eight in 1506. She refused to have him buried and for years traveled around Spain with his coffin, until she was confined in an isolated castle by her son, the Emperor Charles V.

Few anecdotes about medieval relics and the preservation of saints' bodies can compare with the contemporary preservation of the body of Nikolai Lenin. For the half century since his death in 1924, his embalmed body has been permanently displayed in a mausoleum in Red Square, Moscow, during which time it has been viewed by literally millions of visitors.

Even more sensational has been the history of the body of Eva Perón. Maria Eva Duarte de Perón had had a very modest fame as a radio actress in Argentina when she married Juan Perón, the coming strong man of the country. She was still under thirty when Perón became master of the Argentine in 1946. Virtually the coruler of the country, she became famous for her well-publicized personal charity, which consisted mainly of receiving a string of daily petitioners to whom she handed out fifty- or hundred-peso notes that she kept under her desk blotter. The needy were also encouraged to write to her asking the assistance of the "Eva Perón Foundation"; she sometimes received ten thousand letters a day. At the peak of her power the Eva Perón Foundation, chief instrument of her charity, was said to be the largest such organization in the world and to have an annual income of more than $50,000,000. The money was raised by "voluntary" contributions from corporations, rich people, unions, and workers who were sometimes obliged to contribute an entire day's pay to the foundation. The country rewarded her with the official titles "Lady of Hope," "Standard Bearer of the Workers," and "First Samaritan." In the midst of her extraordinary success she died of cancer at the age of thirty-two in 1952, leaving a fortune deposited abroad and said to amount to $800,000,000, about which innumerable rumors have circulated.

Both Eva and Juan Perón, although on very good terms with the Roman Catholic Church—Eva visited the pope in great state,

15

but he did not create her a papal countess as she had hoped—were also interested in spiritualism, much to the distress of the Argentine clergy. After her death Perón declared that she would never be buried. He had "Evita" embalmed by a special "secret process" and preserved her in an immense orchid-colored transparent coffin lined with satin. The funeral, a spectacular outpouring of national grief, took place amidst scenes of frenzy in which several people were killed and more than two thousand injured. Every honor possible was bestowed on the "Lady of Hope," and a movement was started aimed at her canonization.

Eva Perón's body has still never been buried, and when Perón went into exile it traveled with him (he is said to have been supported luxuriously in exile by her hidden funds). Even his two subsequent marriages did not end this extraordinary odyssey; the body was on permanent exhibition in his Spanish exile. (It has been given treatments by the "secret process" of embalming for twenty-one years to preserve it.) When Perón was recalled to Argentina in 1973, Eva's body went with him, "redone" by the embalmer, and with a new dress and updated hair-do.

Where the entire body has been lacking, various portions have survived for veneration. On display in Stockholm is the skull of the Swedish King Charles XII, killed by a sniper at the siege of Frederiksten in Norway in 1718, which shows the huge hole near the right eye caused by the bullet.

At Stourton in Wiltshire, England, seat of the very ancient family of that name who traced their ancestry to Saxon "thanes" (or chiefs), they long preserved the gigantic thighbone of Botolph of Stourton, who lived about the year 1000. As one historian remarked, if any Philistine doubted the origin of this relic, the family could smite him, "not with the jawbone of an ass, but with the thighbone of an ancestor." Other historians who saw the relic thought it derived from a large animal rather than a large Saxon.

Blood, of immense significance in Christian theology and tradition, figures largely in relic collecting. In Vienna the Hapsburg treasury numbers among its countless art treasures, "The Burse of Saint Stephen," an extremely ancient reliquary of gold, silver, and pearls made about the first third of the ninth century. According to tradition, it contained earth soaked with the blood of the archmartyr Saint

Stephen, who was stoned to death in Jerusalem about A.D. 36 (*Acts* 6 and 7), but it has been empty for some centuries.

Blood, as will be related in later chapters, was rubbed up from the steps of the house where the dying Lincoln was carried, and the blood-soaked towels used in the death room were cut up and distributed to collectors. Only a few years ago one of these pieces was sold at auction for $35. Similar relics of Charles I of England, Louis XVI, Marie Antoinette, and many other notables have been sold.

Remnants of the famous need not be natural growth, so to speak, to be attractive to collectors and curators. The descendants of the Duke of Wellington still have the dentures of the "Iron Duke" at their house Stratfieldsaye in Hampshire. The false teeth are of curious construction, the top and bottom teeth being joined together by a spring. At the New York Academy of Medicine are the wooden false teeth of George Washington, who was greatly troubled with his teeth. In the Château de Valençay in France, the country home of the celebrated Prince Charles-Maurice de Talleyrand, is kept the metal device he wore all his life on his crippled foot.

During the United States' War with Mexico (1846–48), the American General Robert Patterson was the happy captor of the wooden leg of the Mexican General Santa Anna (who had lost the original during the so-called "Pastry War" between the French and Mexico in 1838). General Patterson brought the leg home to Philadelphia, where it was installed in a corner of his drawing room along with "other works of art," of which he had a considerable collection. We are not told how Santa Anna made his escape from the Americans minus the leg.

These mementos seem insignificant in comparison with a relic that the monks at the Escorial in Spain showed to the traveler William Beckford, when he visited there in the later eighteenth century. This was nothing less than a feather that had fallen from the wings of the Angel Gabriel when he came to visit the Virgin Mary!

Since the most ancient times human hair has been preserved and treasured; from the seventeenth through the nineteenth centuries it was the most precious and sentimental of personal relics. Locks and even strands of hair were exchanged and collected. One of the most famous poems in the English language, Alexander Pope's *The Rape of the Lock,* has hair as its subject. It describes an actual incident in which young Lord Petre slyly cut off a lock of Arabella Fermor's tresses without her permission, giving rise to an absurd dispute between their families.

There were memorial portraits painted on closely matted hair and encased in jeweled lockets. Even Jane Austen's sensible characters exchanged hair, usually mounted in jewelry. Innumerable eighteenth and nineteenth century miniature portraits on ivory have been preserved, the hair of the subject being shown under the glass in the back. The demand for locks of Lord Byron's hair was so great even during his lifetime that perhaps it is not surprising his later portraits show him balding. The American abolitionist Thaddeus Stevens, who was bald and wore a toupee, was so irritated by one female admirer who pestered him for a souvenir lock of hair that he pulled off his whole wig and offered it to the startled lady. One collector got together locks of hair from the heads of Abraham Lincoln, John Brown, and William Lloyd Garrison and wove them together in commemoration of abolition.

Nineteenth century ladies with time on their hands were fond of gathering locks of hair from various members of one family or from friends and weaving them into wreaths, exactly as one might make a floral wreath. The different shades of hair added variety, and placing them attractively was a test of skill for the wreathmaker. The hair compositions were then framed, usually in deep frames. Hair wreaths of American origin have sold in recent years in the $100–$200 range. They are a curious product of Victorian leisure.

Hair collectors were undeterred even by the decease of one of their subjects: hair was cut off after death for preserving—even the long dead and buried were not immune from such attentions. Horace Walpole had at Strawberry Hill a lock of hair cut off the skull of King Edward IV (who had died in 1483) when his body was exhumed in 1789, during repairs to Saint George's Chapel, Windsor. This lock or another taken at the same time was sold at auction by Stevens in London around 1900 for the solid amount of eight guineas (about $500 today). A twelve-inch lock of the "golden hair" of Mary Tudor, Duchess of Suffolk, taken when her body was exhumed, belonged successively to several famous English collectors, including the Duchess of Portland and

Among personal relics of the famous, clothing ranks high. Hats seem to have a special appeal, particularly when they are regarded as characteristic of the wearer. Few hats can have been more famous than New York Governor Alfred E. Smith's brown derby. *Museum of the City of New York*

the Duke of Buckingham. When the extravagance of the Duke of Buckingham caused his possessions to be sold at a celebrated auction at his house, Stowe, in Buckinghamshire, the lock sold for seven pounds, ten shillings (about $350 today).

The Dorotheum, the famous state auction house and pawnshop in Vienna, founded in 1707 and affectionately known to the Viennese as "Tante Dorothea" ("Aunt Dorothy"), has sold carefully preserved whiskers from the beard of the revered Emperor Francis Joseph, who died in 1916. As later chapters will show, the hair of figures as diverse as Napoleon, Marie Antoinette, John Keats, "Bonnie Prince Charlie" Stuart, and Abraham Lincoln is keenly sought by collectors today.

Even the hair of famous animals has been collected. During the nineteenth century hairs from the mane of the Duke of Wellington's famous horse Copenhagen, who bore the duke in battle and became a national hero in his own right, reached the salesroom. The celebrated Traveller, Robert E. Lee's mount, survived the Civil War and was put to pasture at Washington College, Virginia, when his master became president there. So many people plucked hairs from his mane for souvenirs that he became extremely wary of strangers

Among personal possessions, the apparel of famous people comes first with collectors of

Canes, walking sticks, and umbrellas carried by famous men, made from relic wood or deriving from interesting places, have survived in large numbers and, unless bejeweled, are usually priced for the modest collector. Most date to the nineteenth or early twentieth century. This selection of collectors' pieces shows, *left to right:* (1) walking stick with onion-shaped silver cap engraved "From Pikes Peak Colorado, 12,000 feet above the sea April 13, 1895, J. M. Horton to H. Grube." Since the summit of Pikes Peak is at 14,110, this party probably stopped at about timberline. The wood may well be from the sparse growth there. (2) Silver-headed natural wood walking stick engraved "S.V.," given to an American diplomat by Sténio Vincent, President of the Republic of Haiti from 1930 to 1941. (3) Mahogany walking stick with a sterling silver cap, given as a college prize and engraved on the cap: "Yale Sophomore German, Jan. 20th, 1908." (4) Silver-topped ebony evening stick, once carried by violinist Fritz Kreisler. The head has English hallmarks and is engraved F.K. (5) New York Governor Alfred E. Smith's ebony-handled umbrella with a triple gold ring engraved AES. Canes of this general variety and with the sort of associations listed above are generally on the market at under $100 apiece. *James F. Carr, New York*

relics. Just as the collecting of physical remains. had its foundations in the Christian religious cult, the collecting of clothing and other textiles has its origin in the cloths associated with Christ and His saints. As mentioned earlier, half the churches of medieval Christendom had items from the wardrobe of the Virgin Mary. A number of reliquaries of the Middle Ages contained fragments of the so-called "apron of Christ," a garment He is said to have worn—

with surprising fastidiousness—when He washed the feet of the poor. As late as 1368 Pope Urban V bestowed upon the Holy Roman Emperor Charles IV, as a notable gift, a piece of plain silk said to be from the robe of Saint John the Evangelist.

Handkerchiefs are especially attractive articles of antique haberdashery for collectors, easy to display and pretty, since they nearly always have lace or embroidery. A linen handkerchief of Napoleon's embroidered with the imperial crown and his initial, used by him at Saint Helena and with traces of blood, was sold in Paris in 1970 for $1,100. Sashes, gloves, and stockings are equally popular.

Umbrellas have a long association with high rank in both the Eastern and Western worlds. They began as a sort of canopy carried by attendants and have always had an implication of dignity. The Duke of Wellington's umbrella was sold early in this century for eight guineas (about $300), as was the pink sunshade Queen Victoria used as a child. The superb handles made by Carl Fabergé's firm for the umbrellas of royalty have been avidly collected.

Hats and shoes have a peculiar fascination for collectors; these articles of clothing are by far the most widely collected apparel. Headgear has its remote ancestor—so far as relics go—in one of Christianity's holy relics, the Crown of Thorns, which for centuries was probably second only to the True Cross as an object of veneration. Hats, crowns, caps, bonnets—any head covering is respected and collected. During the nineteenth century an African chief of the Gold Coast visited England, and when asked by British officials what he wanted as a souvenir, begged for one of Queen Victoria's famous widow's caps to use as a crown. The Queen, who (contrary to legend) was not without a sense of humor, sent him one, and he was photographed happily wearing the cap—over which he had placed a top hat!

In more recent times, Sir Winston Churchill was much interested in hats and had a collection of them that is kept today in his country home, Chartwell, in Kent. The late Sir Edward Hallstrom of Sydney, Australia, collected hats worn by famous men. At the auction of his collection in Sydney in 1972, a hat was sold that had been worn by Charlie Chaplin in his early movies (for $225), a hat once worn by President Dwight Eisenhower (also sold for $225), and a white Stetson presented to Sir Winston Churchill by the people of Calgary, Alberta ($312).

As for shoes, the most expensive ever to be sold were Judy Garland's already-mentioned red slippers from *The Wizard of Oz* at $15,000, but many others have been on the market: the comfortable beaded moccasins embroidered with his initials that Lincoln wore were sold at auction in 1952 for $275. And the American Ballet Theatre, among many other dance companies, has been selling toe slippers, worn by and also autographed by famous dancers, to raise funds for their organizations.

Textiles with religious associations include "a piece of the tablecloth of Christ" housed in a reliquary made in Nuremberg in 1518 and now in the Kunsthistorisches Museum, Vienna. The reliquary is a small box of gilded silver studded with precious stones and engraved on the back with a picture of the Last Supper, at which the tablecloth is thought to have been used. "But," as the current catalogue of the museum coolly remarks, "the embroidery is from the thirteenth century at the earliest."

Among textiles other than clothing, flags and banners have become especially dear to relic collectors. In 1971, the Musée de l'Armée in Paris paid no less than $8,000 for an eighteenth century silk standard, embroidered in gold and silver, of the "Compagnie des Gendarmes de la Garde Ordinaire du Roi" (the Royal Guard), from the estate of a great-great-grandson of King Louis Philippe.

The Holy Lance of the Passion can be considered the original metal relic, and secular relics of various metals have followed it in great profusion. Most of these have been objects that are utilitarian in some way: swords, guns, and other weapons, pens, and various implements. Weapons are especially desirable and, because they are usually metal, tend to be well preserved. The sword carried by Lord Cardigan during the ill-judged but celebrated "Charge of the Light Brigade" at Balaclava during the Crimean War was sold in the late nineteenth century for eight and a half guineas (about $350 today), as was the Sudanese spear that killed General "Chinese" Gordon at the siege of Khartoum in 1885 (£30, about $1,200). In armor museums like the Tower of London, there are innumerable suits of armor and other equipment with royal associations, including at the Tower the small armor made for King Charles I when he was a child. At the General George C. Marshall Research Foundation in Lexington, Virginia, there is a sword of Benito Mussolini's so prized by the dictator that he had duplicates made to give to Hitler and Goering. It was captured during the Second World War and given to General Marshall. Also preserved there is the sword presented to Marshall on Graduation Day, 1901, at Virginia Military Institute, when he was first elected captain by Company "A" Corps of

Cadets. The late Sir Winston Churchill's pistol, a .30 Mauser semiautomatic, twelve inches long and engraved "W.L.S. Churchill," the initials standing for Winston Leonard Spencer (Leonard after his American grandfather), was sold at auction in 1971 for $9,800, an auction record for a modern pistol.

Royal armor, when it appears for sale, is easily recognizable by its engraved coats of arms and royal ciphers. Weapons, too, often are marked in the same way and have a considerable written history; they have interested collectors for generations. The Winston Churchill pistol was accompanied by a letter from the firm of Holland, the London gunmakers, detailing its history, and in one of his volumes of recollections, *My Early Life,* Churchill made several references to the pistol. In 1972 Sotheby's sold a pair of pistols said to have belonged to Napoleon, captured from his baggage during the retreat from Moscow. Made by Nicholas Noël Boutet, the foremost gunsmith of the early nineteenth century, they were inlaid with the arms of the Grand Cross of the Légion d'Honneur and other insignia of the Empire.

Historic swords are often marked with lengthy inscriptions, because they afford a large flat surface on the blade for engraving. A magnificently decorated sword presented by the Lloyds insurance firm to a hero of the Battle of Trafalgar was inscribed in gilt on the blade:

From the Patriotic Fund at Lloyds to Robert Redmill Esqr. Capt. of H.M.S. Polyphemus for his meritorious services in contributing to the signal victory obtained over the combined fleets of France and Spain off Cape Trafalgar on the 21st of October 1805.

(This sold in 1966 for $3,000.) Innumerable swords formerly belonging to historic personages have been preserved in museums and private collections. Even Benjamin Franklin, most peaceable of men, owned a sword that he wore—it was obligatory—when he was presented to Louis XVI and Marie Antoinette.

Jewels and jewelry that belonged to famous people are desirable relics. However, historic jewels are prone to metamorphoses. They are recut, changing their weight, and reset, changing their appearance to the point that they are extremely difficult to recognize. Nearly all historic jewels are sold with some sort of dis-

claimer in the catalogue. Recently, an emerald and diamond necklace had the note that most of the emeralds, which were of enormous size, were "thought to have once been in the possession of Tsar Alexander II of Russia." And there was a minor uproar a few years ago when an enormous pearl known as "La Peregrina" ("Traveler"), said to have belonged once to Philip II of Spain, was sold at auction to the actress Elizabeth Taylor, whereupon the exiled Queen Victoria Ena of Spain declared that "La Peregrina" had never left the Spanish royal family and was in her possession.

Rings generally change their form less than historic necklaces, tiaras, and other pieces. Many interesting rings, without especially large stones but with historical connotations, come on the market, and they are the form of jewelry most likely to be within the reach of the average relic collector. A gold ring presented by King Henry VIII in 1540 to the gatekeeper of Windsor Castle was sold in 1970 for $2,000. A ring with an inscription mourning Sir Walter Scott's death in 1832 was sold in 1967 for $50, and a small diamond and emerald ring given by Florence Nightingale in 1904 (at age eighty-four) to her housekeeper as a wedding present sold in 1967 for $250.

Kings and princes have long rewarded courtiers and servants with valuable gifts. In the eighteenth and nineteenth centuries and a considerable part of the twentieth, servants, favorites, diplomats, and military men received gifts in recognition of service. The value of the gift was not only in the hand that bestowed it; many pieces were made of gold and silver and encrusted with diamonds and other gems of value. Presentation pieces were therefore not only symbolic rewards for services rendered; they were actual payments that could be and were turned into cash. When the Duc de Saint-Simon went to Spain as ambassador in 1721 to arrange a double royal marriage, on his departure he was given a miniature portrait of the King of Spain surrounded by jewels. The first thing Saint-Simon did when he got back home was to have the stones valued by the best Parisian jewelers. They were appraised at 80,000 livres (about $20,000 today), "the most expensive present ever given to an ambassador by the King of Spain," Saint-Simon relates complacently in his memoirs. He promptly had the stones removed from the portrait and made up into a decoration for his son. Thousands of similar precious objects,

Desk seals are among the most attractive of personal relics. These two seals belonged to Armand, last Duc de Richelieu, who died at his New York town house in 1952. They bear the arms of his famous family, including those of the seventeenth-century statesman the Cardinal-Duc de Richelieu, an eight-pointed star hung with five crosses. The seal on the left, about two and one-half inches long, is of engraved smoky quartz. The other seal is made of brass with a wooden handle. Seals made of semiprecious stones, gold or silver, or a substance like quartz and identifiable by coats of arms or ciphers, sell for $350 upwards, but seals made of other metals, such as brass, and also identifiable, are often priced at around $100. *James F. Carr, New York*

among the finest workmanship of the eighteenth century, were handed out by royalty, especially in the period from 1750 to 1800. They are preserved in large numbers in museums and private collections today. Examples are often offered for sale on the international art market.

A *carnet de bal* is a dance program in a small case about 2½ x 4 inches; it contains a small ivory tablet and a tiny pencil to jot down the names of partners for each dance. The most distinguished craftsmen of the eighteenth century, including artists such as Fragonard, decorated these elegant trifles that were used as favors at parties. The *carnet* was made of gold, copper, bronze, ivory, tortoiseshell, or ebony, often bejeweled, and with a miniature scene painted on ivory on the side. Across the top was the inscription, frequently in diamonds, *souvenir, de l'amitié,* or *de l'amour,* or some other gallant sentiment. They were extremely expensive then and now. Great ladies collected: the Empress Maria Theresa of Austria was said to own more than six hundred. In a later age the greatest American collector, J. P. Morgan, was extremely fond of them; his collection, regarded as the finest in existence, is at the Metropolitan Museum of Art, New York. *Carnets* directly associated with historical personages, above all with Queen Marie Antoinette and her court, are collected as relics.

Presenting gold and silver boxes was not the exclusive privilege of kings and courts. "Freedom boxes" or "Freedom caskets" are elaborate containers, mostly eighteenth and nineteenth century in date, specially designed to hold a document giving the recipient the honorary "freedom" of the city, meaning that he was an honorary member of the corporation that governed the city. The present American equivalent is the "key to the city." Receiving one of these freedoms from an important city was a great honor. The City of London, for example, bestowed its freedom in the nineteenth century on such distinguished persons in various fields as Dr. William Jenner, the Duke of Wellington, William Pitt, Garibaldi, Dr. Livingstone, Ferdinand de Lesseps, and President U. S. Grant. New York City gave its freedom and freedom boxes to George Washington, John Jay, the Marquis de Lafayette, Alexander Hamilton, and other notables of the Revolution. A gold box with the 1686 seal of the city, showing the famous windmill arms and the beaver, given to General von Steuben is at Yale University. Although boxes from the major cities given to people as important as those mentioned here are seldom on the market, quite a number of freedom boxes in silver or Sheffield plate presented by lesser cities to lesser dignitaries do come on the market at reasonable prices; they are very attractive relics.

The nineteenth century was the great age of orders, medals, and decorations. Unless these are unique items, they are not ordinarily considered relics. Unique medals and decorations are those created for one person and given to him alone. Knights of the Garter, England's oldest and highest order of knighthood, wear a "collar" (i.e., a chain around their necks) and an emblem known as "The George," which is a small statue of Saint George slaying the dragon. "The Great George," twice the size of the regular George, was created by Queen Anne for the Duke of Marlborough in 1702. The Duke of Wellington and Sir Winston Churchill were also given "The Great George"

in their time. These are the only three "Great Georges" ever given; all can certainly be considered relics, and all three are preserved in museums.

John Brown, Queen Victoria's famous servant, was the subject of legend even during his lifetime; his closeness to the queen, his notorious rudeness, and his drinking caused an immense amount of gossip. Entire books have been written on their relationship, including such speculations as that they were secretly married, that she was mad and he her keeper (people said she was, after all, George III's granddaughter), that they tippled together, and other such nonsense. In 1872, an Irishman leaped into the queen's carriage while she was out for a drive and demanded that she sign a document freeing all Irish terrorists, holding a pistol to her head while he was talking. John Brown leaped on the Irishman with great bravery and pinned him to the ground. In reward, the queen had a unique decoration struck in gold for him—the Victoria Devoted Service Medal inscribed "To John Brown, Esq. in recognition of his presence of mind and devotion at Buckingham Palace, February 29th, 1872." This unusual item was sold at auction with two other routine medals of Brown's in 1964 for $1,550.

Elaborate cigar and cigarette cases with the royal arms engraved or mounted were bestowed by various kings. Edward VII of England distributed them among friends and servants, and he and his queen, the beautiful Alexandria, also bestowed their portraits in diamond-set brooches. Pairs of these are sometimes sold at around £1,000 ($2,500). Queen Victoria ordered some ingenious souvenirs for her ladies—gold and drop-pearl pendants, for example, containing (as might be expected) a tiny photograph of Prince Albert and inscribed: "In remembrance of the best and greatest of Princes, from his broken-hearted widow Victoria R. Dec. 1861." The Russian Imperial family, with the curious mixture of sophistication and barbaric splendor that marked their taste, rewarded favored retainers with cigarette cases, picture frames, and desk sets in the rarest materials and of almost incredible luxury from the workshop of Carl Fabergé. Examples of all these types of royal presentation objects are frequently on the art market. Although the items of eighteenth century workmanship and the Fabergé pieces command high prices, royal presentation items in

Relics of silver and gold are often easily identifiable, since the custom of marking such objects with names, initials, or coats of arms goes back for centuries. This superb George I beverage urn, twenty-eight inches high, was made in London in 1720 by Thomas Farrer. It carries the arms of Archibald, first Earl of Rosebery. The family name of the Scottish Earls of Rosebery is Primrose, and their shield shows three roses. The first earl was one of the commissioners for the Act of Union of England and Scotland in 1707. *The Folger's Coffee Collection of Antique English Silver. By courtesy of The Procter and Gamble Company*

jewelry, on the other hand, ordinarily indicate positively that these items are *not* royal possessions but are objects that sovereigns, princes, or other heads of state have given away—presentation pieces. Frederick the Great of Prussia, for example, was a keen collector of snuffboxes, of which he owned about fifteen hundred (his pockets were lined with chamois leather so that the boxes would not get scratched). Among these are probably few if any bearing his own portrait; those set with his portrait encircled with diamonds he gave away. The same is true today of the presentation items given by various presidents to White House visitors which are marked with the seal of the United States or that of the president. These include pens, ashtrays, and cigarette boxes.

Silver marked with royal or presidential arms has often been used by the head of state or his family. (The exception to this rule is ambassadorial silver of the nineteenth and earlier centuries, which is known in some periods to have carried the royal arms.) Royal silver has survived into the present era in very large quantities. The relic collector seldom can know exactly which objects were directly associated with the various heads of state even when they are emblazoned, but it is generally assumed that personal articles in silver such as hairbrushes, powder boxes, perfume bottles, items for the desk, chamber pots, and so on with royal arms, initials, and ciphers were actually used by the monarch or president and may be considered his personal relics.

Furniture with historic associations is, like jewelry, silver, and porcelain objects, usually valuable apart from its worth as a relic, and when pieces of furniture are sold or displayed with a mention of a famous former owner, it is

less precious materials are to be found by the modest collector.

All these royal presentation items have marks of various kinds in addition to their hallmarks. The collector is forewarned that some marks of ownership or provenance are not what they seem. Particularly misleading are items connected with royalty. Royal coats of arms, crests, mottoes, and other heraldic devices, initials and ciphers on silver, porcelain, furniture, and other objects that are basically utilitarian—no matter how expensive the materials—generally indicate that the object was owned and used by royal personages themselves. Portrait miniatures of royalty, views of royal palaces, fêtes, and triumphs found on orders, medals, snuffboxes and other boxes, cigarette cases, picture frames, rings and other

Tazzas were a kind of salver introduced into England in the seventeenth century to be "used in giving beer or other liquid thing to save the carpet or cloathes from drops" (i.e. foam). This is one of a pair of George III silver tazzas made in London in 1804 by Digby Scott and Benjamin Smith. The diameter is twelve and a half inches. The arms are those of the Baron Scarsdale, the family of the Marquis Curzon of Kedleston, Viceroy of India from 1899 to 1905. *The Folger's Coffee Collection of Antique English Silver. By courtesy of The Procter and Gamble Company*

sometimes difficult to tell where the emphasis is falling—on the previous ownership, the craftsmanship, or the intrinsic value. Most of the furniture mentioned in this book will be that clearly collected for its relic value.

The relaxation of great men has produced relics that are much in demand, usually games equipment. Lord Nelson's ivory cribbage board has been sold. The London Museum has a chess set that King James II gave to his admiralty secretary, Samuel Pepys. The Drexel Institute in Philadelphia, a rather unlikely place perhaps, has a chess table (that is, a table with a chessboard inlaid on the top) said to have belonged to Napoleon, who played the game at Saint Helena (and, according to his unwilling and irritated opponents, cheated out-

rageously). Sets used by King George III of England, George Washington, Benjamin Franklin, Robert E. Lee, and others have survived.

Numerous pipes smoked by celebrated men have been treasured. One of the most interesting ever sold was Sir Walter Raleigh's, which reached the salesroom in 1912. It was of natural Virginia myrtle wood, crudely carved by the Indians with a dog's head and Indian faces. The mouth of the forked stem was a whistle used by Sir Walter to summon his servants. According to tradition, this was the pipe he smoked during his captivity in the Tower of London, where he awaited the execution with which England rewarded one of its greatest explorers. The pipe sold for seventy-five guineas (about $3,000).

Comestibles have been preserved as relics. Sir Walter Scott was presented with a petrified oatcake found in the pocket of a Highlander killed on the battlefield of Culloden; he kept it among his military relics at Abbotsford. A dealer in the United States recently offered for sale at $64.50 "a genuine piece of Civil War hardtack, a good, large 2½ x 3 inch piece, very hardened," described further as "the classic type." Hardtack is a kind of biscuit carried as a sort of instant food by soldiers and sailors. This piece was offered with a letter attesting that a soldier had sent it home to his mother from a camp in Maryland. At the Grover Cleveland Birthplace in Caldwell, New Jersey —his father's Presbyterian parsonage at the time the future president was born—there is a

portion of the wedding cake served when Cleveland married Frances Folsom in the White House, 2 June 1886. A minor event of the 1901 auction season was the appearance for the first time of a piece of Queen Victoria's wedding cake—presumably the auctioneers had been waiting for her death, which occurred that year. The cake, then sixty-one years old, sold for the high price of ten guineas (about $400). In 1974, a piece was sold for $154.

At another sale the sandwich box (empty) that the English artist John Constable carried with him on his painting expeditions was sold for but ten shillings.

Daguerreotypes, ambrotypes (a negative on glass), and tintypes (a modification of the

Personal relics include furniture with associations. This desk is the famous one at which Elizabeth Barrett wrote in her home at 50 Wimpole Street; the olive wood chair was used by the Brownings in their apartment in the Casa Guidi in Florence, as was the Dresden china inkstand; across the book lies Mrs. Browning's cross. *Armstrong Browning Library, Baylor University*

Daguerreotypes, because each is unique, are considered relics. All these daguerreotypes show members of the Kip family, long associated with New York City, where the first Kip settled prior to 1643. A tailor by trade, he established one of the most prominent families of the city; the name is still preserved in Kip's Bay on the East River. Four of these daguerreotypes have been tinted by hand, including touches of gold on watches and chains and other jewelry. Alexander Beckers, who made the picture of Mrs. Garrett Kip in her coffin, was a notable early New York daguerreotypist. Thousands of daguerreotypes were made in the 1850s and early '60s, and they are not rare today. Many, perhaps the majority, of the subjects can no longer be identified, however, which seriously decreases their value to relic collectors. Daguerreotypes of identifiable persons such as these members of the Kip family sell for $50 or more; those of unidentified subjects, considerably less.

ambrotype but on black japanned iron) are the only forms of photography that can be considered relics. Each is a unique object, whereas photographs on paper are liable to infinite multiplication. These three forms are usually found with a protective glass covering and encased with a velvet lining between two book-style covers. The covers or cases were made from a variety of materials in the middle of the nineteenth century when these forms of photography were popular. They were often molded from gutta percha (an early form of plastic) and occasionally have elaborate pictorial designs. Enormous numbers of these portraits exist today, but identification even of famous people is difficult. Although many sell for quite modest prices, unquestioned daguerreotypes of really noted people can bring very high prices. In 1972, a daguerreotype of Henry D. Thoreau sold for $2,000, then by far the world record; the following year an extremely fine daguerreotype of Edgar Allan Poe known to have been taken in 1848 sold for the amazing sum of $9,250.

Wood and objects made from it have a central place in any discussion of relics and relic collecting. "Relic wood" is the recognized term for timber deriving from some famous tree or other plant, building, or wooden object that has been cut up and made or carved into a souvenir. Relic wood is liable to almost indefinite subdivision. No one who reads the history of wood relics should ever doubt the miracle of the loaves and the fishes. Almost every wooden relic has multiplied miraculously by splintering.

For instance, through all its vicissitudes, bits and pieces of the True Cross down to the size of mere splinters were being sawed off and distributed by its various guardians to churches and important people. Gradually, most of the places of pilgrimage in the Christian world and most of the royal and noble families of Europe owned fragments of the Cross, causing the irreverent to snicker that if all the splinters were put together they would add up to more than one cross. A reliquary with a particle of the Cross—and there are hundreds in existence now—even had a special name: a *pacificale*. The Imperial Cross of the Holy Roman Empire, made about 1024 and still in existence, had particles of the True Cross set in its shaft. No other religious relic has so captured the imagination, and none other has aroused such competition among collectors. The most unexpected people have desired splinters; even Madame de Pompadour, that Voltairean and eminently commonsensical lady, asked her friend the Duc de Choiseul to obtain for her a piece of the True Cross, which she had set in a crystal heart with rose diamonds.

The True Cross is not the only wooden relic associated with Christ. Among the powerful relics given by Pope Urban V to the Holy Roman Emperor Charles IV in 1368 was a piece of wood from "The Cradle of Christ." The emperor had it encased in a reliquary (still in existence) with a small window through which one can see a silhouette of the cradle above the piece of wood.

Desks, chairs, and other furniture, snuff-boxes, and canes are among the wooden objects associated with notable people that have been collected. In the nineteenth century when many men habitually carried canes or walking sticks and almost any man might own half a dozen, they were much-sought mementos. After the assassination of Abraham Lincoln, Mrs. Lincoln seems to have had an inexhaustible supply of her husband's canes for parceling out to his admirers. She even owned canes of other presidents, and contributed one of General Andrew Jackson's for sale at a charity fête.

Relics of famous places are often of wood. When the Pennsylvania Railroad sold some of its possessions at auction in 1972, a piece of wood from the Conemaugh, Pennsylvania, railroad viaduct was sold. This viaduct collapsed in 1889 during the Johnstown Flood, in which at least 2,000 people were killed.

Relic wood has been carved or turned or joined on the same principle as the splintering of the True Cross. A celebrated example is the Mulberry Tree of Stratford-upon-Avon supposedly planted by Shakespeare in his backyard in 1609, wood from which has been carved into innumerable objects (see chapter 7).

Some relics of this kind are both souvenir and symbol. The Library of Congress preserves a walking stick given by the naturalist John Burroughs to his friend Walt Whitman, which was carved from the root of the calamus plant, a reference to Whitman's "Calamus" cycle of poems.

A nineteenth century English poet named Charles Stuart Calverley wrote—probably with his tongue in his cheek—in a poem entitled "Precious Stones":

> *A clod—a piece of orange peel—*
> *An end of a cigar—*
> *Once trod on by a Princely heel*
> *How beautiful they are:*

Some relic collectors have taken those lines only too literally. Others have collected relics that do not fall even into the fairly broad categories listed above. For example, at Buckland Abbey in Devon, England, Sir Francis Drake's old home, is shown the large side drum (twenty-one inches high and two feet in diameter) that accompanied him on his circumnavigation of the globe in 1577—80 and was used to "instil fear into the enemy" when his ship attacked the Spanish. It is "the earliest English drum in existence."

Also in the class of interesting but unclassifiable relics is a piece of the pavement of the balcony of the old Federal Hall in New York, on which Washington stood when he was inaugurated president, 30 April 1789. This is in the possession of the Museum of the City of New York.

At the David Livingstone Memorial at his birthplace, Blantyre, Lanarkshire, Scotland, can be seen the plaster cast of Livingstone's left armbone, which was crushed by a lion in the bush country of Africa. And at the American Museum of Immigration, opened at the Statue of Liberty in New York Harbor in 1972, is displayed a coat rack used by the bureaucrats at Ellis Island when it was the port of entry for immigrants, and also a desk used by the eye doctors who inspected the newcomers.

In 1973, Sotheby's auction gallery in London sold a spade "in new condition" with which George Bernard Shaw planted a mulberry tree in the public garden at Great Malvern, Worcestershire, on his eightieth birthday in 1936. It had a silver label describing the occasion.

Walnuts from the trees said to have been planted at Mount Vernon by George Washington have been treasured, and during the 1932 bicentennial of his birth, the Boy Scouts of America gathered the nuts and distributed them all over the country for planting.

The true relic hunter is unfazed by cost, size, difficulty of transport, or hazards of preservation if he is determined to have a particular souvenir. A collector recently paid $1,200 for an iron cannon barrel large enough for a twenty-four-pound ball from H.M.S. *Foudroyant*. This inconvenient relic was a souvenir of the immortal Lord Nelson, who used the *Foudroyant* as his Mediterranean flagship. An even more inaccessible relic was found in Rowan Oak, the home of the late novelist William Faulkner, in Oxford, Mississippi. The study wall there had written on it manuscript chapter outlines of a Faulkner novel, impossible to remove. The entire house was therefore purchased in 1973 by the University of Mississippi for $175,000, and turned into part of a university "cultural center."

The palm for being the largest, heaviest, and most expensive relic ever sold certainly goes to London Bridge, which was sold in 1968 for $2,460,000 and moved, all 13,000 tons of it, from London to Arizona. It is said that the removal cost another $1,600,000. Fortunately for the purchaser, the McCullock Oil Corporation, the bridge was 146 years old; otherwise it would have been dutiable under United States Customs on entering the country. It was entered as an "antique," being at the time more than a century old. The 26,000,000 pounds of granite, completely reconstructed, are now the chief ornament of a real estate development called "Lake Havasu City" in the arid stretches of the state of Arizona.

ent
3

American Heirlooms

American historical relics begin with the bones of Christopher Columbus. There have been "excavated" or "discovered" at various times over the last hundred years a multitude of supposed "relics" of discoveries preceding Columbus's in the New World. Runic inscriptions purportedly carved by Dark Age Vikings wandering around on the North American continent have been thick on the ground, according to the amateur archaeologists who have located them. The so-called "Kensington Rune Stone," found in Douglas County, Minnesota, in 1898 is one of the best-known examples. This and many other fraudulent remains, although denounced by every reputable authority as hoaxes, have always attracted a following of believers, and numerous are the publications supporting one runic inscription or the other. "Norse halberds" and "Scandinavian battle-axes" aplenty have also been found, and even whole buildings like the Newport, R.I., Stone Tower supposedly built by Norsemen that inspired Henry W. Longfellow and God knows how many other New England poets to burst into verse. But it is with the remains of Christopher Columbus that American relic collecting really begins. The history of these remains is highly controversial.

No authentic possessions of Columbus are known to exist. The whereabouts of his grave has been a topic of dispute among scholars and politicians for generations. Keen patriotic feelings have been aroused; the honor of having

the burial spot of the discoverer of America is a mighty one in the Spanish-speaking lands.

Columbus died at Valladolid in Spain in 1506, and his body was buried there. In 1541, or shortly thereafter, his body, together with that of his son, Diego Columbus, was removed to the island of Santo Domingo, which the admiral had discovered, and buried in its cathedral. That was Diego's wish. An inscription was placed on the vault but did not remain; it is said to have been removed in 1655, when the island was threatened with an English invasion. When the Spanish government had to cede Santo Domingo to the French in 1795, there was an exodus of Spanish officialdom. In their baggage was the body of the admiral, the Spanish naturally not wanting this great relic of Spanish achievement in the New World to fall into the hands of the French. The remains of Columbus were reinterred in the cathedral in Havana, the most important city in the Caribbean Sea that Columbus had made known to the world.

In 1877, while the cathedral at Santo Domingo was being repaired, the engineer in charge, one José María Castillo, found an urn that he declared contained the true remains of Christopher Columbus! They had never left the island of Santo Domingo—it was the ashes of *Diego* Columbus that had been transferred to Havana. International excitement. Sometime later a silver plate was discovered on the bottom of the urn that seemed—there was some

The two crystal lockets containing relics of Christopher Columbus that appeared at auction in 1973 after nearly a century of controversy about their contents. *Sotheby Parke Bernet, New York*

dispute as to exactly what it said—to identify the remains as those of the senior Columbus.

Later, when the Cuban rebellion began to overwhelm the Spanish regime in the late nineteenth century, the Spaniards packed up the body in the Havana Cathedral again and shipped it to the mother country. It was buried —for probably the fourth time—in Seville. At least *a* body was buried. Was it truly the much-traveled body of Columbus, or had there been a mixup? Accidentally or by patriotic design, some said, an anonymous body had been substituted so that the Cubans could keep the remains of the discoverer instead of sending them to Spain. Feelings ran high and a veritable war of pamphlets broke out, each seeking to prove one of three principal theories:

1. Columbus's body was still in Santo Domingo.
2. It was still in Havana.
3. It was truly in Seville.

All three places show the burial spot of the Admiral of the Ocean Sea. There is no modern consensus on this emotional subject, but most students now feel that Columbus is buried in the Santo Domingo Cathedral.

At the time Castillo found the famous urn, he and the local ecclesiastical authorities took from it some of the dust that was all that was left of the great admiral. This dust was divided into at least eight very small portions. Gift portions were given to the City of Genoa, usually accepted as the birthplace of Columbus, the University of Pavia, where he studied, and to the Pope. Castillo kept two portions, which he also divided. He gave bits to friends in New York City: George Stokes and Mrs. Epes Sargent, wife of a noted writer and spiritualist and herself a medium (did they hope to get in touch with Columbus in the beyond?). Mrs. Sargent placed her dust in a crystal locket worn as a necklace. Stokes further divided his portion— the amount was by now the merest pinch—and one fragment was encased in a gold locket. The Sargent and Stokes lockets later came into the possession of John Boyd Thacher, who wrote an immense biography of Christopher Columbus. In 1973, the two lockets were offered for sale by a Thacher descendant. They were valued at $3,000 for the two, but no buyers were found.

On this vexed question Mark Twain had something to say, as he did on so many others. In *Innocents Abroad* he claims that in Genoa he was shown the skull of Christopher Columbus as a young man and the skull of Christopher Columbus as an old man.

For more than a century after Christopher Columbus's voyages, American history affords

Peter Stuyvesant lost his right leg in 1644 in the naval service of the Dutch West India Company. He had an artificial limb made in Holland to replace it. On his good heel he wore this spur of Spanish type of the seventeenth century, which has descended in his family, still New Yorkers. *Hamilton F. Kean. On deposit, Museum of the City of New York*

few relics for the collector. Such objects seldom date from earlier than the mid-seventeenth century; the age of the discoveries left its traces on maps and in books rather than on the landscape. One of the very few artifacts of the period is preserved in New York City—in two places. The charred remains of Manhattan's earliest recorded fire are those of the Dutch Captain Adriaen Block's ship, which burned on the island in 1613. They were turned up in 1916, by workmen excavating under the street surface at the intersection of Dey and Greenwich streets, where a subway extension was being laid. When the ship, which was called *The Tiger,* burned, Greenwich Street was the west shoreline of Manhattan. Some of the timbers found are now in the Museum of the City of New York. The remainder of the oak prow, keel, and frame still repose about twenty feet down at Dey and Greenwich, and it is unlikely they will ever be exhumed since the World Trade Center buildings have been erected on top of them.

Despite plentiful legends and tales told in the family circle about objects handed down from the days of the *Mayflower,* there are few artifacts of the Pilgrim era in New England that can be specifically associated with known persons. There is, for example, only one known portrait of a *Mayflower* Pilgrim; in Pilgrim Hall, Plymouth, is a portrait of Edward Winslow, governor of Plymouth Colony, believed to have been painted in London in 1651. A little furniture of the period remains and is believed to be authentically Pilgrim. The wickerwork cradle preserved in Pilgrim Hall was probably brought on the *Mayflower* by William White, in preparation for the birth of his son Peregrine, which occurred aboard the ship while it was anchored in Plymouth harbor in 1620. And chairs believed to have belonged to Elder William Brewster and Governor John Carver have given their names to the "Brewster" and "Carver" types of chair familiar to collectors of early American furniture.

In the colonial history of America, items made from relic wood abound, however. Numbers of boxes, canes, and even pieces of furniture have been made from trees famous in American history. Wood from the tree under which William Penn made his treaty to buy land from the Delaware Indians on 27 October 1682 has been employed in an array of objects, many of which are held by museums in Pennsylvania, but others are occasionally found—identified —on the market.

Several wood relics derive from a tree that is perhaps the most famous in New York City's history. In 1647, Peter Stuyvesant imported a pear tree from his native Holland and had it planted on his estate in the Bouwerie, at the present-day northeast corner of Third Avenue and Thirteenth Street. The tree survived not only the director-general but his estate, and became an object of veneration for New Yorkers of the eighteenth and nineteenth centuries as a living relic of Dutch rule. The diarist Philip Hone wrote sentimentally of the pear tree and reverently preserved one of its rather sparse blossoms under glass. The tree perished in 1867, victim of a traffic accident when two wagons collided at the corner and laid it low. It was presumably at that time that pieces of its wood were used in various ways. At the Museum of the City of New York, for example, is a land grant from Peter Stuyvesant that has been framed in the wood, and some pieces are preserved at the New York high school that bears Stuyvesant's name. (An effort in the 1950s to plant another pear tree on the historic spot failed when the Parks Department assured the antiquarians that a pear tree could no longer survive in Manhattan's air.)

It is the years of the American Revolution that are rich in relics. Most of the colonists who were in rebellion were fully cognizant of the historical importance of their actions—the Declaration of Independence shows that clearly —and they were great keepers of mementos. But Herman Melville's grandfather must have been the only member of the "Boston Tea Party" who preserved until the end of his long life (he did not die until 1832) a bottle containing tea leaves from that celebrated excursion. He was also said to be the last American to wear the cocked hat that had been universal among well-to-do colonials of the eighteenth century.

The variety of relics of the American Revolution is endless, including arms said to have been carried by various heroes, bits and pieces of other military equipment found on battlefields, parts of uniforms (complete uniforms are extremely rare, as are other textile items, such as flags), and stones or wood from historic forts. Much fine silver and furniture was produced in this period of American history. Although such pieces may have had notable

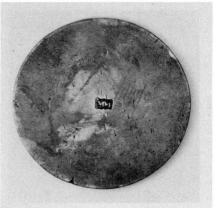

The notarial seal of Richard Harison, who held the office of Recorder of the City of New York at the turn of the nineteenth century. Between 1686 and 1831, the recorder was second only to the mayor in the government of the city. The seal bears Harison's personal coat of arms. The reverse shows one of the marks "MM" used by Myer Myers, who was president of the Silversmiths' Society in 1746 and a leader in Jewish affairs in the City. *New-York Historical Society*

owners, their appearance on the market at high prices is primarily because of their rarity and value as antiques.

It would be difficult to choose the most celebrated relic of the Revolutionary years, but the top candidate is probably the Liberty Bell. The bell that came to be called by that name was cast in 1751 in England for the State House in Philadelphia (now Independence Hall) long before the Revolution was in men's minds. Its celebrated crack developed shortly after its arrival in the colonies. That was repaired and the bell was occasionally rung, but the mending was never really successful. The last time it tolled was to mark Washington's birthday in 1846. By then the crack was so wide that the bell could not sound again without the distinct possibility of its disintegrating altogether.

About 1840, the bell began to be used as a symbol by the abolitionists in their antislavery campaigns because of its apt inscription, "Proclaim liberty throughout all the land, unto all the inhabitants thereof," although the inscription had been written originally in an entirely different context. The bell became known as the "Liberty Bell' about that same time, when the Philadelphia novelist George Lippard wrote a story in 1847 about a (fictional) old bell-ringer who supposedly rang the bell on the Fourth of July 1776 to hail the Declaration of Independence. Since then its fame has been secure. It is little known today that the Liberty Bell once traveled great distances in the United States by train. Between 1885 and 1915, it was often sent on tour, and wherever in the country it stopped, it was greeted by droves of visitors. Travel, however, weakened the bell along the crack, and by the time of the First World War it was decided that its touring days were over. The bell has since remained in Philadelphia, where it is illuminated each night. Over a million people come to visit it each year.

The Liberty Bell is very likely the most reproduced of all American relics. For more than a century it has been reproduced in miniature in metal, glass, plaster, and other materials, and in recent years has even been reproduced full-size by an English foundry for sale to institutions. One of the most popular forms of miniature reproduction has been "Liberty Bell banks," which are usually cast-iron still banks. Although the connection between the Liberty Bell and money remains obscure, there is no question that manufacturers have found reproducing it in the form of banks highly profitable because, after a century, they are still being made. Nineteenth and early twentieth century metal or glass Liberty Bell banks sell currently for around $25 to $35. They are far from rare. The bell in the form of a paperweight has also been endlessly reproduced; examples sell today for about the same figure as the still banks.

Relic wood of the Revolutionary era has been widely used and the objects made from it often sold to raise funds for the restoration of important sites and for similar causes. Pieces of wood from the historic North Bridge at Concord, Massachusetts, where "the shot heard round the world" was fired in 1775, have been fashioned into canes with a small inserted plaque giving their provenance. Such canes—and those from many other Revolutionary locales—are currently selling at around $75 to $100.

Americans have always enjoyed commemo-

Annie Oakley, the sure-shot, appeared between 1885 and 1902 in Buffalo Bill's touring "Wild West Show," along with Indian scouts, cowboys, sheriffs, and Sitting Bull. She gave this watch to Buffalo Bill (William F. Cody) during their triumphal appearance in London in 1889. London was but one stop on what has been called "the most successful European tour ever made by any American company." At one performance the Prince of Wales, later Edward VII, rode shotgun as Cody drove during the staged Indian attack on the stagecoach that was the high point of the performance. *Sotheby Parke Bernet, Los Angeles*

rating their Revolution and its heroes, and various anniversaries and centennials have inspired a mass of patriotic objects that are very widely collected. Commemorations began early in the history of the republic, and much of this material is now well over a century old. In 1856, for example, Boston marked the unveiling of a statue by Richard Greenough of Benjamin Franklin, who had been born in Boston and made it his home until he was seventeen. Among other events was a parade five miles long with floats made and run by the apprentices to various trades, apprentices regarding "Poor Richard" as their patron saint. Many of the floats had shops in active operation. The bakers had an oven and threw hot cakes and bread to the crowd. The printer's car had a press and threw out facsimiles of the first issue of the Boston *Courant* on which Franklin had worked. There was an electric machine to give volunteers a light shock, and thousands of kites were distributed to the crowds. Events such as this were recorded in many commemorative items including programs, china, small boxes, buttons, and in this case the kites and the facsimiles. All these are collector's items today.

Interest in the history of the American West is perennial, and Western Americana affords opportunities for the collector of relics, souvenirs, and mementos at almost every level of price. The common impression of a thinly settled country linked until recent times only by horse-drawn traffic and long-distance railroads is correct. It does not follow, however, that artifacts of the frontier are especially rare. Genuine remains of the early life of the Plains and Rockies are not difficult to find, and the demand by collectors for those items is being met continually by new searches.

For many years—and increasingly today—a prime source for Western Americana has been the western "ghost town." Raiding ghost towns for the household and business effects left behind in them has become a sport, especially in California, where an unusually large number of such towns exists. Some of these once had considerable population and therefore plenty of appurtenances. The dry climate throughout the American West has been favorable to preservation. In New Mexico, for example, a century-old abandoned coal-mining town had until recently over one hundred buildings standing, many of them furnished. The raiders like to call themselves "pot hunters," and regard their

scavenging as a wholesome outdoor activity. In fact, since most ghost towns have an owner—federal or state agencies, ranchers, mining companies, railroads—removing objects from them is theft. In addition, souvenir hunters are guilty of much vandalism and have wantonly destroyed many historic sites throughout the West. For years the isolation of most of the towns acted as their best protection, a sort of first line of defense against "pot hunters," as it were, but the "dune buggy" and "snowmobile" have unfortunately opened up new areas to the despoilers. According to a 1973 report in *The Wall Street Journal,* even cemeteries have been looted—for tombstones and metal coffin fixtures.

Western Americana collectors seek such artifacts as old whiskey bottles, apothecary jars, musical instruments, moustache cups and other china, billiard tables, faro tables, and other gambling equipment—any of the nineteenth century everyday objects to be found in ghost towns, down to the porcelain doorknobs.

The western states produced incalculable wealth, especially from railroads and mining, and some of the surviving relics are far from being old whiskey bottles. Decorative and commemorative items in solid silver or gold are particularly plentiful in western collecting. John Mackay, a Dublin-born immigrant who discovered the "Big Bonanza" mine in Nevada, used a small portion of the wealth it produced to commission Tiffany & Co. of New York to make a silver table service for him and his family, supplying them with 14,719 ounces of Nevada silver as raw material. Tiffany employed, it is said, two hundred silversmiths on the job. The result was a Victorian silver service of extraordinary weight—there were 250 ounces of silver in a pair of candelabra—and alive with American and Irish motifs, including the shamrock. It was exhibited at the Paris Exhibition of 1878. The service remains in the hands of Mackay's descendants except for a selection of pieces they gave to the University of Nevada in 1959.

Few collectors, of course, would want an entire service like this even if it were available, but single pieces of Western Americana in silver and gold, trophies, presentation items, inlaid guns, and even poker chips in precious metals are ideal for the collector interested in the West.

The bloodier episodes of western history exert a notable fascination on a large number of collectors. Guns of all kinds are therefore

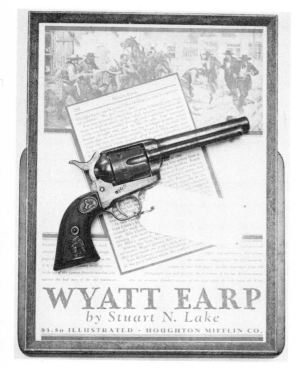

WYATT EARP
by Stuart N. Lake
$3.50 ILLUSTRATED · HOUGHTON MIFFLIN CO.

A western Americana relic with a famous gun-fighting history is this .45 Colt S. A. revolver made in 1881, the handgun carried by Marshal Wyatt Earp in his pursuit of the outlaw "Curly Bill," which has been the source of so many Westerns. *Sotheby Parke Bernet, Los Angeles*

very much in demand and, indeed, are at the head of all western memorabilia. Many examples definitely qualify as relics from their ownership by the famous—usually, in Western history, the infamous—or their part in a well-known encounter in its history. There has been a market in such guns for many years, but they have only recently arrived in the important salesrooms. The Los Angeles division of the international auction house Sotheby Parke Bernet held a landmark sale in this field in 1973. The high point was the Wyatt Earp gun, illustrated here, but there were many other guns with picturesque stories attached, including a second gun that once belonged to Earp. This was described as a "Stevens 10 gauge D. B. shotgun used by Wyatt Earp to kill Curly Bill Brocius and by Heck Thomas to kill Bill Doolin," and was sold along with the note calling it the "one and only used in the killing of

stage robber." Earp and Thomas were United States marshals, the others outlaws. The note refers to the long-wished-for demise of Doolin, whose gang had terrorized western roads for years. The shotgun fetched the very high price of $10,000.

Not all the historic guns sold at auction are at such a rarefied level of price. A pair of Smith and Wesson revolvers used by a performer called "Two Gun Nan" in a trick shooting act were sold in 1973 for a much more moderate $200.

The popularity of western arms is so great that series of modern reproductions of handguns have been issued by important manufacturers for the collector trade. Colt has produced revolvers in series with names like "Pawnee Trail," "Frontier Scout," "Fort Riley," "Colorado Gold Rush," "Lawman" (with guns named for Bat Masterson, Pat Garrett, and other notable fighters), "Nebraska Centennial," and so on. Winchester has also issued rifles in series—"Canadian Centennial," "Theodore Roosevelt," "Buffalo Bill," "Montana Territorial Centennial" (1964), and others. All these guns have either a silver plate set in the butt identifying the commemoration or a barrel inscribed with the same information. They are of course modern commemorative items and not relics.

Not all the relics of western gunslingers are firearms. A pair of silver-decorated spurs was accompanied by an affidavit stating that they were taken from Emmett Dalton when he stood trial for armed robbery about 1910. Dalton said at that time that he had won the spurs from Billy the Kid (William H. Bonney) and that the Kid had had the spurs made to order in New Mexico at a cost of $25. At a sale in 1973 they brought $525.

A rare memento of the rambunctious days of early Arizona that appeared on the market was a tooled leather belt with an engraved silver buckle, a presentation to "Buckskin Frank" Leslie on the first day of the year 1881. Buckskin was a bartender at the Crystal Palace in Tombstone and a friend of Wyatt Earp. He, according to documentation sold with the belt, "killed a number of people and served the local law both officially and unofficially." This unusual piece sold for $2,500.

Wells Fargo, a name practically synonymous with the trans-Mississippi West, was originally a money and transport joint-stock enterprise organized on 18 March 1852 as an express and banking business to serve California, then at the height of its gold rush prosperity. The Wells Fargo Company has issued equipment and presentation items since its founding that are considered relics by collectors of Western Americana. An increasing band of enthusiasts is working on collections of Wells Fargo material, and large groups of this material have begun to appear in the important salesrooms.

Drivers and shotgun riders on the Concord stagecoaches run by Wells Fargo carried—out of dire necessity—double-barreled shotguns and often a "Wells Fargo Colt" pocket pistol as well. More interesting relics are the presentation pieces that Wells Fargo gave to employees and officers of the law who fought off or captured bandits. These were not only of handsome craftsmanship, but of considerable monetary value. One watch, now in the Wells Fargo Bank History Room in San Francisco, is encased in two pounds of Nevada silver. Rifles such as that shown here, engraved with the scene of the exploit for which the presentation was made, a miniature silver treasure box given to an employee of the company, service pins also given for employee anniversaries, the commemorative medal issued to each employee on the company's fiftieth anniversary in 1902, all are prime pieces for Western Americana collectors. Many are extremely valuable: at an auction a Wells Fargo ironbound wooden stagecoach treasure box with the original lock and key, made sometime between 1870 and 1880, sold for $1,100. It is not difficult to imagine what a unique gold snuffbox made by Tiffany for honoring the president of Wells Fargo in 1864 might bring.

Among the less expensive Wells Fargo relics are the following, along with some recent (1973) prices. All these are marked with the name of the company or with the initials "W.F. & Co."

- Signs: $150 to $200, more for those in fine condition
- Smith and Wesson or Colt Revolvers made for Wells Fargo (very much in demand): $500 to $1,000 (or more)
- Mail pouches and bags: $75 to $100 or more depending on condition
- Employee badges: $10 to $25
- Scales for weighing freight: $100 to $200
- Brass or lead sealing devices used to impress

the company's name on steel straps binding packages: $25 to $75
- Brass padlocks on money chests: $50 to $75
- Horse blankets: $100
- Fiftieth anniversary medals, in solid silver inscribed with the name of the employee: $200 to $300. (These were originally presented in leather boxes embossed and gilded, now rare.)

As is the case with most Western Americana, some of the Wells Fargo material sold is downright bizarre. One auction lot was described as

a collection of materials pertaining to the famous attempted robbery of a Wells Fargo mail car by Ben Kilpatrick, the "Tall Texan" of Butch Cassidy's "Wild Bunch" and his partner Ole Beck at Eldridge, Texas, 12 March 1912, and the man who killed them both, Wells Fargo messenger David A. Trousdale.

This lot included many letters, Trousdale's Wells Fargo fiftieth anniversary medal, and "a wooden ice mallet used by Trousdale to crush the skull of Ben Kilpatrick during the aborted robbery."

A strong caveat to collectors of western Americana, including Wells Fargo memorabilia, concerns metal relics of the Old West. In the mid-1960s and possibly earlier, there began to be sold at antique shops, "tourist attractions," and other souvenir outlets a series of metal badges, tokens, watch fobs, tags, and (especially) belt buckles with the names and emblems of famous companies, among them

(*opposite page, top*) Wells Fargo & Co. presented its employees with specially made mementos as a recognition of outstanding service. This Henry rifle with a silver plate was presented to Stephen Venard in 1866. *Wells Fargo Bank History Room, San Francisco*

(*bottom*) The Winchester rifle presented to William F. Cody ("Buffalo Bill") at Fort McPherson in 1870, when Cody was only twenty-four years old and serving as scout for the Fifth U.S. Cavalry. *Sotheby Parke Bernet, Los Angeles*

Along with gold seekers, merchants, sailors, and writers, San Francisco of the gold rush era attracted a criminal element from near and far. The crime and disorder grew so bad and police protection was so inadequate that in 1856 citizens formed a Vigilance Committee to secure some peace. Each member of the Executive Committee wore a medal for purposes of identification, the eye signifying that the vigilantes never slept. This is Vigilante Medal No. 1, belonging to William T. Coleman; it is an important relic of early-day San Francisco. *Robert L. Coleman*

Mayor Robert A. Van Wyck used this silver spade to turn the first earth at the excavation of New York's first subway (then called, rather awkwardly, "The Underground Rapid Transit Road") on 24 March 1900. The first section was built from City Hall Park north to Grand Central Station. *Museum of the City of New York*

Wells Fargo. Typical examples of these "relics" are:

Indian Police badges (often "Apache")
Wells Fargo badges (often "Special Agent")
Brothel tokens (supposedly issued to customers by madams in houses of prostitution, to keep cash out of the "girls' " hands)
Conductor badges from western railroads, notably the Atchison, Topeka, and Santa Fe
Tags supposedly issued by Wells Fargo to mark boxes, including coffins
KKK tokens, supposedly issued to members of the Ku Klux Klan
Belt buckles marked Levi Strauss (the maker of Levis), Wells Fargo, or with the names of western railroads, and even Coca-Cola. Also, Civil War military buckles
Lawmen's badges, a favorite being "U.S. Marshal."

In 1973, stories began to appear in the antique-world press warning collectors against these productions. As yet, not all have been identified. The archives of the companies whose names these objects carry ought to be able to verify their own products and to separate the genuine from the spurious modern reproductions. Unfortunately, the archives of most of the companies have either been lost, destroyed, or shed little light on the history of what was truly routine nineteenth century business equipment. Until all the phony material has been identified, the western Americana collector will do well to exercise extreme caution in buying any such metal memorabilia.

The Wells Fargo Company of the present day decided to make its own authentic brass-buckled leather belt, and began to issue these legitimate reproductions in 1973. The examples are serially numbered. On the reverse of the buckle is the 1973 copyright date, a serial number, and the words "Officially authorized and produced by specific order of Wells Fargo & Company." The leather belt is lettered: "This belt handcrafted exclusively for the official Wells Fargo belt buckle." The belt and buckle were priced at around $15. It is likely that other companies will issue similar items.

American history is rich in memorabilia of famous buildings and events, and the collector should keep an eye out for such relics. A good example is a lock used on the gates of the great

A mayor of the City of New York used to have the privilege of a pair of street lamps placed before his private house. This iron lamp was designed by the architect Stanford White for the house at 9 Lexington Avenue of Abram S. Hewitt, who was mayor in 1887/88. The charming custom of "Mayor's lamps of honor" lasted until 1909, when they were abolished as an economy measure. At that time there were still nine pairs standing in the city. *Museum of the City of New York*

1904 Louisiana Purchase Exposition held in Saint Louis. Some of these brass locks, measuring about three by two inches, with the name of the exposition cast on them were for sale in 1973 for about $25. Relic wood is still being used for the production of souvenirs. When the White House was remodeled during the administration of President Truman, some of the wood removed from the historic building was used to make presentation items. Truman had a gavel made from it, which he presented to Sam Rayburn when Rayburn passed Henry Clay's record and became the Speaker of the House of Representatives with the longest period of service. Donors to the General

Douglas MacArthur Memorial in Norfolk, Virginia, receive a sterling silver plaque mounted on Virginia heart pine wood from Riveredge, the home of Mary Pinkney Hardy, the general's mother.

Other examples of famous American wood include mementos of the following:

- The Charter Oak at Hartford, Connecticut, where the Connecticut Charter of 1662 was concealed from the British governor, Sir Edmund Andros, in 1687. (The tree fell in 1856.)
- The Old Belfry on the Green at Lexington, Massachusetts, from which the bell summoned the minutemen at the beginning of the Revolution. The belfry was separate from the church.
- Holy Trinity Church (known as The Old Swedes Church) in Wilmington, Delaware, built in 1699, the oldest surviving Swedish church in what was New Sweden.

The alert collector of Americana not prepared to spend large sums should look out for relics not connected with the most important names. Many of these are extremely charming and perhaps surprising. It has long been the custom, to cite an example from naval history, to have new ships christened with a bottle of champagne, which is slung in a fine mesh bag to prevent the glass from flying when the champagne flows. These mesh bags are usually of fine gold or gold-tinted weave and are strung with broad silk ribbons on which the name and date of the occasion are given along with the name of the christener. Ordinarily such a bag was given to the lady who broke the bottle, as a souvenir. Many have been framed. The Museum of the City of New York owns an important bag and ribbons given to Alice Tracy Wilmerding, daughter-in-law of the then secretary of the navy, when she christened the famous battleship *Maine* on 18 November 1890.

Typical items of local American interest not necessarily associated with a very famous person are the batons carried by marshals in local parades. Some of these are very handsome productions in fine wood with inscriptions in silver or gold lettering; they are rarely priced today at more than $100. Policemen's clubs used to be presented either to mark a promotion or a notable performance on duty. Some very fine presentation clubs were made for members of the New York City Police Department in the early twentieth century. Ebony clubs with ivory turnings and of course an inscription about the event sell for less than $100 today. Even more unusual items are the special badges struck for officers. A few of these were made in solid gold and placed in fine presentation boxes. In gold they are of course much more expensive today than the other items, selling up to $300. Other badges and medals, unless remarkably elaborate, are under $100.

Each event of public interest seems to produce its relics almost instantaneously. During the "Watergate" hearings in Washington in 1973/74, the members of the Senate Watergate Committee carefully preserved the artifacts of the sessions; one senator meticulously filed "the doodles and the notes I made during the hearings." They were also overwhelmed with gifts. The chairman, Senator Sam Ervin of North Carolina, received more than twenty gavels, including one five times larger than the average gavel, and another made by the Cherokee Indians of North Carolina.

Most relics are kept in shrines, whether these be called museums, historic sites, birthplaces, or whatever, and a striking phenomenon of the present time is the marked increase, in the United States, in the number and variety of these shrines. New museums filled with relics of one or more notables or of a celebrated event are opening all the time in this country. Although there is certainly no shortage of genuinely great men in the course of American history, the cult of personality here is reaching into some extraordinary byways. There are entire museums devoted to men, no doubt of honorable achievement, whose names and accomplishments are far from being household words, even regionally. In Salt Lake City, for example, there is the "Lester F. Wire Memorial Museum and Historical Association." Lester Wire invented the electric traffic light, and the Memorial Museum contains not only his personal memorabilia but a traffic signal collection.

One would think that few Americans, males at least, would care to be reminded of military conscription, but the General Lewis B. Hershey Museum at Tri-State College in Angola, Indiana, honors the government official whose name was synonymous for thirty

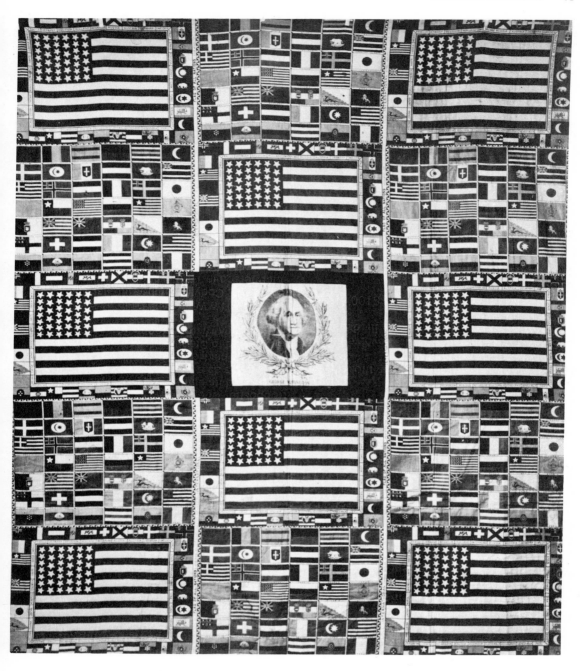

This spectacular quilt measuring seven feet by six and one-half feet was made in 1876 for the centennial of the Declaration of Independence. The portrait of George Washington is surrounded by eight thirty-nine-starred American flags, each in turn framed by numerous small flags of other countries of the world with their names embroidered alongside. The entire quilt is made of commemorative handkerchiefs stitched together. *Pamela Ackerman and Bette Klegon, New York*

years with "the draft." The museum's collections depict the history of conscription in America from colonial times to the present and display mementos of General Hershey's career, including the famous lottery bowl used during World Wars I and II to draw the numbers of eligible draftees.

A modern shrine to a famous person is often his birthplace, sometimes his longtime home or the place he did his most important work, or sometimes the place of his death, especially if the death was violent—Ford's Theatre, for example, where Lincoln was shot, and across the street "the house where Lincoln died." Other factors may affect the choice: Washington's birthplace, although an historic site, is not a shrine because the house was not preserved—the one on the grounds now is a reconstruction—but Mount Vernon, where he lived many years, is.

The United States surpasses most countries in preserving sites associated with her famous men. It is true that in Vienna there are two houses shown as Beethoven's residences, but in this country it is not unusual to have three or more memorials or museums to one person. President U. S. Grant, for example, is honored as follows:

Grant's Birthplace at Point Pleasant, Ohio

The Grant Schoolhouse in Georgetown, Ohio, where he went to school

The U. S. Grant Museum in Vancouver Barracks, Vancouver, Washington, where he was stationed in 1853

Grant Cottage at Mount McGregor, New York, near Saratoga, where he died and where are preserved the fans and tumbler used during his last illness and the pencils and pads he used for his messages when he could no longer speak

The General Grant National Memorial (better known as Grant's Tomb) on Riverside Drive, New York, with a museum containing memorabilia.

All these are in addition to numerous shrines commemorating every stage of his Civil War service, including two at Appomattox alone!

Americans have sometimes been accused of neglecting their literary men, but consider the following:

The Edgar Allan Poe Foundation, Inc., administers a Poe Museum in "the oldest house in Richmond," built about 1688.

(*above and opposite page*) Barbara Fritchie was an aged resident of the town of Frederick, Maryland, a strong partisan of the Union during the Civil War, who, according to a famous story, waved a Union flag defiantly at General Thomas "Stonewall" Jackson when he ordered his troops to fire on it in her window in September 1862. When the aged Barbara protected the flag with her body, "Jackson's nobler nature" was said to have asserted itself, and he blushingly withdrew his order. John Greenleaf Whittier, a strong Union sympathizer for all that he was a Quaker, wrote a famous poem about the patriot lady (Whittier spelled it "Frietchie"). Unimaginative historians have doubted the entire incident, but the poem has been a great favorite—everyone knows the lines: " 'Shoot, if you must, this old gray head, But spare your country's flag,' she said." Barbara Fritchie's house, full of relics, has been preserved and has been open to the public since 1927. *Barbara Fritchie Home, Frederick, Md.*

The Edgar Allan Poe Society of Baltimore, Inc., shows the house in which he lived from 1832 to 1835 and wrote his first short stories and also cares for his grave in Westminster Churchyard.

The Richard Gimbel Foundation for Literary Research has preserved Poe's house on Seventh Street in Philadelphia, where he lived from 1842 to 1844 and also preserves much memorabilia.

The Poe Cottage in Poe Park on the Grand Concourse, Bronx, New York, where Poe lived from 1846 to 1849 and where his wife died, is cared for as a memorial.

The Sam Rayburn Library in his hometown of Bonham, Texas, includes a reconstruction of his House of Representatives office in Washington, complete with the memorabilia the Speaker had accumulated during his long tenure. *The Sam Rayburn Library, Bonham*

These shrines are more dignified and instructive memorials to important American writers than the plans of New Bedford, Massachusetts, to honor Herman Melville by constructing a giant statue of Moby Dick, fifty feet of foam concrete rising from a pool of turbulent water, in a downtown shopping center called Melville Mall. Other attractions will include a "harpoon sculpture" and a "whale-spout fountain."

In America, downright criminality is no deterrent to commemoration and enshrinement. Raynham Hall at Oyster Bay, Long Island, which was the British headquarters on the Island from 1778 to 1780, preserves the four-poster bed on which Major André, the British spy who conspired with Benedict Arnold to betray the American colonists, slept. Some of

the relics in these museums are highly incongruous. An unexpected souvenir preserved at the Museum of the City of New York is an elaborately bound Holy Bible that belonged to, but was presumably unread by, William Marcy "Boss" Tweed (1823–78), one of New York City's most prominent municipal larcenists. The museum also owns his handsome cane, which is topped by a bejeweled Tammany Hall tiger's head in recognition of the political backing that got him into office.

More distressing are the museums, historic houses, and other sites associated with desperados who were no Robin Hoods. By a curious process of sentimentalization (assisted in many cases by the motion pictures), places like the Jesse James House in Saint Joseph, Missouri, where the outlaw was shot, are preserved. In the state of Kansas there are lots of similar sights: at Meade, a "Dalton Gang Hideout Museum" displays furnishings used in 1887 and an "escape tunnel" from the house to the barn. At Coffeyville, a "Dalton Defenders Memorial Museum" founded in 1954 holds items relating to bank robberies by these thugs in 1892. At Dodge City the Boot Hill Museum (on West Wyatt Earp Street) is on the original site of Boot Hill, where numerous felons were buried, and none too soon in the opinion of their fellow citizens. Also in Kansas, which is rich in recollections of lawless days in Mid-America, at Cherryvale is a replica of the home of "The Bloody Benders," a nasty family of four, notorious for their systematic murders of travelers along the Osage Trail in 1872 and 1873. All these museums preserve grisly mementos of the various rough customers. One alien, Francisco "Pancho" Villa, is commemorated, or at least recollected, in a "Pancho Villa Museum" at Columbus, New Mexico, a border town he attacked in 1916, brutally murdering many citizens. Also in New Mexico is Lincoln, which recently received a grant from the state government to finance research among its old buildings because it is the town with the doubtful honor of being Billy the Kid's headquarters. Finally, the Historical Museum of the Union Pacific Railroad in Omaha displays the skull of "Big Nose" George Parrott. He was a Wyoming badman with a special weakness for robbing Union Pacific trains.

Worthier Americans than these are of course commemorated by shrines and historic sites. The presidential libraries and memorials will be dealt with fully in the next chapter, but there also is an increasing number of foundations honoring other political figures, such as the Sam Rayburn Library at Bonham, Texas, and the Eugene V. Debs House at Terre Haute, Indiana. This last contains some unusual memorabilia. Debs, a leader in the organized

labor movement, made an antiwar speech in Canton, Ohio, on 16 June 1918. For this speech, which came over a year after the United States had entered the First World War, he was arrested and convicted in federal court at Cleveland under a wartime "espionage" law. Sentenced to ten years in jail, he began serving his term at the federal prison in Moundsville, West Virginia. While incarcerated, he carried on an extensive campaign of writing, composing articles and letters on a small and clumsily made wooden table, and running for president in 1920 on the Socialist Party ticket. He drew nearly a million votes. He was pardoned on Christmas Day, 1921, by President Harding. The little wooden table is preserved in the Debs House.

Literary figures are very widely honored: the William Cullen Bryant homestead is shown at Cummington, Massachusetts; his mother's boardinghouse at Asheville, North Carolina, made famous by Thomas Wolfe, is open; there is a Willa Cather Pioneer Memorial at Red Cloud, Nebraska, her childhood home; and the cabin of Joaquin Miller, "Poet of the Sierras," is preserved at Canyon City, Oregon. But Americans who have achieved in nearly every field are honored: at Farmington, Maine, "the Homestead of Lillian Nordica" contains the heirlooms of the American opera singer who was born Lillian Norton in that town. There are museums dedicated to generals, suffragettes, and scientists. And there is already a Neil Armstrong Museum at Wapakoneta, Ohio, honoring the first man to step foot on the moon. Each of these places has its collection of relics.

Visiting such shrines can be very useful to the relic collector. Although the objects he sees will not be available for purchase, he can get a good idea of what authentic relics exist and clues as to how relics offered to him will look if they are authentic.

4
United States Presidents

The aura that has come to surround the presidency of the United States means that relics of the presidents have been and are today more avidly collected than any other American personal artifacts. It is no exaggeration to say that surviving relics, souvenirs, and mementos of the thirty-seven men who have held the presidency mean more to most Americans than those of any scientist, writer, artist, religious leader, or other prominent American, no matter what his noteworthy achievements. This is shown, among other ways, by the immense crowds who visit every shrine connected with the presidents. The principal places associated with the holders of the office, homes such as Mount Vernon, Monticello, and others, each count more than a million visitors a year. The same is beginning to be true of the enormous presidential libraries that have been built or are under construction. Although Americans have always had a natural interest in their heads of state, their lives and relics, the phenomenon has grown with the continual strengthening of the presidency in the twentieth century and shows no sign whatever of abating.

There are now six "presidential libraries" (which are actually also museums): the Herbert Hoover Library at West Branch, Iowa; the Franklin D. Roosevelt Library at Hyde Park, N.Y.; the Harry S. Truman Library at Independence, Missouri; the Dwight D. Eisenhower Library at Abilene, Kansas; the Lyndon B. Johnson Library at Austin, Texas; and the John F. Kennedy Library in the planning stage for Cambridge, Massachusetts. All these were originally built with private funds and contributions; the running expenses, however, which are huge, have become a charge on the taxpayers through the National Archives, which administer this ocean of paper and relics. There are also other presidential libraries that are run by private groups, such as the Rutherford B. Hayes State Memorial in Fremont, Ohio, administered by the Ohio Historical Society.

The federally run libraries attract the most attention and visits. Each has become a shrine to the president whose manuscripts and relics are housed there, and in American fashion each has become surrounded by "tourist attractions," souvenir stands, and other roadside clutter living off the visitors. Sometimes the "souvenirs" are grotesque. Before his death President Lyndon Johnson gave $50,000 toward purchasing land around his Texas home to make a Johnson State Park. "Mr. Johnson," said his spokesman, "became upset on learning that cheap souvenir stands were springing up near the LBJ Ranch, some of them selling 'cow chips' for twenty-five cents and asserting that they came from the LBJ Ranch."

Not all the interest in the new presidential libraries has been uncritical by any means. The architectural writer Ada Louise Huxtable has pointed out that "what started out as a rational, scholarly depository for documents has grown into a public-relations monster." There is no dispute that the newer edifices have be-

Historical societies in the United States are the guardians of relics of many statesmen of this country. Several are custodians of presidential papers. The Stark County Historical Society in Canton, Ohio, houses the manuscripts and memorabilia of President William McKinley. *The Stark County Historical Society, Canton, Ohio*

come Pharaonic: the planned John F. Kennedy Library in Cambridge is literally a pyramid, eighty-five feet of glass. Its planners expect 12,000 visitors daily.

Relics, of which all these libraries are chock full, play an increasing part in their displays. The Lyndon B. Johnson Library contains 31,000,000 documents, 500,000 photographs, and 500,000 feet of movie film, and a replica of his Oval Room office in the White House. It also contains such relics of his life and presidency as:

The wedding dresses worn by his two daughters

The plumed hat actress Carol Channing wore in a White House performance of *Hello, Dolly!*

The ballet slippers worn by Maria Tallchief when she danced for LBJ, autographed by the ballerina.

At the "Little White House" in the resort of Warm Springs, Georgia, where President Franklin D. Roosevelt often stayed from 1924 to 1945, and where he died, are preserved, among other relics:

His wheelchair

His collection of ship models

The dog chain for his famous Scottie, Fala

His 1938 Ford convertible with special hand controls.

For the relic collector the surprising result of the construction of these huge libraries, with their massive accumulations and their determination not to let anything relevant get away, is that relics of presidents who served before the twentieth century are generally easier to find than those of the more recent men. And generally more interesting, since few important artifacts seem to escape the archivists who now administer the presidential heritage.

Collectors' demand for presidential relics is very unequally divided among the presidents. There must be few ardent collectors of memorabilia of Millard Fillmore or John Tyler. Such is the mystique of the presidency, however, that sometimes surprisingly high prices are paid for relics of the least esteemed presidents. But there is no question that relics of Washington and Lincoln are more in demand among collectors than those of the other presidents and sell for more substantial prices. The other presidents in strongest demand are probably Jefferson, the two Roosevelts, Grant, Eisenhower, and Kennedy.

The reputation of George Washington was immense for about the last twenty-five years of his life—he was forty-four when the Revolution came, and he died at sixty-seven—and grew greater very soon after his death. Esteem for him was widespread in Europe, too, and he received innumerable foreign visitors, many of whom carried home with them some relic of the general-president or gave Washington something that he preserved, such as a snuffbox. Many items in both categories have come on the market. Also, a very large number of Washington relics passed out of the possession of the Washington family during the nineteenth century through sales, usually at auction, by his collateral descendants. The destruction of the Civil War in Virginia played its part in the scattering of Washingtoniana. The sacking of Arlington, home of Mrs. Robert E. Lee, great-granddaughter of Martha Washington, was typical. The estate of Mount Vernon fell on evil times, the contents were dispersed, and it was not until 1853 that The Mount Vernon Ladies' Association of the Union began to restore it and to gather the belongings that had been in the house in Washington's time.

A listing of a few of the auction sales with lots described as "the property of President Washington" will give some idea of how many Washington relics have been sold:

In 1876, books from his library were sold, many with his beautiful armorial bookplate and/or his signature. Some of these and others have come back on the market. They are very much sought for by rare book and autograph collectors and bring very high prices, often $5,000 or more.

An auction in 1890 was described inaccurately as "The Final Settlement of the Estate of General George Washington." It included a considerable amount of china, silverware, and glass from Mount Vernon, and some more important relics, such as Martha Washington's Bible with her signature.

In 1891 more silverware, glassware, and china came to the salesroom (possibly this was a reappearance for some of it), along with one of Martha's slippers, Washington's violin, a mahogany chair used at the Continental Congress, and such esoterica as the needle book of Nellie Custis, Washington's stepgranddaughter.

In 1917 the Anderson Galleries in New York held an auction of "historical relics of George Washington" for one William Lanier Washington, described as a direct descendant of two of the President's brothers (there were many cousin marriages in the clan) and the owner of the family heirlooms. The sale, which had only eight-eight lots, was very successful. William Randolph Hearst, then at the height of his magpie activity, was a heavy buyer. Washington's shoe buckles, sword buckles, whist counters, wineglasses (*more* glassware), pants, coat buttons, and snuffboxes were sold. The leading bookseller of the day, George D. Smith, purchased for several hundred dollars a pair of Sheffield candlesticks "used by General Washington on his desk at Mount Vernon." Encouraged by such success, W. Lanier Washington held another sale three years later at the American Art Galleries of "statuary, medallions, snuffboxes, watches, clocks, silver, and other relics or memorabilia of or belonging to George Washington." This sale contained 445 lots and was also successful. Typical prices were $125 apiece for coat buttons, $370 for shoe buckles, and an unbelievable $210 each for some pink seashells said to have been bought by the President to help out an indigent sailor. The sale also contained another pair of Sheffield candlesticks from the desk at Mount Vernon. George D. Smith, who had purchased the first pair, had a furious argument with W. Lanier Washington, which terminated by Smith's falling dead. Undeterred by what most consignors would have regarded as an omen, Washington went right ahead and had another sale in 1922, this time of 487 lots of his ancestor's belongings. By this time suspicion about the regular flow of Washington relics to the salesroom had become so widespread that the 1922 sale was the last consigned by W. Lanier. Although it is possible that some of these Washington relics were genuine, since W. Lanier was a member of the family, a provenance of a Washington relic that includes W.

The Rutherford B. Hayes State Memorial in Fremont, Ohio, called "The First Presidential Library," consists of the President's home, his tomb, and a library and museum, all administered by the Ohio Historical Society. Among many important relics of Hayes's presidential years (1877–81) is this 1880 mahogany sideboard used in the White House, on which are displayed pieces from the famous Hayes china service painted with American flora and fauna. *The Rutherford B. Hayes Library, Fremont, Ohio*

Young Fanny Hayes played with this well-equipped doll house, made for her in 1878. She was one of the children of President Hayes and his wife Lucy (Ware) Hayes, who unfortunately has gone down in history under the name "Lemonade Lucy" because she was a strong advocate of temperance. She was also the first college-educated woman in the White House and the mother of eight children. *The Rutherford B. Hayes Library, Fremont, Ohio*

The arms of the family of George Washington—three stars—appear in the lower right of the shield on this George II salver made in London in 1759 by Ebenezer Coker. It is sixteen inches in diameter. *The Folger's Coffee Collection of Antique English Silver. By courtesy of Procter and Gamble Company*

Lanier Washington as a previous owner inspires little confidence today.

Many Washington relics that are not suspect exist, of course, at Mount Vernon and other places associated with the President. At the Jonathan Hasbrouck House in Newburgh, New York, from which the general commanded the Continental Army, are preserved pieces of cloth from the general's garments, a lock of his hair, and the razor and its hone that he is said to have used there.

Washington was a Freemason, and a number of relics are preserved by Masonic lodges. The Alexandria, Virginia, Lodge has another razor, a glove, a pruning knife, a pocketknife, and a bedroom clock that was stopped at 10:20 P.M., 14 December 1799, the moment of his death. The Grand Lodge of Maryland owns the desk on which he laid his resignation of his commission from the U.S. Armed Forces.

One of the most important relics in American history is connected with both Washington

President and Mrs. Washington used a table service of porcelain made for them in China and decorated with the emblems of the Society of the Cincinnati, an organization (still active) composed of American and French officers of the Revolutionary War and their descendants. The device on this soup plate is Fame trumpeting while suspending the badge of the Order. The service was bought by Washington in 1786; it consisted of about three hundred pieces and cost the President $150. It descended in the Custis family of Virginia and belonged to Mrs. Robert E. Lee. Much of it was destroyed by Union troops during the Civil War. Surviving pieces are very highly valued. *The Campbell Museum, Camden, N.J.*

and Freemasonry. On 30 April 1789, when he was being inaugurated—"introduced," it was called then—as first President of the United States at the ceremony at Federal Hall in New York, it was discovered at the last moment that no one had remembered to provide a Bible for taking the oath. Happily, Chancellor Robert R. Livingston, who was Grand Master of the New York Lodge, knew there was a Bible at Saint John's Masonic Lodge No. 1, on Broadway a little above Wall Street. That Bible was sent for in haste and was used by Livingston to administer the oath to Washington. It has survived and was used in the inaugurations of Presidents Harding and Eisenhower as well. The Bible is now on display in Federal Hall, New York, at Nassau Street and Wall, which replaced the original building in 1862, and is called by most New Yorkers by its earlier name, "The Sub-Treasury."

The Alexandria Lodge had made for Washington the trowel with which he laid the cornerstone of the U.S. Capitol in 1793. Masonic ceremonies were used on that occasion. The trowel is still in the possession of the Alexandria Lodge.

Today, the collector can occasionally find a piece of porcelain from the famous service made for Washington in China (one piece is illustrated); the price is likely to be in the thousands of dollars. Well-authenticated locks of hair usually sell for around $1,000, and a fair number appear on the market. If documented, they are quite likely to be genuine, as it is known that a considerable number of locks and hairs were taken during Washington's lifetime by friends and admirers.

Many Washington relics have very good provenance. Since he was famous during his lifetime, people were proud of their contacts with him and recorded them. At a 1973 auction a Washington lot was described with its provenance thus:

A lock of George Washington's hair in a blue and gold enamel locket. With an affidavit signed by Annie Kellogg McIntyre and notarized, stating that the lock came to her husband through his grandfather, James McIntyre, who had been given it as a token of friendship by De Witt Clinton. Clinton inherited from his uncle, Gen. George Clinton.

The locket had been fitted into an expensive morocco case with an original autograph signature of George Washington and a miniature portrait of him painted on ivory.

The President's silver sugar tongs sold in 1972 were engraved with his easily identifiable crest and motto, and in addition had attached by a wide ribbon a card on which was written in a nineteenth century hand: "Genl Washington's sugar tongs with his crest inherited by me from my grandmother Eliza Parke Custis— E. S. Goldsborough (nee Rogers)." The Custis family descends from Washington's stepchildren.

In modern times the Washington relics have been the subject of much scholarship. A "Note on Memorabilia" published by The Mount Vernon Ladies' Association of the Union declares: "No activity at Mount Vernon is pursued with greater energy and persistence than research relating to memorabilia associated with General and Mrs. Washington in their domestic life." The published results of these endeavors make fascinating reading for the relic collector. Washington, for example, delighted in fishing; the Ladies' Association have traced his tackle and it now reposes with its documentation at Mount Vernon.

A great array of mementos of the Washingtons have survived, such as pincushions made from the curtain fabric at Mount Vernon, cuff links with examples of the Washingtons' hair woven together, fragments of Mrs. Washington's dresses, and objects made from the wood of his coffin when it was replaced by a marble sarcophagus in 1837. It is known that Upton Herbert, who was the first resident superintendent of Mount Vernon, had at least four small pine boxes fashioned from the coffin's wood, with mother-of-pearl inlays and locks. Miniatures of the sarcophagus were made in silver. An example about seven inches wide was sold at auction in 1972 for $1,300.

Relics of Abraham Lincoln have proliferated more than those of Washington or indeed of any other president. If a student were to select one American as the most collected, he would certainly have to choose Lincoln. Huge collections of Lincolniana have been formed by universities and foundations; many private collections have been made and some are still in the process of formation. No period of Lincoln's life is without its memorabilia. His wartime leadership, the circumstances of his death and the troubles of his widow and family after he died, the extreme grief felt by the people of this country at his assassination, his unusual and intriguing personality, all contributed both to the emergence of a Lincoln cult and the collecting of relics, true and spurious.

One of the most famous collections was the enormous accumulation of Lincolniana brought together by Oliver R. Barrett. The collection was Barrett's lifework and so extensive that Carl Sandburg, who studied it for his life of Lincoln, wrote an entire book about it— *Lincoln Collector. The Story of Oliver R. Barrett's Great Private Collection* (New York, 1950). It was sold at auction by the Parke-

Abraham Lincoln used this paperweight, which is about six inches high, on his desk in the White House. Its provenance is very good: Major Stackpole, a steward in the presidential mansion at the time of Lincoln's death, was an earlier owner. *The Lincoln National Life Foundation, Fort Wayne, Indiana*

Bernet Galleries in New York in 1952. Few sales can have been more eagerly anticipated. The collection was rich in letters and other manuscripts, and they brought the highest prices. There were many important relics, most of them with excellent provenances. Great interest was shown in a silver watch that Lincoln gave to his cousin Dennis F. Hanks. Hanks, who long survived Lincoln, loved to tell stories

about his illustrious relative and to describe a trip he made to Washington, D.C., to visit him. It was on this visit, in 1864, that the President gave Hanks the watch, which ever after was his most precious possession. In 1891, at the age of ninety-two, Hanks made an affidavit describing the watch in great detail and narrating the story of his visit and the gift. He concluded: "I am a full cousin of Abraham Lincoln, and taught him to read and write." At the Barrett sale the watch sold for $1,600, the highest price for any relic.

The sum of $1,300 was realized by a handsome watch chain made of California gold, presented to Lincoln by a committee of the Union Pacific and Central Pacific railroads, who were urging the government to build the transcontinental railroad—lobbyists, in other words.

The seal of the President of the United States used by Lincoln while he was in the White House, a most attractive relic, brought $650. A quill pen, also said to have been used by Lincoln as President, sold for only $65. During the 1920s another, believed to be the pen with which he signed the Emancipation Proclamation, had brought $1,600.

An axe handle carved with "Abraham Lincoln" and "New Salem 1834" was sold for $300 with the affidavit of one of his boyhood neighbors giving a lengthy history of the relic and affirming positively: "There is no dought but what it is jenuine."

A piece of the tablecloth upon which he ate his wedding breakfast in 1842 was sold for $30.

A crimson silk Bible bookmark embroidered with a cross, Lincoln's name, and "Executive Mansion, Washington, D.C. [the name 'White House' was not used then] Dec. 6, 1864," sold for $650.

In the Barrett Collection and in many other Lincoln collections, relics of the assassination of the President take first place in human interest. Literally from the instant of his death, relic collectors were after Lincoln souvenirs. There is the famous story of the boy found scrubbing up Lincoln's blood from the steps of the house to which he was carried after the shooting, and selling it to collectors. Lincoln died in the boardinghouse room of one William Clark, who was a stenographer for the War Department. Clark was apparently not a sensitive person, as there is in existence a letter in which he describes the horde of visitors who wanted to see his room and calmly remarks that he is continuing to sleep on the mattress on which Lincoln died, "and the same coverlid covers me nightly that covered him while dying."

Since the assassination in Ford's Theater on 14 April 1865 is the focus of Lincoln collecting, it is interesting to know what an advanced collector like Oliver Barrett owned relating to that evening. Among other items were:

- The playbill showing *Our American Cousin* as the event of the evening. This item, which was not unique, sold for $175. Copies sell for somewhat more now. It has been reprinted in an excellent facsimile of which the collector should be aware.
- A ticket to the theatre, sold for $25; today the tickets bring twice that. Most of the audience appear to have saved their stubs.
- A piece of the dress that the actress Laura Keene was wearing sold for $70.
- A piece of the U.S. flag draped over the Presidential box that night sold for $85.
- The key to the box brought $150.
- The fan used by Mrs. Lincoln that night, bloodstained, sold for $70.
- Mrs. Lincoln's veil brought $210.

The funeral of Lincoln was the occasion of a national hysteria unparalleled in American history. For days the funeral train made its way slowly from Washington to Springfield, Illinois, where Lincoln was buried, past literally millions of Americans. Funeral services were held in various cities amidst the most extravagant scenes, which combined grief with showmanship.

During the period of national mourning for the president, every manufacturer in the country seems to have issued black-bordered textiles, including handkerchiefs, bookmarks, ribbons, and so forth, and thousands of badges, tokens, and medals were also issued. All these items are on the market today; many may be purchased for under $20. They are commemorative items rather than true relics or souvenirs, but making a collection of them gives the collector an unusual glimpse of a tragic event in American history.

A paralysis seems to have overtaken official Washington immediately after the President's death. In the White House they lost their heads altogether. Lincoln's widow, the strange, unsympathetic, and probably unbalanced Mary Todd Lincoln, remained in her room, but the doorkeepers admitted anyone who said he had come to pay a condolence call, and huge crowds prowled through the house—aimlessly, since Mrs. Lincoln received no one. It is known that much of the Lincoln china and silver and apparently other possessions as well were carried off during this mourning period. A letter of Mrs. Lincoln's written a few months later shows the conditions in the White House at that time. A friend had asked for a lock of the President's hair, and Mrs. Lincoln replied in part:

I enclose a very few hairs from my beloved husband's head. I regret I have so few to spare you as I have only a bunch as large as one of your fingers. I was told before I left Washington that quite a quantity was cut off to be reserved for me [and] was placed in the wardrobe in the guest room. As some officers were present at the time it was presumed it was taken.

Mrs. Lincoln, who had a mania for possessions of all kinds, especially clothing, had many souvenirs to distribute, and for years she was dispensing locks of hair (despite the letter above), canes, and other memorabilia. She gave the suit worn by Lincoln the night of the assassination to Alphonso Dunn, a White House guard and doorkeeper. It descended in the Dunn family and was kept by them until 1967, when it was purchased for the Lincoln Museum now established in Ford's Theater. She gave one friend a snuffbox that had belonged to both Henry Clay and her husband and a cane made from the wood of Fort Sumter.

In the first year of her widowhood, Mrs. Lincoln depended heavily on one Elizabeth Keckley, an important name in the annals of Lincoln collecting because she issued affidavits of authenticity on certain Lincoln relics that came into her possession. Elizabeth Keckley, described at the time as "a Negress" or "a mulatto," was not exactly Mary Lincoln's servant. She was an adept seamstress who made many of Mrs. Lincoln's dresses; Mrs. Lincoln came to regard her as a friend and frequently said so. Few people can have been more cruelly betrayed by a "friend." In 1867, Mrs. Lincoln, who was extremely extravagant and at the time nearly bankrupt despite Lincoln's substantial estate, had the unfortunate idea of selling her enormous wardrobe under

Mary Todd Lincoln had an interest in fine clothes that bordered on a mania. During the worst times of the Civil War she would rush to New York to see the latest fashions, and more than once got into severe financial straits by purchases for her wardrobe. This shawl of black Chantilly lace belonged to her and later to her daughter-in-law, Mrs. Robert Lincoln. *The Lincoln National Life Foundation, Fort Wayne, Indiana*

her own name. The sale was actually advertised in New York City. Mrs. Lincoln put Elizabeth Keckley in charge of the entire business, writing her at least twenty-four letters, mostly long, about the sale and its necessity that are so emotional they make painful reading even today. The advertisement brought such unfavorable comment about Mrs. Lincoln that it had to be canceled, although some sales

had been made. This was the famous "Old Clothes Scandal." Soon after, Elizabeth Keckley published for profit Mrs. Lincoln's twenty-four letters to her in a book called *Behind the Scenes,* in which she utterly betrayed Mrs. Lincoln's trust. The publication of the book, of course, marked the end of their relationship. As far as is known, Mrs. Lincoln never mentioned Elizabeth Keckley again, ex-

cept once in a letter to refer to her derisively as *"the colored* historian."

The collector can easily see from this summary that numerous relics of Lincoln and his family were scattered about, and there is reason to believe in the authenticity and provenance of the greater number of those that are around today.

Forgers have been known to add their mite to the Lincoln memorabilia, and controversy has cast a shadow on a number of well-known "Lincoln relics." There was long exhibited and often described in print a flat stone inscribed with the names of Lincoln and a girl named Ann Rutledge, who was supposedly his first love. It is now generally thought that the story of Lincoln's romance with Ann Rutledge had almost no basis in fact and was inserted by William H. Herndon in his biography of Lincoln to spite Mary Todd Lincoln, whom he hated. In 1900, when interest in the story was at its height, one William L. Green found on the townsite of New Salem, Illinois, a stone lettered with the legend "A Lincoln Ann Rutledge were betrothed here July 4, 1833." This object, under the circumstances suspiciously

(*above*) Columbia, Tennessee, in the bluegrass country was the home of President James Knox Polk. Local boosters liked to call Columbia "the dimple of the universe." This is the sitting room of the Polk house. The circular center table is inlaid with a mosaic of colored marbles representing the American eagle surrounded by thirty white stars for the then states. *James Knox Polk Memorial Auxiliary, Columbia, Tenn.*

(*opposite page*) Mrs. Polk (Sarah Childress) used this handsome fan decorated with miniatures of Polk and the ten presidents who preceded him. On the reverse is a painting of the Signing of the Declaration of Independence. Among other relics, the house also has the ball gown worn by Mrs. Polk when she carried the fan. These are unexpectedly luxurious items, since Mrs. Polk had the reputation of being a strict Presbyterian who would not tolerate drinking, dancing, or even card playing while she was mistress of the White House. *The James Knox Polk Memorial Auxiliary, Columbia, Tenn.*

pat, was noticed by Carl Sandburg, most famous of Lincoln's twentieth century biographers, who wrote noncommittally: "And there is in existence, for what derivations may be made from it, a stone from the New Salem neighborhood, 'dug up' in 1890 near the Lincoln & Berry store, by the grandson of Bowling Green [an early friend of Lincoln], according to affidavits." This relic was apparently too good to be true even for the Lincoln faithful: at sale in the 1950s it went for only $75.

The presidents after Lincoln have apparently all been great accumulators. Since most lived before the founding of the presidential libraries (which begin with Hoover) with their careful hoarding of all memorabilia, there has been a flow of relics available from these administrations. A typical relic of this era is a wreath of flowers taken from President Grant's coffin and

framed in a shadow box frame with a piece of the American flag used on that occasion, recently for sale at $250. Freedom boxes, keys, cups, and all kinds of other gifts made to presidents by governments, organizations, or private persons exist in large numbers.

A visit to one of the homes of the presidents of the time, such as Theodore Roosevelt's Sagamore Hill in Oyster Bay, Long Island, New York, shows what quantities of memorabilia exist. The twenty-three rooms of the house are crammed with objects such as a cribbage board made of elephant tusks, an inkwell made from a rhinoceros foot, a bedspread of Chinese silk (gift of the Empress Dowager of China), andirons made from shells and cannon balls of the Spanish-American War, and even a dinner gong framed in four-foot-high tusks from elephants shot by Roosevelt in Kenya in 1909.

Something of the same maudlin atmosphere that prevailed at the time of Lincoln's death was also in the air at the assassinations of Presidents Garfield, McKinley, and Kennedy. These men could hardly be compared with Lincoln except that they were also murdered, but there were elaborate funerals and the manufacture of mourning souvenirs on all three occasions. Most of the mourning ribbons, badges, and medals sold at the time are available: the collector can usually take his pick for less than $20.

The puzzling circumstances of Kennedy's murder and the widespread belief that the findings of the Warren Commission were somehow unconvincing brought the relics of that occasion great and continuing attention from all over the world. Many sensational books and articles came out. Offers were received for Lee Harvey Oswald's gun, which had been seized by the government; his widow had many bids for memorabilia of her husband; and letters and documents by all the principal actors in the bizarre drama reached the market. More than one collector or entrepreneur wanted to buy the Texas School Book Depository Building from which Oswald fired. It is still standing, and as of 1973 an attempt to designate it a Texas State historical site had failed. Thousands if not millions of visitors had come to Dealey Plaza in Dallas, scene of the assassination.

President Rutherford B. Hayes used this 1877 carriage during his term in the White House. *Rutherford B. Hayes Library, Fremont, Ohio*

(*opposite page, top*) The funeral train of the assassinated President William McKinley was seen by hundreds of thousands of Americans as it bore the body of the president from Buffalo, New York, where he died on 14 September 1901, to Washington for a state funeral, then to Canton, Ohio, where he was buried in this immense tomb. McKinley, who was good-hearted and amiable, was much loved during his lifetime, and after his death many commemorative items of all kinds were issued, as they had been for President Lincoln. *The Stark County Historical Society, Canton, Ohio*

(*bottom*) The reconstruction of President McKinley's study at Canton is filled with memorabilia of his White House years. *The Stark County Historical Society, Canton, Ohio*

(*above*) President Woodrow Wilson was born in Staunton, Virginia. His first Christian name was Thomas, and he was called "Tommie" throughout his boyhood. This is his first nursery, with original furnishings, including his crib. *Woodrow Wilson Birthplace Foundation, Staunton, Va.*

(*left*) Among the relics at the Birthplace is the Wilson family Bible, which records the president's birth 28 December 1856. The portrait of the president's father, the Reverend Joseph Ruggles Wilson, a Presbyterian minister, hangs above the reading stand. *Woodrow Wilson Foundation, Staunton, Va.*

(*opposite page*) The sitting room of the Wilson Birthplace contains the family's musical instruments. *Woodrow Wilson Foundation, Staunton, Va.*

Kennedy shrines have already developed in addition to the projected library for his papers. The house in Brookline, Massachusetts, where he was born in the master bedroom on 29 May 1917, is a National Historic Site and open to the public. The National Park Service's official booklet on the house seems to have succumbed to the sticky sentimentality that afflicts most writers about such places. It declares, for example, "in this house John F. Kennedy learned the basic skills each man must learn: to walk, to talk, and laugh and pray." His bassinet and christening dress and other remembrances of the president's infancy are on view.

The National Archives announced in 1973 that it had purchased for $1,000 the emergency medical equipment used by the team of doctors in Parkland Hospital, Dallas, to which the dying Kennedy was taken on 22 November 1963. The material was described as the contents of "Trauma Room 1," and it was implied that these grisly relics might someday be put on public display.

The armor-plated automobile in which Kennedy was riding when he was shot was rebuilt after his death and returned to the White House. Later, it was sent to the Henry Ford Museum in Dearborn, Michigan, which has a large collection of historic vehicles, and there it was refurbished and restored as well as possible to the state in which it was used by Kennedy.

The more sensational columns of the world press remain fascinated with Kennedy and his widow. After Jacqueline Kennedy married the Greek millionaire Aristotle Onassis, there were repeated stories that employees of the couple had been discharged for stealing Mrs. Onassis' personal belongings and selling them to relic collectors. Since many of the principals in the Kennedy history are not only living but comparatively young, it may be expected that numerous relics of the president and his family will be displayed, discussed, and possibly sold in the future. Kennedy commemorative material such as plates, ingots, and medals continues to be issued in great profusion.

The distinctive table china used in the White House during the various presidential administrations long afforded the modest collector an opportunity to own an attractive relic of a president. Pieces from the services have now, however, become rare and exceedingly expensive. Several books have been written on the White House china, cataloging the sets used over the last century and a half. Recent (1973) prices quoted for pieces of presidential china range as high as $5,000 for a single plate from the Lincoln service, short sets (six plates) from the Harrison service at over $5,000, and from the Hayes service at over $3,000. This last is particularly noted since the decoration reproduces more than sixty drawings by the artist Theodore R. Davis of the flora and fauna of the United States.

From the Lincoln service on, much of the presidential china was made by the firm of Haviland & Co. in Limoges, France, founded by Americans. Since at least 1876, reproductions of presidential china have been made by Haviland and other firms and sold to collectors. In May 1969, Haviland began to issue a series of White House china reproductions commencing with a copy of the famous Washington service of China Trade procelain, followed by plate and cup and saucer reproductions of the Lincoln service (originally made by Haviland in 1861), and plates of the Grant, Hayes, Harrison, and other services. These are issued as collectors' commemoratives in editions said to be limited to 2,500.

Silver or plated ware used in the White House is seldom, if ever, available on the antiques market.

Canes made of relic wood associated with the presidents and the White House are likely finds for the collector, as shown in the case of Lincoln.

Pens, especially the fountain pens used by modern presidents to sign bills, are often moderately priced (under $100) because so many of them exist. In the twentieth century there is so much legislation for the president to sign— and some presidents have been so anxious to distribute instant souvenirs during the ceremonies attending the signing of bills—that it may be confidently expected many more pens will be for sale.

Some amusing souvenirs of modern presidents are being created by employing genuine relics, exactly as they were in the nineteenth century. In 1973, the Belle Springs Creamery Co. of Abilene, Kansas, offered a modestly priced ($3.50) paperweight containing brick bits from the chimney that serviced the creamery's coal-burning boilers, which were stoked during the summers from 1906 to 1910 by a young future president, "Ike" Eisenhower.

5
Relics of Royalty

The regalia of monarchy have fascinated commoners for thousands of years, and relics of royalty have long been preserved. Objects belonging to kings, especially those used in their coronations, have extremely ancient mystical associations that are dimly remembered even now. One can see in the preservation and exhibition of the possessions of royalty and even nonroyal heads of state such as modern presidents, lingering traces of the awe for "such divinity doth hedge a king."

During the expansion of Europe there was a fascination with the trappings of primitive royalty sent back by explorers and colonists. Hernando Cortés presented to his ruler Charles V, Holy Roman Emperor, various curiosities from his conquest of Mexico in 1519/20. Among them was a feathered shield that had belonged to Montezuma, Emperor of Mexico. It became part of the Hapsburg possessions and is still kept in Vienna with other relics of the conquest of the Aztecs, among which is one of the finest Mexican codices or pictorial manuscripts. In the nineteenth century when the Hapsburg Archduke Maximilian became Emperor of Mexico, his initial enthusiasm about the country led him to ask his brother, the Emperor Franz Josef, to return some of the Mexican treasures from Vienna to Mexico. Franz Josef refused to give up the Aztec codex or the shield, but he did send back the original manuscript of Cortés's first report to Charles V on the conquest.

Another interesting survival of a savage monarch is the feather cloak of King Kamehameha I of Hawaii (1737?–1819) now on display at the Bernice P. Bishop Museum in Honolulu. Kamehameha I was a bloodthirsty chieftain who conquered all the Hawaiian Islands and made them into something like a kingdom. Chiefs in the Islands wore elaborate cloaks made from the feathers of various prized birds as symbols of their leadership. Nearly one hundred examples of these have come down to the present day, but the Kamehameha cloak is unique because it is made of the feathers of the *mamo* bird (*Drepanis pacifica*), which is found only on the island of Hawaii itself. It is a black bird with a few feathers of a deep yellow above and below the black tail feathers and on the thighs. The circular feather cloak is fifty-six inches long and 148 inches wide at the base, composed entirely of *mamo* feathers but for a few red *iwi* feathers around the neck. It weighs only six pounds. The feathers per square inch have been counted by a patient researcher, and it has been computed that about 450,000 feathers were required to make the cloak. Since a *mamo* bird furnishes only about six or seven suitable feathers from his body, about 80,000 birds must have been plucked to make the cloak. Although it was apparently begun during the seventeenth century, its fabrication occupied the tenure of eight of Kamehameha's predecessors as chief. Captain James Cook saw

65

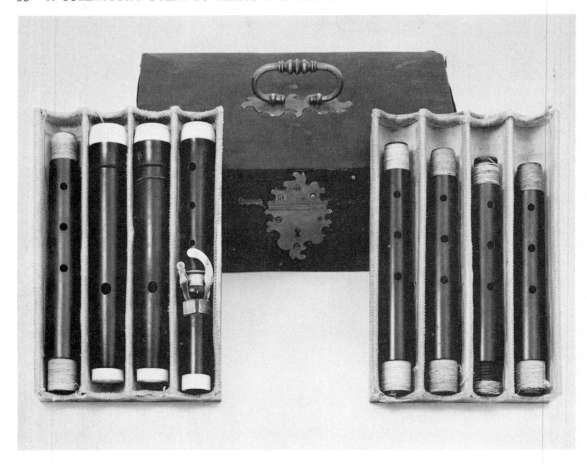

One of the finest historical relics sold in decades was this two-keyed ebony flute formerly the property of Frederick II, "the Great," King of Prussia, who was a capable performer on the instrument and the composer of numerous flute sonatas and concerti. These compositions are still in the active musical repertory and some are available on recordings. The king was greatly grieved when he could not play the flute in his old age because he had lost so many teeth. *Sotheby & Co., London*

cloaks like this during his 1778 visit, when he was killed by natives whom he found stealing. He compared the cloaks to "the thickest and richest velvet, which they resemble, both as to the feel, and the glossy appearance."

In the nineteenth century James Jackson Jarves saw the Kamehameha cloak and made some ingenious calculations about it:

A piece of nankeen, valued at one dollar and a half, was formerly the price of five feathers of this kind. By this estimate the value of the cloak would equal that of the

purest diamonds in the several European regalia and including the price of the feathers no less than a million of dollars worth of labor was expended upon it at the present rate of computing wages.

It was used, by members of the dynasty that Kamehameha founded, to decorate the throne on public occasions until the Hawaiian monarchy came to an end with Queen Liliuokalani in 1893.

An unusually large assortment of relics of the Hawaiian royal family may be seen by the public. The Iolani Palace in Honolulu, Queen Emma's Summer Palace, also in Honolulu, and Hulihee Palace in Kailua Village on the island of Hawaii all have furniture, china, medals, and decorations. The Summer Palace shows royal clothing (including the wedding dress of Queen Emma) and the cradle of Albert Edward Kauikeaouli, Prince of Hawaii, who died at the age of four.

Other exotic royalty with notable relics includes the sultans of Turkey, whose sovereignty ended as recently as 1922. As all visitors to the celebrated Topkapi Palace in Istanbul know, the sultans were especially fond of jewels and bejeweled objects. Most of the relics of the dynasty that come on the market are dazzlingly decorated swords, pistols, and the like. An occasional jewel, generally of immense dimensions, is sold that was formerly in their great storehouse. Sultan Abdul Hamid II (1842–1918), who was deposed in 1909, owned perhaps as many famous precious stones as any single man who ever lived; the "Hope" diamond and the "Star of the East" were among them. He also owned an enormous diamond of over seventy carats known as "The Idol's Eye." It was discovered in the celebrated

Golconda diamond mines of India about 1600. The prince in whose domain it was found was heavily in debt to the British East India Company, who seized it to settle the debt. It disappeared for about three hundred years, and like so many large stones, was said to have been discovered again as the eye of an idol. It then came into the hands of Abdul Hamid II. When the Turkish Empire showed signs of collapse early in this century, Abdul Hamid sent it by messenger to Paris for safekeeping. The messenger stole it by means of a faked robbery. After other adventures, the stone finally came into the possession of the New York diamond dealer Harry Winston, who sold it to an American woman, May Bonfils Stanton, daughter of the publisher of the Denver *Post*. She lived on an estate near Denver that was a copy of the Petit Trianon at Versailles, with French furniture, tapestries, paintings, and an array of jewels that included the "Libertador I" diamond and other huge stones. She wore "The Idol's Eye" as the pendant of a necklace set with forty-one round diamonds weighing over twenty-two carats and forty-five baguette diamonds weighing an additional twelve. When it was sold (1962) after her death for the benefit

Farouk, last king of Egypt, counted among his possessions this jade-handled whisk of ostrich and peacock feathers decorated with diamonds and turquoises, the whole 32½ inches long. Sold at the Farouk dispersals in Cairo in 1956, it reappeared in the salesroom in 1956, when it sold for $2,500.

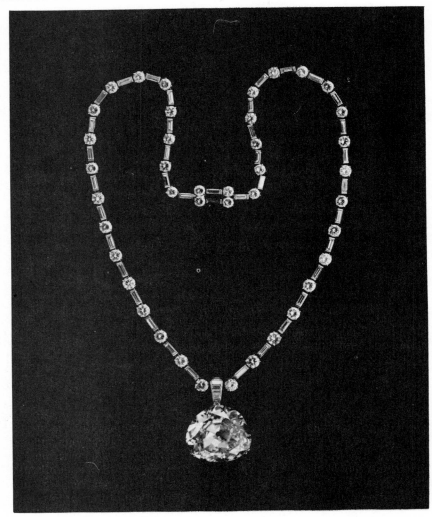

The famous seventy-carat diamond known as "The Idol's Eye" is a relic of Near Eastern royal families and American millionaires. It is now the pendant in a necklace and in 1973 was valued at over $1,000,000.

of various Roman Catholic charities, it brought the then world's record of $375,000. The "Libertador I" sold for $185,000.

Abdul Hamid II owned numerous lesser baubles, among them an unusual Golconda diamond of a light golden yellow color weighing over ninety-five carats, which sold in 1961 in London for a mere $23,000.

The possessions and collections of the late King Farouk of Egypt (died 1965) are now scattered all over the world. The strange monarch, whose grotesque appearance and bizarre behavior are thought by his biographers to have been the result of an unusual glandular disorder, was a royal magpie, and when he was expelled from Egypt in 1952, there were literally tons of objects to be disposed of by the new government. He had collected—seriously —stamps, coins, medals (there were 8,500 gold coins and medals and 164 pieces struck in rare platinum), glass, Korans, clocks and watches, and objects by Carl Fabergé, but he also accumulated with equal enthusiasm cigarette cards, postcards, walking sticks, ashtrays, and razor blades. The collections included unusual things made especially for him, such as a fleet of flaming red automobiles and a solid gold holder for his Coca-Cola bottle. The army decided to sell the whole lot except Farouk's Egyptian antiquities, which were sent to the National Museum. A staff came out from Sotheby's London salesrooms to catalogue and auction off the royal belongings. The sales, which began in February 1954 and lasted for weeks, were held at the Kubbah Palace in a carnival atmosphere with bands, refreshment stands, and general nonchalance. One visiting collector saw army guards playing ball with a Fabergé Easter egg that brought $20,000 at the sale. The strongly puritan Moslem element who had taken over the country were offended by the king's collection of erotica, and it was segregated into one part of the palace. The army permitted buyers who spent over £ 5,000 to tour "the secret museum." Most of the "erotic art" consisted of American nude postcards and paperback books; the showpiece was a copy of *Fanny Hill.* Western visitors were

Royal relics often include fine china. This pair of Staffordshire creamware soup plates carries the arms of the English Duke of Clarence (later King William IV). The arms portrayed are heraldically incorrect, as coats of arms on china often are, china painters being but little versed in the involved language of the herald. The plates were probably used by William and his mistress, the Irish actress Dorothy Jordan, by whom he was ten times made a father. These children were given the family name Fitzclarence. *Campbell Museum, Camden, N.J.*

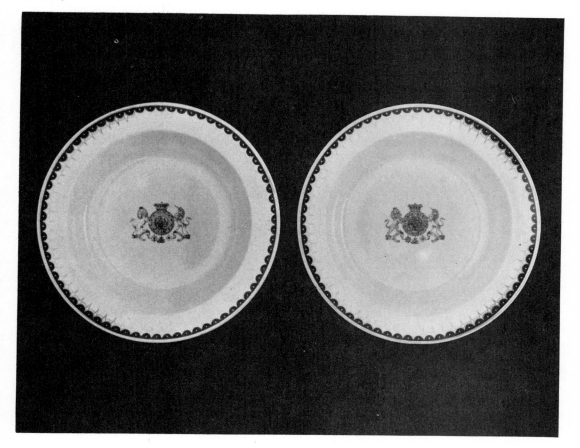

Another soup plate with royal provenance is this remarkable piece of Polish faïence with an oriental pattern that was ordered by King Stanislaus II Poniatowski as a gift for Sultan Abdul Hamid I of Turkey in 1776. A Turkish inscription in the design tells the story of the gift. Stanislaus II, sometime lover of Catherine the Great, was the last king of an independent Poland. *Campbell Museum, Camden, N.J.*

badly disappointed! The entire sale brought only about £700,000 (then about $2,000,000) and contained some great bargains for smart buyers. Possessions of other members of the royal family—as a result of the Moslem system there were no fewer than 370 princes at the end of the monarchy—were also disposed of by sale.

In Europe up until the time of the Second World War, numerous dynasties, even those that had lost their sovereignty during the First

War, preserved royal heirlooms in hundreds of residences. In Germany, especially, the custom was observed of keeping sacred the room in which a member of the family had died; it was locked immediately after the death in order to preserve it exactly as it was at the moment of expiration. Princesses from other countries used to be horrified when they married into German royal families and found the palaces with sometimes dozens of these death chambers. Queen Victoria also observed this unpleasant custom. When Prince Albert died, his rooms at all the royal residences were kept exactly as they had been during his lifetime; and they were photographed so that when upholstery needed renewing, it could be prepared to match that used during his lifetime. Even more chillingly, the dead prince's clothes used to be laid out and hot water brought to his rooms each morning.

Princess Marie Louise, Queen Victoria's granddaughter (one of her forty grandchildren), married into the German princely house of Anhalt, and although the marriage was annulled apparently because it was never consummated—"She returns as she went," said Queen Victoria succinctly when the princess came back to England—Marie Louise lived for some years surrounded by relics of the dynasty. The Anhalts owned thirty-six castles crammed with possessions. One, for example, had the relics of Frederick the Great's famous general, Prince Leopold of Anhalt-Dessau, known in military history as "The Old Dessauer." Marie Louise recalled:

We would use his silver for our picnics, solid silver plates and knives out of his traveling canteen. There was also a most marvelous tent with a wonderful Persian carpet belonging to him . . . We had our supper sitting on it and eating off his silver plates.

The most august and important store of royal relics in Europe has been and is the Hapsburg treasure now kept in the Kunsthistorisches Museum in Vienna. It contains religious relics, some of which have been mentioned earlier, coronation regalia, vestments and royal garments, jewels and decorations. The most important are the Insignia and Regalia of the Holy Roman Empire, transferred to Vienna from Nuremberg and Aix-la-Chapelle during the Austrian retreat before the Napleonic

armies. The treasury has sustained some losses: after the First World War the members of the imperial family going into exile took their personal jewels; Italy demanded and got (Austria had been on the losing side) the insignia and vestments Napoleon used when he was crowned King of Italy; and in 1932 Hungary got the relics of the Order of St. Stephen, including a great diamond-studded cross of the order worn by the Empress Maria Theresa as queen of Hungary.

Two of the relics in the treasury were considered "the inalienable heirlooms of the House of Habsburg," and were the subject of a pact among the sons of the Holy Roman Emperor Ferdinand I in 1564, by which these two objects would not be bequeathed to any individual member of the family but would be considered in perpetuity as the property of the entire house, not to be sold, pledged, or taken out of the country. One was "The Agate Bowl," a dish twenty inches at its greatest width, believed to have been made at Trier in the fourth century A.D. It was sometimes identified with the Holy Grail. The other inalienable object was the "Ainkhürn" (horn of the unicorn), actually a tusk of the narwhal (*Monodon monoceros*), an Arctic mammal, the male of which has a spirally twisted tusk. The unicorn had an important place in the legends of the Middle Ages because it was identified with Christ: it could be caught only by a virgin as Christ was born of a virgin.

Among the minor trophies of the imperial dynasty is a "Golden Rose Tree," deriving from the custom of the pope's consecration of an engraved gold rose tree about two feet high each year on "Rose Sunday," the fourth Sunday in Lent, which was sent to a personage of high rank. The one in the treasury was sent by Pope Pius VII to the Empress Carolina Augusta of Austria in 1819.

The relics of the Bourbon dynasty in France have suffered greater depredations than those of almost any royal house. During the French Revolution, every royal residence was ransacked and many of them totally destroyed, with the loss or at least dispersal of the accumulated treasures of a family whose kings descended from Hugh Capet, who became ruler of France in 987 (Louis XVI and Marie Antoinette were called "Citizen Capet" and "Citizeness Capet" during their trials by the Revolutionary Assembly). Even the bodies of the French kings buried at Saint Denis chapel in Paris were turned out of their coffins and their dust scattered. The Revolutionary commissioners conducted a series of sales at Versailles in which incredible quantities of furniture, clocks, linens, pictures, and other royal possessions were knocked down, mostly for very low prices and quite frequently to foreign bidders. From this period date the beginnings of the great English collections of French royal furniture and objects of art that still fill entire rooms in museums.

Among the former royal possessions and collections that came on the market at that time was the armory of King Louis XIII. Like so many Bourbons, he was a passionate huntsman and all his life was devoted to arms and armor collecting. He is known to have owned more than three hundred guns. When he used one he personally cleaned it. The breaking up of his famous *cabinet d'armes* at the time of the French Revolution was a landmark in the collecting of antique weapons. Nearly two centuries afterward guns from the armory of Louis XIII still appear at auction and are absorbed into new collections. In 1973, the Metropolitan Museum of Art paid $300,000 at auction, a world record for a weapon, for a flintlock fowling piece' that had once belonged to the king.

Queen Marie Antoinette became a cult figure from the moment of her execution in 1793. Her dignity at her farcical trial and her courage on the scaffold seem to have obliterated the memory of her silly interference in the government of France during the previous decade. Her relics have attracted numerous collectors. The Empress Eugénie, wife of Napoleon III, had great admiration for Marie Antoinette, with whom she appears to have identified herself, although she lost only her throne. She led the restoration of Versailles to an appearance similar to that of Marie Antoinette's time. Proust had his fictional Baron de Charlus collect the hats of the queen and her ladies, which he displayed in a cabinet in his green drawing room. During the nineteenth century and particularly toward its close, any relic of Marie Antoinette that came on the market aroused great interest. In 1886, a consignment of lace that had been collected by a Miss Gamble was sold for the benefit of Girton College (for women) at Oxford. A lace "flounce and Berthe of point-de-Venise" with coats of arms and the initials of Marie Antoinette believed to be from her wedding dress sold for £236; in terms of

today's purchasing power that was probably over $5,000.

Jewels once belonging to Marie Antoinette have been in the collections of many famous buyers. The late American heiress Marjorie Merriweather Post frequently wore the pair of pear-shaped diamond earrings that were found sewed into Marie Antoinette's pocket when she was arrested at Varennes, attempting to escape from France. The earrings are now at the Smithsonian Institution. Many pieces of furniture commissioned by Marie Antoinette and found on the inventories of the palaces have come onto the market. These are not collected primarily as relics; their high prices are a reflection of the fact that eighteenth century French royal furniture is the finest ever made. The name of Marie Antoinette, however, still means something: in 1973 there was a lawsuit in New York State Supreme Court between a collector and a furniture dealer over a "kidney shaped travel, dressing and writing table made of ebony and ivory with mountable legs and secret drawers" said to have belonged to her. It had been sold by the dealer to the collector for $22,000 with the "false and negligent representation," said the collector, "that the table had been made for and had once belonged to Marie Antoinette."

Curious reminders of the French queen are the porcelain bowls in the shape of one of her breasts called *bols-sein*. The story is that the breast cups were modeled from her bosom and used by her guests to drink milk at the Petit Trianon while they were playing at being dairymaids. Be that as it may, the Sèvres porcelain factory long reproduced the model with a biscuit base formed by three rams' heads. The cup is about five inches in diameter. Nineteenth and twentieth century examples sell currently at around $400 to $500.

The fascination of the queen for the public is still strong. New biographies often appear, and in 1955 a great exhibition in Paris marked the bicentenary of her birth. Nearly one thousand relics were exhibited to throngs of visitors. They included twenty-two of the huge white diamonds originally in the famous "Diamond Necklace of Marie Antoinette" about which so much has been written, a mauve silk waistcoat she embroidered for her son, the young dauphin, the wooden spoon she ate with while in prison, and—as the final exhibit—part of a black silk stocking the Queen wore to her execution, exhumed with her remains in 1815.

Masterpieces of the cabinetmaker's art were created for French royalty of the eighteenth century on a scale never since equaled. Jean-Henri Riesener, one of the favored furniture makers of Queen Marie Antoinette, made this handsome console table for her. The high prices paid by today's collectors for such pieces are usually a reflection of their value as objects of art and not of their former ownership. *Sotheby Parke-Bernet, New York*

Relics of Bonaparte rule in France are discussed in chapter 6.

Among British royal families the Stuarts merit a section to themselves (see text later in this chapter) because their relics are by far the most generally collected. The royal possessions and collections were dispersed after the execution of King Charles I in 1649; at the Restoration eleven years later, even the regalia had to be reconstituted for the Coronation.

Relics of earlier kings and queens survive mainly in the collections of the great English houses, often as gifts from various monarchs to their subjects, or souvenirs of their residence there. At Sudeley Castle in Gloucestershire, for example, the home of Catherine Parr, last queen and widow of King Henry VIII, there are many objects that belonged to the queen, including her needlework. Catherine Parr had received from her stepdaughter Queen Elizabeth I a manuscript the eleven-year-old Elizabeth wrote for her in 1544 in her finest italic hand. The vellum manuscript, which is entitled "How We Ought to Know God," now in the Bodleian Library, Oxford, is one of several calligraphic manuscripts known to have been written by Elizabeth, who was proud of her handwriting. She was also proud of her skill with music, and her virginals (they were a sort of primitive desk-piano) emblazoned with the arms of the Boleyns, the family of her unhappy mother, are still kept in the Victoria and Albert Museum, London. Hatfield House in Hertfordshire has some very personal relics of the great queen: her gloves, straw gardening hat, and a pair of silk stockings said to be the first worn in England.

The Hanoverian dynasty never inspired much enthusiasm, and no premium has been placed on relics of the Georges, although scarlet breeches worn by King George II at the Battle of Dettingen were once sold at auction for the high price of ten guineas (about $500 today), as were George III's pale blue brocade dressing gown (twenty guineas) and his razor (three guineas), and the shoes worn by George IV at his coronation in 1820 (five guineas). Some of the finest English silver was made for the Hanoverian kings, and many pieces of it have been sold for record-breaking prices in recent years, but as in the case of Marie Antoinette's furniture, the prices are primarily for craftsmanship—and with silver, weight—rather than as relics.

Queen Victoria did not particularly care to be reminded of her ancestors. She was sensitive on the matter of her grandfather George III's madness, and there had been so much trouble with her uncles and aunts during her childhood that they were not a pleasant topic for reminiscence either. She was slightly more interested in her Stuart ancestors, probably because of her affection for Scotland, their country, and added to the collection of Stuart relics at Windsor. She doted, however, on preserving relics of her own enormous family (nine children and forty grandchildren before she died). The hair of her children and grandchildren was

set in gold lockets, numbers of which hung from her bracelets. On birthdays and other days of family commemoration, she always wore special brooches or other pieces of jewelry given to her by members of the family. Although little of this jewelry is ever on the collectors' market, various relics of Victoria are occasionally available. A most unusual tea service of sixty-four pieces, each with a transfer-printed snapshot of the Queen and her family in informal poses, was sold in 1971 for $375; the only other known set is in the royal collection at Windsor Castle.

The first member of the British royal family to take a real interest in its relics was Queen Victoria's granddaughter-in-law, the late Queen Mary. As her biographer James Pope-Hennessy wrote: "She was a pioneer amongst the modern royal family in this field." In 1904, the Cambridge branch of the royal family began to disperse its family possessions, and Queen Mary commenced "to collect, to preserve, to docket" the Hanoverian memorabilia. Identification of the numerous objects in the various palaces was in itself a life's work, and the Queen spent years at what she described as "my one great hobby." She also collected herself, mostly small objects of vertu—jade, Fabergé, enamels, and other bibelots. Her interest may be summed up in what she wrote in 1948 at the time of the birth of the present Prince of Wales: "I gave the baby a silver gilt cup and cover which George III had given to a godson in 1780, so that I gave a present from my great-grandfather to my great-grandson 168 years later."

Other royal memorabilia are in use by the reigning family of Great Britain. When Princess Anne was married in 1973 her wedding ring was made from the same nugget of Welsh gold from which came the rings of her grandmother, mother, and aunt. She carried a bouquet with a cutting from a myrtle bush grown from a sprig from Queen Victoria's wedding bouquet in 1840.

Lost causes have their charms. For generations collectors have eagerly sought memorabilia of the royal house of Stuart, the Southern Confederacy, the Romanoff dynasty, and others of history's well-known lost causes. No lost cause has attracted more devotion—thousands died or were exiled for it—than the restoration of the Stuarts to the throne of England. "Jacobitism," as it became known in

At Traquair House in Peeblesshire, said to be the oldest inhabited house in Scotland, are preserved some important relics of Mary, Queen of Scots, including (as shown here) her rosary, crucifix, and purse. In the background can be seen part of the cradle in which Mary rocked her son, later James VI of Scotland and I of England, during a visit in 1566. *Scottish Tourist Board, Edinburgh*

the seventeenth century, after the Latin form of the exiled King James II's name, played a major role in British history for a century, and for generations more rallied romantics to the most romantic of lost causes despite a succession of feeble Stuart pretenders. Stuart relics are the most widely collected royal souvenirs.

The earliest Stuart to become the object of devotion was Mary Queen of Scots, and countless relics of her have been preserved, mainly from her long captivity in England (1568–87), when Roman Catholics and many Scots came to regard her almost with veneration. Locks of her hair, described as "brown in the shade and golden in the sun" in her youth, but darkening as she grew older, have been preserved. The queen excelled, like most ladies of her time, at handwork. (Her enemy Elizabeth of England was an exception: she hated doing needlework even as a little girl.) Many pieces of Mary's embroidery survive and an entire book has been written on her needlework. Babies just walking were at that time put into leading strings to keep them from walking into the open fires. Mary embroidered such a set of leading strings consisting of three broad rose-colored silk ribbons, four feet long, with Psalm XCI, verse 11 ("For He shall give his

angels charge over thee neither shall any plague come nigh thy dwelling") for her baby son James VI of Scotland (later James I of England). These are in a private collection. A cloth of silver purse and other work she did during her captivity have survived; at Scone Palace in Perth, Scotland, is a whole set of bed hangings worked by the queen.

When the romantic cult of all the Stuarts grew in the late nineteenth century, prices increased for such relics as came up for sale. At the great auction of the possessions of he Scottish Duke of Hamilton in 1882, referred to

These four pieces of jewelry are mourning commemorations of King Charles I of England, the Stuart Martyr. From left to right, they are a heart-shaped pendant, three and three-quarters inches long with rubies and rose diamonds set with a portrait of the king; a toothpick with an enameled hand holding a ring; another pendant with an enameled portrait of Charles I; and a scepter, four inches long. All were made about 1680. *Christie's, London*

as "The Hamilton Palace Sale," a commemorative coin known as the "Cruikstone Dollar" was sold. It had been struck on the occasion of the marriage (her second) of Queen Mary with her cousin Henry Stuart, Lord Darnley, in 1565, and was set in a frame made of the wood of a yew tree under which the royal couple were said to have courted. The frame was inscribed with a lightly rakish verse:

When Harie met Marie under this yew tree
What Harie did to Marie I'll no tell to thee.

Lord Darnley was regarded as the handsomest man of his time, athletic and lusty. He was noted for his fine penmanship, an art then much prized, and for his playing on the lute. Mary fell in love with him on sight. Part of his attraction for her was undoubtedly his remarkable height: he was over six feet one inch tall, unusual for a man of that era. Mary herself was nearly that tall and was accustomed to towering over most men. It took her, however, only a short time after her marriage to discover that Darnley—for all his beauty and accomplishments—was faithless, bad-tempered, and alcoholic. The "Cruikstone Dollar," relic of Mary's short-lived love, was sold at the Hamilton Palace auction to Lord Moray, also a member of the House of Stuart, for £168 (in today's terms not less than $4,000).

According to Lady Antonia Fraser, the queen's latest biographer, the government of Elizabeth I took such steps to prevent Mary's body and belongings from becoming objects of veneration after her execution in 1587 that a "doubtful light" is cast on the many relics dating from that time. Her clothing was burned instead of becoming the perquisite of the executioner. One of the most touching relics is a silver handbell, four inches high, used during her captivity and given by Mary to one of her favorite attendants just before her death. Perhaps the most important relic of the queen is her magnificent gold rosary and crucifix, which she bequeathed at her execution to the Countess of Arundel. It is now in the possession of the leading Roman Catholic peer of England, the Duke of Norfolk.

From earlier periods of her life, numerous relics of the Queen of Scots are preserved in both public and private collections. The British Museum has her signet ring, the Victoria and Albert Museum has the veil worn at her trial, and the Royal College of Music has a very curious relic, the guitar of David Rizzio, her private secretary and a bass singer, who was murdered by Lord Darnley. A casket that may have contained the celebrated letters proving Mary's connivance in plotting the horrible death of Darnley—he was blown up with gunpowder—belongs to the Dukes of Hamilton. The "Casket Letters" themselves, about which historians have almost shed one another's blood, disappeared long ago.

Still more relics have been preserved of Mary's grandson, Charles I of England—"King and Martyr," as he was called by the Stuart adherents after his execution by Cromwell's parliament. Gloves, a hat, shirts, and a boot worn by Charles as a boy are in the London Museum. For his trial the king had been brought to London from the Isle of Wight, where he had been incarcerated at Carisbrooke Castle. Several relics are still at the castle: a prayer book, a nightcap, and a piece of cravat. The chair covered with red velvet in which he sat at his trial is in the Victoria and Albert Museum. At the Ashmolean Museum, Oxford, is a quainter relic: a specially reinforced flat-brimmed hat made for John Bradshaw, president of the court at the trial, presumably for protection from the king's adherents.

In the time between his sentencing by the court and his execution, the king gave away the few personal belongings he still possessed. His son James, Duke of York (afterward James II), was given a curious invention made by Richard Delamaine, who had been the king's mathematics tutor years earlier. It was a large double ring of silver with figures engraved on it, which could be used both as a sundial and a slide rule "resolving many questions in arithmatick."

The king was beheaded "in Whitehall," the part of London between the Thames River and Saint James's Park that is now government offices. The exact spot where the scaffold stood has long been a topic of violent antiquarian dispute. Benjamin Disraeli said he could detect a bore when he began to discuss on which side of Whitehall the king was killed. The date was the thirtieth of January 1648, as the calendar was then (Old Style), when the new year began in March; by present reckoning it was 30 January 1649. Charles wore two shirts to his execution because the day was cold and he did not want to shiver; the people—and there were thousands of spectators—would think he was shivering with fear. Both these shirts have been

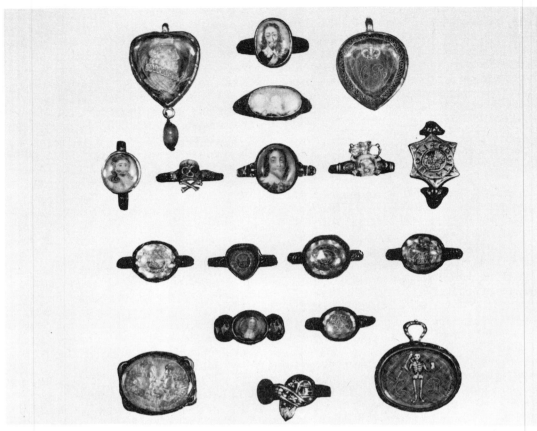

Among these gold pendants and rings are many mourning jewels commemorating King Charles I, who is frequently portrayed, several times in company with his wife the French princess Henrietta Maria. The skulls, death's-heads, and skeletons are common devices. Several pieces are inscribed in English or Latin "Remember the 30 of Jann. 1648." By today's reckoning, the date of King Charles's execution was 30 January 1649. Until the eighteenth century the New Year began in England in March, January being the eleventh month. Another popular inscription on Stuart mourning jewelry was "Preparéd be to follow me." *Christie's, London*

preserved: one is in the royal collection at Windsor, the other at Longleat House.

On the scaffold the king gave his "George," the jeweled insignia of the Order of the Garter, to his chaplain, Bishop Juxon, with the famous single word: "Remember." The Parliamentarians, anxious that cult objects be held to a minimum, took the "George" from Bishop Juxon, but at the Stuart Restoration in 1660, it was recovered by King Charles II. When Charles's brother James II was ejected from England by the Glorious Revolution, he took it with him. From him it descended to Prince Charles Edward ("The Young Pretender") and finally to his wife, the Countess of Albany, who sold it in 1810 to an emissary of the Marquess Wellesley, Wellington's brother and then British Minister of Foreign Affairs. It has descended in the Wellington family, and this major royal relic is still in their possession.

These Stuart relics and mementos include a peachstone (see photograph on page 80); also a book-shaped pendant two and a half inches high, which contains a silver gilt portrait of King Charles I and a piece of bloodstained cloth, undoubtedly from the clothing worn by the king at his execution. Beneath this the two lockets honor the Martyr (at left, with skull) and (right) King Charles II. The bottom row includes a medallion of Charles I, fine cut glass portrait three and a one-quarter inches high of Prince Charles Edward Stuart, "The Bonnie Prince," and an ivory pipe stopper (tamp), three inches high, in the form of a cavalier. *Christie's, London*

This unusual relic is a peachstone carved with a portrait of Charles I, painted and carved on the reverse (see photograph, page 79, upper left) with the badge of the Order of the Garter, set in a gold pendant. Carved about 1640, it is signed by the artist Nicholas Briot with his initials. It is about an inch and a quarter high. At the Sloane-Stanley sale at Christie's in 1973, this important piece of Stuart memorabilia sold for the very high price of $8,600.

The scene around the scaffold after the king's head fell was indescribable. Those who wanted to dip their handkerchiefs in the royal blood were admitted on the payment of a fee. The guards tore up and sold pieces of the boards into which the blood had soaked and handfuls of blood-spattered sand. Locks of hair were cut off and sold. The king's small body—he was only five feet four inches tall—was hurried away and embalmed, and all requests for hair were refused by the surgeon.

Soon miracles of curing the sick were being reported from the blood-soaked cloths, and the king was regarded as a martyr. The Parliamentarians were alarmed and tried to outlaw physical reminders of the royal martyr. A concerted effort—fitting, in view of their iconoclastic attitude toward the depicting arts in general—was made by the Puritans to destroy statues and pictures of the king. The bronze statue of the monarch by Hubert Le Sueur in the gardens at the Palace of Whitehall, where Charles was executed, was sold to a contractor, ostensibly for him to melt down for the metal content. Either a devoted royalist or a singularly farsighted businessman, the contractor buried the statue rather than melting it. At the same time he sold to the public pocketknives said to have been made from the metal. At the Restoration of the monarchy eleven years later, he triumphantly unearthed the intact statue that stands today in Whitehall.

Great interest has always been felt by collectors in relics of the execution. As long ago as 1825 one of the most important Caroline relics was sold at auction: the prayer book with his name written in it that the king used on the scaffold. It had become a possession of the diarist John Evelyn, a devout monarchist, who wrote on it: "This is the Booke which Charles the First M.B. [Martyr Beatus] did use upon the Scaffold xxx Jan. 1648, being the day of his glorious martyrdom." The prayer book fetched £105, probably $5,000 today. In 1898, the blue silk vest worn by the king on the day of his execution (over the two shirts) came up for sale at Stevens's Rooms, London, having descended for generations in the family of his physician. It brought 200 guineas (about $6,000). At the same time a nail from the scaffold was sold for six and a half guineas ($200 today).

Admiration of the king was so great that his relics were split up the way those of the old saints had been: one Legitimist family owned one of his white leather gloves; its mate belonged to another family.

In 1971 an important relic of Charles I reached the salesroom: his "travelling library," a set of fifty-eight small volumes of the classic authors fitted into a trunk made for them, sold at Sotheby's for $15,000. And in February 1973 a large collection of Stuart relics formed by Major Cyril Sloane-Stanley was sold at Christie's for the impressive total of $42,000, demonstrating the great interest still existing in these pieces. Among the lots were a gold pendant set with a peachstone portrait and a woven silk garter (see the illustrations).

Perhaps it should be added that relics have been sold at auction of Charles I's greatest opponent: Oliver Cromwell. Huntingdon is the locality most closely associated with Cromwell. At the museum dedicated to him there are scores of relics, including the hat he wore at the Dissolution of the Long Parliament in 1653, swords, his boots, stirrups, and spurs, and a cannonball from the battlefield of Marston Moor, where he defeated the royal forces. In 1910, one of Cromwell's swords sold at auction in New York for $1,500, and J. P. Morgan once owned his leather tankard, but Cromwell collectors have always been a tiny minority. Several copies of a death mask of Cromwell have changed hands; one of them is now in the National Portrait Gallery, London. The body of Cromwell, incidentally, was dug up when the Stuarts were restored and was beheaded.

King Charles II, for all the rakish associations of his reign, has never been popular with collectors, although his waistcoat, table napkin, and other memorabilia have been on the market, and there is a wax effigy of him—probably carried in his funeral procession, as was then the custom—in Westminster Abbey dressed in robes of the Order of the Garter.

The romance of the Stuart pretenders to the throne of England begins with the deposing of Charles's brother, James II, by the Glorious Revolution in 1688. Because of the large number of the disaffected, especially in Scotland, who believed that James and later his son Prince James ("The Old Pretender" or to the Jacobites "James III") and his grandson Prince Charles Edward Stuart ("The Young Pretender," or "Bonnie Prince Charlie," to the Jacobites "Charles III") were the rightful kings of England, a spirit of rebellion grew up which not only resulted in serious uprisings in Scotland against the Hanoverians in 1715 and 1745 ("The '15" and "The '45" in Scottish history), but gave birth to an entire secret Jacobite cult.

Jacobitism consisted not only in actually plotting against the *de facto* government of Great Britain but in endless more or less surreptitious jibes at it. When drinking a toast, the Jacobite passed his wineglass over a dish of water to make a silent homage "to The King over the water" (this custom was said to account for the unpopularity of finger bowls at the English court as late as the time of Queen Victoria!). When King William III was thrown by a horse that had been startled by a mole, and later died, Jacobites toasted the mole as "the little gentleman in a black velvet coat."

"Jacobite glasses"—i.e., wineglasses engraved with Stuart emblems such as the White Rose and the plant known as "Jacob's Ladder" or slogans such as "Redeat" ("May he come back")—were produced in great numbers and today constitute an entire field in glass collecting classified as "Old Pretender glasses," "Young Pretender glasses," and so on. A fine "Old Pretender" glass recently sold for $2,500 was inscribed "Send Him soon Home / To Holyruood House [the Scottish royal palace in Edinburgh] and that no Sooner / than I do wish Vive Le Roy." During the reign of King William III and for years after, there were also "Williamite" goblets, which were of course used openly and proudly. A typical goblet was engraved with a portrait of the king and inscribed "The Glorious and Immortal Memory of King William and his Queen Mary and Perpetual disappointment to the Pope the Pretender and all the Enemies of the Protestant Religion" (sold in 1962 for $2,200).

Glasses are by no means the only Jacobite souvenirs. Even pincushions were embroidered at the time of Bonnie Prince Charlie's uprising in '45 with the motto "God Bless P. C.," and personal relics of the three pretenders were treasured as almost sacred objects. The Stuart hopes were really ended at the Battle of Culloden in 1746, when the Bonnie Prince was defeated by the Hanoverian Duke of Cumberland, although there were plans for new uprisings for another decade. The Bonnie Prince was in hiding for six months in the Highlands of Scotland before he could get away to the Continent. Numerous relics, mainly gifts from the prince to the faithful who sheltered him at frightful risk to themselves, are still preserved from this time, including his "sporran," the purse affixed to the front of the Highland kilt (which the prince wore during his concealment), his dagger, gloves, and so on. A famous Jacobite family, the Gordons of Kildrummy Castle, sold their relics of the Bonnie Prince in 1898, when his yellow satin vest brought $300 and two gold rings given by the prince to Gordon retainers, $250 each. Since then, many relics have reached the market and more may be expected as ancient Scottish families die out.

The most important relic of the Bonnie Prince to be sold in years was his camp canteen used at the Battle of Culloden and captured there by the Duke of Cumberland, who gave it to his favorite aide-de-camp as a reward for carrying news of the victory to London. The canteen was a silver container in the shape of a

flask, seven inches high, engraved with Prince of Wales feathers (he regarded himself, and was regarded by the Jacobites, as Prince of Wales, since the Old Pretender was still alive in 1745), that held full equipment for eating in the field: knives, forks, spoons, spice containers, and so on. It had been made for him in Edinburgh in 1740. This interesting relic, sold by a descendant of the aide-de-camp to whom it had been given, brought $20,000 at auction in 1962.

The Young Pretender's brother, Henry Benedict Stuart, was born in Rome, never saw the British Isles, and spoke English as a foreign language. He became a cardinal in 1747, to the fury of his brother, who realized that not only was the Stuart succession now reduced to himself alone—and he never had any legitimate children—but that the action emphasized the Roman Catholicism of the Stuart pretenders and probably cost the allegiance of Protestant Jacobites, who up to that time had been fairly numerous. The brothers did not see each other for the next nineteen years. Henry Benedict took the name Cardinal York (which the Italians transformed into "D'Orck" or even "D'Orco") and, enriched by pensions and grants from the popes and the kings of France and Spain (the Spanish king gave him real estate in Mexico), he passed his life in luxury in Rome and nearby Frascati until the French Revolutionary wars made him a refugee from the anticlerical French troops. When Napoleon ordered the Papal States to pay a heavy indemnity in 1797, Cardinal York contributed two magnificent family heirlooms: a solid gold shield given by the Austrian Emperor to King John Sobieski of Poland, the cardinal's ancestor, in commemoration of his defeat of the Turks before Vienna in 1686, and "The Great Ruby of Poland," a gem the size of a pigeon's egg. Shortly after this, the cardinal became a refugee from Rome and so destitute that King

George III, out of sympathy for this last of the Stuarts, sent him financial aid.

After the death of the Young Pretender in 1788, Cardinal York was regarded by the Jacobites as "King Henry IX of England." Medals were struck to commemorate his "reign," and he was addressed—at least by his servants and tactful visitors—as "Majesty." He was not, however, recognized by the popes, who had grown tired of the endless pretensions and costly failures of the hapless Stuarts, although they had sacrificed the British throne for Roman Catholicism. When this last of the Stuarts died in 1807, he disposed of many relics in his will. He left to the Prince Regent of England (later George IV) a diamond cross worn by Charles I and a ring that had been part of the ancient royal regalia of Scotland. A friend received the veil of Mary Queen of Scots. A great jewel known as the "Stuart Emerald" was left to one of his cousins. The "Stuart Emerald" was sold at auction in 1971, with a long account of its romantic history, for $130,000. It had been mounted by that time as a pendant brooch with diamonds and pearls.

Cardinal York's pretensions to the British throne passed by descent to the royal house of Savoy, then to the house of Austria-Este, and finally to the house of Wittelsbach, the Bavarian royal family. None of these princes made any attempt to assert the Stuart claim to Great Britain, but British Jacobites followed them faithfully if from a distance and without taking any treasonous action. The cult of the Stuarts became entirely romantic. Queen Victoria herself did not scorn her Stuart connections (except the lecherous King Charles II, of whom "the Queen did not approve"), and at her favorite palace of Balmoral in Scotland she used the Royal Stuart tartan for carpets and the Dress Stuart tartan for curtains and slipcovers, with an effect that was by all accounts

This long garter of the Stuart period could be worn either "crossed" or tied in a bow. The vogue for decorating embroidered garters with religious or political "posies" was at its height in the second half of the seventeenth century. "The Rump" refers to the celebrated remnant of the Long Parliament that survived Colonel Pride's Purge of December 1648 during the English Civil War. *Christie's, London*

startling. The handsome Prince Albert wore the Stuart kilt when he went deerstalking, although since he had skinny legs Highland dress was, as a court lady delicately put it, "not quite flattering to His Highness."

There was a certain increase in sentimental interest in the Stuarts in the late nineteenth century, especially in the upper classes in England and America. The "Order of the White Rose" was revived in 1886 in England and spread to the United States, where its president (called "Prior") was for many years Ralph Adams Cram, architect of the Cathedral of Saint John the Divine. A great Stuart Exhibi-

tion was held in London in 1889, in which many notable relics of the house were shown. It was an active period for collecting—many of the collections since on the market (for example, the Sloane-Stanley Collection mentioned above) were formed at this period. The Jacobite movement expired at the time of the First World War, however, for the excellent reason that the then "Pretender" was Prince Rupprecht of Bavaria (Jacobite "Rupert I"), field marshal in the German Army and commander of the Northern Group along the Western Front; and for an Englishman or American to follow him was treason.

6

Souvenirs of Heroism: Military and Naval Relics

Napoleon first acquired note on the thirteenth Vendémiaire 1795, less than two months after his twenty-sixth birthday, when he stood off a Parisian mob charging the Tuileries Palace. Within a very few years he had become the most famous man on earth; he still was when he died in his island prison on Saint Helena in 1821. He himself said: "I am not a man, but an event." Small wonder that from his young manhood people whom he encountered, no matter how briefly, preserved objects he had owned—even fleetingly. Reverence for his relics has never slackened, but certain high points have marked its progress: 1840, when his remains were reburied in the Church of the Invalides in Paris; during the Second French Empire, 1852–71, when his nephew occupied the throne; the 1920s, marking the centenary of his death; 1940, the reburial of his only child, Napoleon II, beside him; and 1969, the bicentenary of his birth. The present time is one of important Napoleonic studies and great interest in his relics.

As a result of the persistence of the Napoleonic legend, relics and mementos of the emperor exist today in large numbers and are very widely dispersed. Frédéric Masson, who devoted his whole life to Napoleonic studies, wrote that to form a definitive list of the Napoleonic relics it would be necessary to search "the whole of Europe, and," he added in apparent surprise, "even the United States." Masson published an inventory of the emperor's wardrobe, which is available in English

(see Bibliography). The inventory and Masson's detailed historical notes are indispensable to the collector and are also fascinating reading; they give an incomparable description of what the emperor actually owned and used on a daily basis. In the "Personal Clothing" section, for example, one learns that, contrary to most artistic depictions, he did not invariably wear a gray overcoat; he owned six cloth overcoats of various colors and had two new ones made each year. Three, the inventory briefly records, were "burned in Russia." One learns, too, that even at Saint Helena he still had eighty-seven shirts of the finest linen, which were so valuable he bequeathed them in his will—half a dozen to his son, and twenty-seven each to his executors.

For the Napoleonic collector, such information can be extremely useful when he is offered items said to have belonged to the emperor. A great many hats said to have been worn by the emperor seem to find their way into the salesroom, but from Masson's prodigious researches in the official records one learns that he owned more than fifty recorded hats during his public career. As anyone who studies the Napoleonic legend knows, any person into whose hands an imperial hat came probably kept it. Many have been sold; it is not unlikely that more will come up for sale.

There is a visual richness about many Napoleonic relics that increases their attractiveness to collectors. The First Empire was an era of great craftsmanship, heavy and dazzling mate-

85

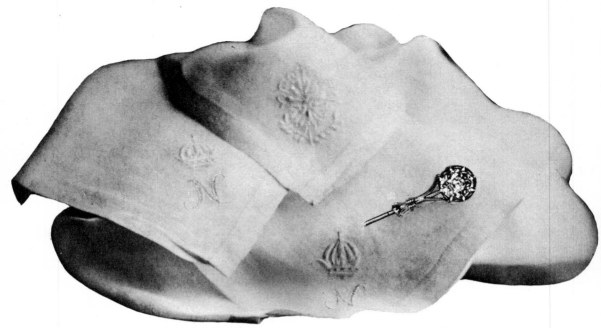

Napoleon's silk cravat and diamond tiepin sold at auction in Amsterdam in 1970 for $6,800. *Paul Brandt, N. V., Amsterdam*

rials, and striking motifs. Innumerable sumptuous articles were made for use and display. The emperor himself was but little interested in the trappings of glory except insofar as they emphasized his power and augmented his glory. Superb articles of furniture, jewelry, and plate were created for him, his family, and his courtiers in the classical (then called "antique") style that is unmistakably "Empire," but personally his tastes were simple. His soldiers ransacked Europe and the Near East for art treasures from the past, but, again, the collections were for glory. The emperor himself showed little interest in memorabilia. He was given various historic relics, including the sword of the Polish patriot John Sobieski by the City of Warsaw, but seldom did he personally collect a relic. He revered Frederick the Great of Prussia, as any soldier might. After the Battle of Jena in 1806, when all Germany lay at his feet, Napoleon visited Frederick's little palace of Sans Souci at Potsdam, where he appropriated Frederick's sword for himself. He carried this relic with him to Saint Helena.

Even Napoleon, however, was not aloof from the nineteenth century mania for hair souvenirs. He had the Empress Marie Louise's hair woven into a chain worn with a gold watch, and in his will he ordered a similar chain made of his own hair for his son, the King of Rome. A lock of the infant's hair was sent to his father at Saint Helena. The emperor kept it carefully in his dressing case alongside a lock of Josephine's hair sent to him at Elba after her death.

Artifacts of the imperial period are called indiscriminately "Napoleonic," "First Empire," or merely "Empire." A group of craftsmen are famous for their imperial commissions: Abraham Louis Breguet for clocks and watches; Nicholas Noël Boutet for firearms; and many silversmiths, including Odiot and Biennais, whose shop was called Au Singe Violet (At the Purple Monkey). Their productions were usually ornamented with the well-known series of decorative motifs associated with the Empire. The Napoleonic cipher (his initial N), eagles, and bees are the emblems most commonly employed.

The imperial use of the bees—incorporated in an amazing variety of objects—is an interesting story. At the commencement of his reign, Napoleon sought an emblem that would symbolize the energy and productivity of his new French Empire and was distinctive and new, but not too new. He wanted to erase the memory of the lilies that had for centuries been the royal mark of the legitimate French dynasties of Valois and Bourbon and were the rallying point for those in opposition to the new Empire. So he turned to the more distant past. Like Hitler a century and a half later, he cunningly used a symbol to remind his people of their ancient days of supremacy. Hitler was always talking about the First Reich (the empire of Charlemagne) and the Second Reich (the Prussian empire) as forerunners of his own Third Reich. Napoleon went back even farther, to the first dynasty of French kings, the Merovingians. This royal family, a thoroughly unpleasant lot given to succession by parricide, had begun with Childerich I in the misty dark ages of European history, when France was not yet converted to Christianity. Childerich died a pagan in approximately A.D. 481. In 1653, his grave was found near Tournai in Belgium. In it were three hundred mummified bees, apparently symbols of his royalty. They were given to King Louis XIV as French royal property. (A few of them are still preserved in Paris in the former royal collections at the Cabinet des Medailles.) Napoleon adopted this antique symbol as his own, and bees are found in gold, silver, precious stones, embroidery, and a hundred other ways in Napoleonic art and antiques.

Among the many categories of Napoleonic relics, the showiest and best known are the arms, the silver, and the jewels. Although these are beyond the reach of the average collector, a short description of some examples helps complete the roster of Napoleonic relics.

Collectors of firearms dote on those produced during the Napoleonic era. It was one of the great ages of gunmaking, particularly of presentation arms and pairs of dueling pistols. These last, engraved and decorated and laid with all their equipment in elaborate velvet-lined rosewood cases, also heavily decorated in silver, have become especially famous. Pairs of Empire dueling pistols sell for $5,000 upward; those by Nicholas Noël Boutet are more expensive.

A pair of imperial presentation pistols made by Boutet, the butts inlaid in silver with the insignia of the Grand Cross of the Légion d'Honneur and also richly decked with eagles, crossed arrows, shields, and other martial emblems, sold in 1972 for nearly $50,000. They

were said by the auction house to have been captured by the Russians during the French retreat from Moscow, which may very well be true. Enormous quantities of equipment were in fact taken by the Russians from the stores the French brought to Russia and had to discard. Around 1900 the saddle and bridle used by the emperor himself in Russia were sold at auction for £90 ($2,000 to $3,000), and as the Masson inventory shows, he also lost some of his clothing in the course of that prolonged debacle.

Silver made for the emperor and his family is usually easily recognizable by its weight and its coats of arms and imperial motifs. All the Bonapartes had luxurious tastes or acquired them, and they were especially fond of silver table services of extraordinary heaviness. Even at Saint Helena the emperor had so much silver plate that he could sell five hundred pounds of it for expenses—the English in effect were causing him to pay for his own captivity—and still have masses left for daily use.

As for the imperial family, a fair example of their taste for luxurious table accoutrements is the celebrated gilded silver dinner service ordered by Napoleon's sister Pauline Bonaparte and her husband Prince Camillo Borghese. The service was created by the Parisian silversmiths Martin Guillaume Biennais and Jean Baptiste Claude Odiot in the very early years of the nineteenth century. After the collapse of the Bonaparte and Borghese fortunes—Pauline sold her diamonds to assist her brother during his exile on Elba—the service passed through various hands. In the early part of this century it was in Chicago—among the innumerable possessions of the American collector Edith Rockefeller McCormick, the daughter of John D. Rockefeller, Sr., and the wife of Harold Fowler McCormick, the "Reaper King." After her death the service was sold at auction in New York in 1934. It is not known how many pieces it originally numbered, but even at the time of the auction it still consisted of no fewer than 1,600, weighing upwards of 11,700 ounces or about one-third of a ton of silver. In addition to the usual complement of plates, serving dishes, and flatware, the count included cake baskets, coasters, and twenty-three mustard spoons, among other implements. In that grim Depression year, the service brought a total of $57,535—or about $35 a piece. It was divided into many lots at the sale and so became scattered all over the world. Individual items, especially examples of the plates engraved with the Borghese arms, have come back onto the market at much higher prices in small lots or even as single pieces. Recently, individual plates from this famous service have sold for $500 to $750. They are typical and important relics of the Empire style and the Bonaparte family.

The Bonapartes were great travelers, not always by their own choice. Many of them visited the United States, and Joseph Bonaparte, the emperor's brother, lived for twenty years in New Jersey. Wherever they went they were accompanied by luxurious traveling services for eating, drinking, and the toilet, which were produced in large numbers in the restless Napoleonic era. The *nécessaire* for eating and drinking consisted of silver plates and flatware, tea- and coffeepots, silver or glass containers for coffee, tea, and condiments, porcelain cups and saucers; the more elaborate contained dish warmers, covered serving dishes, spirit lamps, and kettles. These last were also executed in silver or gilded silver. But there was no limit to what could be included for the rich patron. The emperor's own traveling cases often combined the articles used at meals and in another tray—the traveling cases were fitted like small chests of drawers—toilet articles such as razors, sponge boxes, nail scissors, and a mirror. One of the imperial cases contained 109 separate useful articles. An elaborate traveling eating service given by Pauline Borghese to the emperor may be seen in the Metropolitan Museum of Art, New York.

Toilet services, some for traveling and some for stationary beautification, delighted the ladies of the imperial household. The Empress Josephine, who was madly spendthrift even for an empress, had a sumptuous toilet service made for her in 1804–1808 that included a mirror of solid silver weighing more than ninety pounds and forty other articles in the same metal. The Josephine toilet service brought nearly a quarter of a million dollars when it was sold in 1959 in Switzerland. Other traveling services have been sold for much less, including one of Napoleon's tea and coffee sets for $25,000, but no complete set is likely to sell within the reach of the average collector.

The same statement is true of Bonaparte jewelry, which exists in most of the great jewel collections of the world, public and private, and frequently changes hands. A sumptuous diamond necklace the emperor gave to Marie Louise was among the incredible jewels of the late heiress Marjorie Merriweather Post and often worn by her. Some of the most magnificent jewelry ever made was created for the Bonaparte women; probably only the jewels of the Russian imperial family have been more fabulous. Napoleon loaded both his wives with jewels. One of Josephine's tiaras is shown. Pauline Bonaparte also owned spectacular jewelry; one of her diadems was sold in Geneva in 1970 for $28,500.

The taste for bejeweled boxes for snuff, candy, toothpicks, and other small articles still flourished in Napoleon's time, although it was shortly to fade away. Like eighteenth century royalty, the emperor usually bestowed the boxes on his courtiers as a sign of favor, except for the tortoiseshell *bonbonnières* in which he carried licorice. On Saint Helena he still had over fifty *bonbonnières* and snuffboxes to bequeath to his son. Most of these had been given to Napoleon himself by royalty, foreign governments and cities, and, surprisingly, the pope.

The years on Saint Helena are in some respects the focus of the unfailing interest in Napoleon's life and relics. Relics reminiscent of his trip aboard the ship *Bellerophon* to England, where he threw himself on the mercy of the British, and the *Northumberland,* which carried him to Saint Helena, have been particularly attractive to collectors. A naval telescope, formerly the property of Sir Thomas Devon, who was on board the *Bellerophon,* has been sold, as well as an ivory inlaid chessboard and men used by the emperor and the captain on board.

At Saint Helena, Napoleon was surrounded by a motley and quarrelsome entourage of courtiers and servants, many of whom had, strangely enough, hardly known the emperor in the days of his rule. As Napoleon's health declined—he probably died of ulcers, although there were persistent rumors of poison—and he made his will, the thoughts of most of his attendants seem to have turned to mementos of the dying emperor. Even during his lifetime few visitors left Saint Helena without souvenirs. Dr. Barry Edward O'Meara, a young Irish physician in British service, was sent away by Sir Hudson Lowe, governor of the island (another Irishman), whom he later accused in a famous book, *Napoleon in Exile, or A Voice from St. Helena,* of attempting to murder the emperor. O'Meara took with him a desk used

EMPRESS JOSEPHINE'S TIARA
1805
GIFT OF NAPOLEON I TO THE EMPRESS JOSEPHINE

No woman in history ever received such gifts from a lover as Josephine received from Napoleon. As has been truly said, when he placed the crown of the empire on her head at the Cathedral of Notre Dame on 2 December 1804, he gave her the world. In addition to the great imperial crown, the empress owned other splendid jewels, among them this famous diamond tiara that was a gift from the emperor in 1805. It is now the property of the international jewelry firm of Van Cleef & Arpels, which also owns a tiara of Napoleon's second wife, the Empress Marie Louise. *Van Cleef & Arpels, New York*

by the emperor, which has recently been on the antique market. Several of Napoleon's other attendants left, and each carried souvenirs as well as reminiscences, which most of them published.

After Napoleon's death in great pain—partly because the British did not provide competent doctors—the most ghoulish scenes took place. The emperor had made an elaborate will disposing of most of his portable property to his young son, but with instructions for his staff to divide among themselves other belongings. The French and even some of his British captors practically came to blows over the imperial possessions. Directly the emperor expired, Dr. Francesco Antommarchi, his medical attendant, made a death mask. This is the famous portrait of which copies in various metals and terra-cotta may be bought today. The original, which is perhaps the most important surviving Napoleonic relic, belongs to the present Bonaparte pretender to the French throne. Even the Anglican minister on the island was not ashamed to admit filching an imperial eggcup, a toast rack, an armchair, some buttons from the emperor's uniform, and a lock of his hair, all of which he sold profitably in London. But then the same minister had to be forcibly ejected from Napoleon's funeral service when he tried to conduct a simultaneous Protestant service, whereupon he rushed ahead of the funeral procession to consecrate the burial grounds according to his own rites.

Perhaps the most notorious relics are those carried off from Napoleon's deathbed by the Corsican Abbé Vignali, who had been sent to the island by Cardinal Fesch, Napoleon's uncle, although it is not known that the emperor had ever expressed any desire for a priest. Vignali did not scruple to raid the emperor's possessions for a whole raft of relics: silverware, blood-stained linen used during the last illness, a pair of the famous white breeches (one of twenty-three pairs the emperor had on Saint Helena), a handkerchief with his initials, a copy of the Antommarchi death mask, and, most gruesome, small pieces of the emperor's flesh taken during the postmortem. The relics stayed together in the Vignali family for generations and were repeatedly authenticated and described by historians. In 1924, they were bought for $2,000 by Dr. A. S. W. Rosenbach, an American bookdealer, who kept them for many years and derived plentiful newspaper publicity from his ownership. He had them cased in blue morocco leather boxes lined in velvet. The most recent public appearance of the Vignali relics, still complete, was in 1970, when they came up for sale at Christie's rooms in London. Although enthusiastically greeted by the newspapers, the relics could not meet a too-ambitious reserve of $40,000 and failed to find a new owner at the sale. No doubt they will appear in a new blaze of publicity after a few years have passed.

The most important Napoleonic relics escaped the souvenir hunters at Saint Helena, since the emperor's will left the most valuable objects to his relatives. Some of these have come on the market in the course of the last century in the settlements of various princely estates, but the main bulk have descended directly to the present Bonaparte pretender to the French throne, Prince Napoleon, who lives in Switzerland. They include the badge of the Légion d'Honneur the emperor wore at Austerlitz, his regalia as a Freemason, the silver night lamp used during his final illness, the original Antommarchi death mask, and the clock that was stopped at the moment of his death, 5:49 P.M., 5 May 1821.

In 1840, the Napoleonic cult was already so strong that even the Bourbon king of France, Louis Philippe, wanted to make a gesture toward it. He had the idea of bringing Napoleon's remains from Saint Helena and reinterring them in Paris. After some reluctance the English gave up the body, and Louis Philippe sent his own son, the Prince de Joinville, who happened to be a sailor, to escort the body to France. The great day was 15 December 1840, when with immense ceremony, the burning of incense, and the booming of cannon, the body was laid to rest at the Invalides. Victor Hugo wrote that the day was "brilliant as glory, cold as the tomb," and there were literally millions of hushed spectators.

Because of his unique place in the hearts of Frenchmen, questions about Napoleonic relics can be touchy matters. The horde of Napoleonic scholars are a disputatious lot and testy arguments have developed among them over such questions as whether the emperor wore a hat at the Battle of Marengo and, if so, was it the one piously preserved in the family of his veterinary, who was present? Patriotic feelings, too, are easily excited; whenever a Napoleonic relic is likely to leave France, there is an uproar. In the year 1929, when Americans were offering heady prices for nearly every antique in Europe, the art dealer Sir Joseph Duveen bought a famous "Marshal's table" that had been made at Napoleon's command at the Sèvres porcelain factory. It was four years (1806—10) in the making and showed Napoleon in his coronation robes surrounded by thirteen of his marshals, all portrayed on Sèvres plaques.

An old photograph of the Invalides in Paris, where the body of the Emperor Napoleon was placed in 1840. Exactly a century later the body of his son Napoleon II was brought from Vienna and entombed beside his father. *James F. Carr, New York*

Stendhal paid a visit to the factory in early 1810 when the table was nearing completion. The artist Isabey, "who displayed," said Stendhal nastily in his diary, "nothing but a servile character being polite out of self-interest," showed them the table

which really gives a notion of perfection, especially in the portraits of Marshals

Soult and Pontecorvo; the Princes of Eckmühl and Neuchâtel are the least well done. This charming work, which has already cost 58,000 francs, I believe, is soon to be baked, which may shatter it.

The porcelain was not shattered in the firing, and this First Empire masterpiece survived to cost Duveen 400,000 francs ($20,000) a century later. When the news of this purchase got out, the French were upset and became even more so when it was revealed that Duveen had bought the table for the noisy newspaper publisher William Randolph Hearst. The table was then legally "preempted" by the Fench museums, the price being met, oddly enough, by another American, the francophile Edward Tuck, long resident in France and a great benefactor of monuments that the French themselves neglected. He bought and restored Malmaison, Josephine's country house, at enormous cost, and the "Marshals' table" was placed there.

Since the 1960s interest in Napoleon and his relics has increased sharply. During 1969, the bicentenary of his birth, there were important exhibitions. Scholars in the medico-legal department of Glasgow University analyzed a lock of his hair with a good provenance preserved at that institution and discovered traces of arsenic, giving some new publicity to the old suspicion of death by poisoning. Many sales of Napoleonic relics were held, especially of course in Paris, and the best items realized high prices indeed.

A silk cravat and a diamond tiepin removed from the emperor's coach by a hussar on 19 June 1815, during the flight after the Battle of Waterloo, were sold by the hussar's great-granddaughter in Amsterdam in 1970 for $6,800. A fragment of one of Napoleon's nightgowns brought $200, and a small piece of wood from the emperor's coffin, handsomely mounted in an ormolu and ebony obelisk in the Empire style, sold for $3,000. The most notable relic and the one most discussed at the time of sale in 1969 was one of his famous hats. The story with it was that on 20 September 1814, while the Emperor was in exile on the Island of Elba, he went for a ride on a windy day and a gust of wind blew his hat into the sea. It was retrieved but stained and battered, so he gave it to one Mencio, who was his librarian. This well-authenticated relic was sold in 1967 for a mere $3,400. In the bicentennial year it came up for sale again. Representatives of Moët & Chandon, the champagne company, and Courvoisier, "the brandy of Napoleon," fought a salesroom duel and drove the price up to $31,000 before Moët & Chandon victoriously carried off the relic.

Today, the most common Napoleonic items that the relic collector can find for modest sums include twigs taken from the laurel tree planted on his grave at Saint Helena, which were often carried off the island by visitors who carefully preserved them. They usually sell today for around $50, depending of course on the provenance. Many bits of his snuff were caught up during his lifetime and kept by people near him; these have sold in recent years for around $50 also. Locks of hair are also not too expensive; few in recent years have made more than $250 unless accompanied by an autograph letter. Pieces of wood from his coffin, not mounted (as was the example mentioned above), are in the $100 range. Examples of all these items are found encased in lockets, brooches, rings, and other jewelry.

The French—Bonapartist and others—have a deep affection for the emperor who never reigned: Napoleon II, called "L'Aiglon" ("the eaglet"). The only child of the first emperor and the Austrian Archduchess Marie Louise, he was born in 1811. His birth marked the zenith of the Napoleonic fortunes. The City of Paris had the honor of providing the heir with a cradle fit for a baby monarch. This architectural wonder is still on exhibition among the Hapsburg treasures in Vienna. Immense in size, it is loaded with symbolic figures executed in silver: Justice, Strength, Paris, the rivers Seine and Tiber (the baby's title was King of Rome), and of course the Napoleonic eagles and bees, the whole draped in red velvet. The infant king did not actually sleep in this edifice; the cradle used is in the Palace of Fontainebleau (his baby dress belongs to Prince Napoleon). The Empire of the French collapsed when the King of Rome was just four years old. He was handed over by his nonchalant mother, the Empress Marie-Louise, to his Austrian kinfolk; in Vienna he became Franz, Duke of Reichstadt. Neglected by all his august relatives, he died of tuberculosis at the age of twenty-one.

Not forgotten by the French people, however, he has always been a cult figure. In 1900, Sarah Bernhardt enjoyed one of her greatest triumphs in Edmond Rostand's *L'Aiglon.* in which she played the twenty-one-year-old boy although she was at that time a fifty-five-year-old woman with only one leg. There is even a French opera about L'Aiglon. Relics of the King of Rome are extremely rare, as are his letters, and are scarcely ever seen outside museums and libraries. In 1940, in a gesture he considered conciliatory but that was intensely annoying to the French, Adolf Hitler ordered the body of the King of Rome brought from conquered Vienna to conquered Paris, and Napoleon II is now interred beside his father in the great edifice of the Invalides.

The Napoleonic Wars produced thousands of relics, souvenirs, and mementos other than those associated directly with the emperor. Among these are commemorative silver, medals (about 2,000 were issued to honor the emperor and his many relatives, hundreds more by his opponents), arms, and "prisoner of war art."

Of Napoleon's two greatest opponents, the relics and personal possessions of Arthur Wellesley, first Duke of Wellington, have been preserved in massive accumulation by his descendants. The most interesting and important are now on public display in the museum at Apsley House, Wellington's magnificent home at Hyde Park Corner, London.

Because his personal life was less organized than Wellington's, and because he died in battle rather than surviving for half a century, as did the general, the relics of Horatio Nelson have been much more scattered. There have been the family possessions in the line of the Viscounts Bridport, descendants of Nelson's brother, and numerous private collections, including an important one formed in recent years by an American, Mrs. John G. McCarthy, now placed in the Portsmouth Royal Naval Museum, where Nelson's H.M.S. *Victory* is also preserved. There is a Nelson Museum in Monmouth, England. Many other maritime museums have Nelson memorabilia of varying amounts and importance.

Quantities of Nelson material have been sold at auction. In the early part of the century his cocked hat, silver watch, shoe buckles, hair, and many other relics went into private collections; some of these may well come back on the market. A gold locket has been sold that King George III gave Nelson with a lock of the royal hair and a portrayal of their meeting on board the H.M.S. *Vanguard* worked in ivory and mother-of-pearl. A particularly splendid relic was his wine flagon engraved "Nelson to Emma. In commemoration of the victory of the Nile. Vanguard, September 29, 1798. My fortieth birthday." Emma, of course, was the famous Lady Hamilton, Nelson's mistress; most Nelson collections also contain some souvenirs of this romance.

Disputes have arisen over the authenticity of some of the Nelson relics as is inevitable when there is a strong emotional tie to objects. The Union Jack that flew over the *Victory,* Lord Nelson's ship on which he died, was believed to have been presented to his aide-de-camp Lieut. William Rivers. In the late nineteenth century a descendant of Rivers sold the flag for 120 guineas (today's $6,000). Some contemporary accounts of the Battle of Trafalgar, however, say that Nelson's crew "tore his flag, the Union Jack of the *Victory,* to pieces, each retaining a fragment as a memorial of his beloved chief." Some of these fragments, properly ensconced beneath glass, have also been sold to collectors.

After Nelson's great victories in the Napoleonic Wars, collections of money were organized by Lloyds, the London insurers, to provide funds for wounded men and their dependents. Sometimes, in the case of Admiral Nelson himself and other officers, the money was laid out for the purchase of silver suitably inscribed in commemoration of specific persons and their heroic actions, or swords, also engraved. These items are known as "Lloyds Patriotic Fund" antiques. Classified by students as to what they cost at the time they were issued —for example, "hundred pound type sword"— they are heavily decorated with military and naval emblems and elegantly engraved. The most desirable are those commemorating the Battle of Trafalgar, which sell for up to $5,000. Those issued to mark other battles are usually considerably cheaper.

Many unusual medals were issued in Nelson's time. For instance, one of the admiral's friends, Alexander Davison, had a medal made up on his own to celebrate the Battle of the Nile. It was not official, but every officer and man who served was presented with one of these bronze decorations. They were the sort of thing that no one ever throws away and are not particularly rare now. They sell, depending on condition, for around $100 to $200. Many have been punched on the edge to admit a cord for wearing them around the neck, no doubt because they were not official issue and could not be worn on the chest. Davison had another medal executed in pewter for the men aboard H.M.S. *Victory* at Trafalgar, engraved with Nelson's famous signal: "England expects every man to do his duty." These are more expensive, like everything connected with that decisive engagement, selling now for up to $500. Matthew Boulton, a Birmingham manufacturer, also issued a Trafalgar medal in various metals. Examples sell today for $200 to $300 unless they are inscribed with the name of a specific sailor (more desirable for collectors, as the service record of the individual can be traced), in which case they can bring as much as $500. All these medals and many, many others have been studied and described, and there are reference works on the subject. They are an attractive area of specialization for collectors interested in the history of warfare in the Napoleonic era. The admiral himself would have approved of such sentiments: at the Battle of Copenhagen, when asked to cover up the medals on his uniform so the enemy would not spot them, he refused, saying, "In honor I gained them, and in honor I will die with them."

"Prisoner of war art" consists of objects made—ordinarily carved—out of wood or bone by military and naval men incarcerated by the enemy. The term is usually reserved for objects made by French captives in British prisons during, roughly, the 1800–1815 period, the Napoleonic wars. Typical objects are utensils, dominoes, "playing cards" (bits of bone carved with numbers and figures and occasionally painted), and ship models. The models, which are sometimes extremely elaborate, are the most collected. A good one with rigging can cost $2,000 to $3,000. Most of the objects are much cheaper: sets of dominoes and cards and other gaming equipment can sometimes be bought for under $100. Except for the ships, sometimes named and dated, most "prisoner of war art" is difficult to date and usually there is no hope of identifying it as to specific carver or locality. Obviously, from a substance like soupbone (often used for carving), it is difficult to draw any conclusions as to date and place; and other hand-carved items are often passed off as "prisoner of war art." Nevertheless, it is an interesting area of military collecting.

Few relics of American wars before the Civil War are generally available to collectors of militaria. Memorabilia of the American Revolution are particularly scarce except in the form of objects made of relic wood, some of which have been mentioned earlier. Relics of the War of 1812 and of the War with Mexico usually take the form of presentation swords or silver.

Probably the most important surviving relic of the wars of the early republic is the "Star

Scrimshaw and other carvings in ivory form an important group of American relics. Shown here is a nineteenth-century Chinese ivory portrait bust of an American junior merchant marine officer, which is four and one-half inches high on a one-inch wooden base. The eyes are set with blue mother-of-pearl. *James F. Carr, New York*

Spangled Banner," which was made in 1813 and is now on display at the Smithsonian Institution in Washington, D.C. During the War of 1812, the commandant of Fort McHenry wrote to his superior:

We, sir, are ready at Fort McHenry to defend Baltimore against invading by the enemy. That is to say, we are ready except that we have no suitable ensign to display over the Star Fort, and it is my desire to have a flag so large that the British will have no difficulty in seeing it from a distance.

Mary Pickersgill of Baltimore did her best to meet the commandant's requirement, sewing a flag together that measures thirty by forty-two feet. Her home in Baltimore, where she made the flag, is now known as "The Flag House." It was the sight of this enormous flag waving over the fort that inspired Francis Scott Key to write the words to the national anthem.

No shortage exists of relics of the Civil War: its artifacts are relatively common and for the most part relatively inexpensive. A Civil War relic must be spectacular indeed to command a high sale price. In the 1960s an extremely important American Civil War flag brought the then record price for a flag of $16,240. American flags can usually be dated by the number of stars displayed. This one had twenty-seven in a diamond-shaped pattern in the center, flanked at each end by five stars arranged vertically. It was known to have been presented by the Union General Benjamin F. Butler (known in the South as "Beast" Butler because of his behavior in the occupation of New Orleans) to Abraham Lincoln for his approval just three days before the assassination of the President.

Memorabilia of the Civil War other than that associated with Abraham Lincoln do not often bring high prices, and battlefield souvenirs are usually quite inexpensive (under $25). A rule of Civil War collecting is that, generally speaking, Confederate military material always commands a premium over the equivalent Union items, less of it having been made and much more of it destroyed. There would be even less but Confederate families, like losers in general, were more careful about preservation than the winners.

Collectors of Civil War relics will want to add to their collections military memorabilia that can be traced to a specific officer or soldier whose war record can then be added for better documentation and greater interest.

Among the varieties of moderately priced Civil War relics are the following:

Swords and sabers, $75 to $200, unless specially decorated or inscribed presentation items. Swords carrying engraved references to important officers and their actions can be $500 up.

Knives from the Civil War era are extremely popular with collectors. Many of the pocket-

General Robert E. Lee was wearing this French-made sword and scabbard at the surrender at Appomattox Court House on 9 April 1865. *The Museum of the Confederacy, Richmond*

knives that have an array of blades for various purposes (sometimes as many as a dozen) can be bought for $50 to $75. The "Bowie" knives are more expensive, up to $100.

Buckles, usually brass, from Civil War uniforms are attractive items, not especially rare, selling for $25 and up today. The collector should, however, be alerted to the fact that buckles are now being reproduced in facsimile, aged by a chemical process, and sold as original Civil War equipment.

Insignia such as brass cap emblems sell for around $20. There is a demand for buttons from uniforms, but the prices are generally modest—under $10. The rarer buttons—those of the Confederate Navy, for instance—sell for somewhat more.

One of the most desirable items of equipment is the cartridge box. Good examples sell for $50 and up. Metal cases for carrying messages are more expensive. Less attractive equipment, such as knapsacks and canteens, is usually priced at under $20.

Many collectors have searched the battlefields of the war for artifacts with surprisingly successful results. Some have used metal detectors to locate items like spurs, knives, camp forks and spoons, insignia, and bullets. Even the latter are sought by the more devoted collectors and currently sell for around twenty-five cents each.

Fascinating mementos from the Civil War era are bits and pieces of actual history, such as:

• A piece of the first shell fired into Fort Sumter on 12 April 1861. One of these little pieces of shrapnel sold recently for $100.
• A nineteen-pound cannon ball found on Seminary Ridge at Gettysburg battlefield, now mounted on an inscribed wooden block. This was offered recently for $100.
• A linen patch from the American flag hoisted on Fort Beauregard at Port Royal, S.C., after its capture on 7 November 1861 sold in 1973 for $100.
• A fragment of the Confederate flag that floated over Fort Sumter during its bombardment by the Union forces in October 1863. An example sold for $100.
• A gavel made from a limb of a tree with a bullet embedded from the Battle of Antietam (valued about $50).
• A wooden cross made from the scaffold on which John Brown was hanged.

• A small wallet belonging to John Brown taken from his person when he was searched after his capture at Harpers Ferry, Virginia, on 18 October 1859. Sold for $30 in the 1950s. (His camp knife and fork and many locks of hair have been sold. Examples of the latter are usually accompanied by a letter from his wife certifying the hair as his; they sell modestly [under $100].)
• Canes made from flooring "carefully selected" from under the desk at which President Lincoln sat in his White House office during the Civil War.

Virtually all the more famous participants in the Civil War have shrines of one sort or another with a slight edge to the Southerners. At Washington and Lee University, where Robert E. Lee was president and where he is buried in the Lee Chapel, many relics are preserved and his basement office kept just as it was during his tenure. At Beauvoir, the rather elegant estate near Biloxi, Mississippi, to which Jefferson Davis retired, many of his possessions have been preserved in the main house and in the Library Cottage, where he wrote *The Rise and Fall of the Confederate Government*. On prominent display is the coat Davis was wearing the night he was captured by the Union forces, which, as the catalogue of the collection remarks, puts to final rest "the false report that Mr. Davis was disguised in woman's clothes at the time of his apprehension."

Of the "little wars" of the Victorian era and the two great wars of the twentieth century, multitudes of relics are available to collectors. Some very amusing items came up for sale immediately after or even during the Victorian wars. An ancient and much weather-beaten top hat worn by the Boer leader "Oom" (Uncle) Paul Kruger was captured during the English—South African War and was sold in London in 1900, while the conflict was still in progress, in a great sale of "Relics of the South African War," for the high price of £25 (today's $1,000).

In addition to the usual guns, presentation swords, batons, uniforms, and other militaria, there is from the First and Second World Wars a category of collected items referred to as "Battlefield Art." These are comparable to the "Prisoner of War Art" of the Napoleonic items: they are objects made by servicemen from the detritus of war. An example is a lamp base formed by using pistol and rifle bullets among which an artillery shell is inserted as a stem; the "shade" is a helmet. This was made from a battlefield of the First World War. Unfortunately, any relic value of such objects is greatly reduced because they are seldom identified as to place, date, or maker, and there is additionally no reason, considering the enormous amount of war matériel available in the United States, why they cannot be made today. All this considered, it is surprising what prices are asked by dealers for "Battlefield Art" objects: the lamp mentioned was sold for $150.

In the natural course of events, relics of the Second World War are only just now coming on the market in large numbers. In early 1974, Christie's sold at auction the "Free French" pennant that was flown on General Charles De Gaulle's automobile from his arrival in England in June 1940 until his departure in 1941 for North Africa. The faded blue, red, and white pennant, somewhat frayed, was consigned by the general's wartime chauffeur, whose wife had embroidered a Cross of Lorraine on it. Museums and shrines of various kinds are being opened, and no doubt most of the principal figures of the war will each have his shrine. Already open is an Admiral Chester Nimitz Center in the admiral's hometown of Fredericksburg, Texas, which houses not only his own personal relics but such oversized war souvenirs as torpedoes, antiaircraft guns, fighter plane fuselages, and a Japanese tank. A memorial has opened at the battleship *Arizona* in Hawaii, which attracts more than a million visitors a year, and there are plans for a Pearl Harbor Memorial Museum to be located where the war began.

Among the various areas of specialization within the modern military field the collecting of Nazi memorabilia undoubtedly leads. The personal taste of Adolf Hitler has been aptly described as "chocolate-box." His preference in painting was for the storytelling German painters of the nineteenth century like Carl Spitzweg, and his taste in architecture, as is well known from the memoirs of Albrecht Speer and others, was for the grotesquely monumental and derivative.

Hitler was well aware of the emotional importance of national relics. Although Austria was his native country—it is said that the greatest Austrian accomplishment was to convince the world that Beethoven was an Austrian and Hitler a German—he did not hesitate to ransack it after the 1938 Anschluss. He was anxious to increase the importance of the city of Nuremberg, where the Nazis held their great annual rallies, and to emphasize its history, so he ordered the Schatzkammer or Treasure Room in Vienna to surrender the coronation regalia of the German emperors and despatch it to Nuremberg. It is easy enough to understand that, but one wonders why he had such odd religious relics hauled from Vienna as the links "traditionally believed to be from the chains that bound Saints Peter, Paul, and John." These and other relics and the regalia were recovered by Allied troops after the war and restored to Vienna.

Genuine relics of Hitler himself are rare. His Third Reich ended in such destruction, especially in Berlin, where he met his own end, that few objects survived. Add to that the fact that for years after the Second World War, it was unpopular and even dangerous in Germany to own such memorabilia, and one can see that not many personal belongings of Hitler are around for collectors. The few that are sold generally command high prices.

Some of the pictures painted by Hitler during his years in Vienna before World War I, when he was attempting to support himself with his artwork, were sold at auction during the 1960s. They then brought only a few hundred dollars. Their interest lies only in the hand that painted them because they belong to the postcard school of art.

The brown uniform cap Hitler allegedly wore in the Munich Beer Hall Putsch of 1923 was sold at auction in that city in 1973, to a collector, for $3,750.

For years, what is described as "Adolf Hitler's personal silver service" has been coming on the market; in fact, nearly thirty years after World War II was over, advertisements continued to appear offering pieces of it for sale. This silver (actually plated ware) is flatware stamped with Hitler's initials and the Nazi spread eagle holding a swastika and further stamped (whether always is not known) "WMF 80." It has never brought very high prices. As of 1973, knives, forks, and spoons of various sizes sold for only about $75 apiece, and sometimes less. Very large quantities of this tableware were apparently made for the dictator's various residences, including the Berlin Chancellery, where there was a great

(*opposite page and above*) Relics of war are not always swords, guns, and other militaria. During the Spanish-American War of 1898, the Spanish Caribbean fleet was virtually destroyed off Cuba on 3 July 1898 by the American fleet under the command of Rear Admiral William T. Sampson. The Admiral sent the secretary of the navy a famous telegram in which he said, "The fleet under my command offers the nation as a Fourth of July present the whole of Cervera's fleet." The Spanish Admiral Pascual Cervera and the officers of his fleet who had been captured when their ships went down were interned at the United States Naval Academy at Annapolis, where by orders they were treated "as guests." Many of them formed friendships with the American families stationed at the academy and letters and photographs were exchanged for years. Mrs. Wise, wife of an American admiral, had all the Spanish officers autograph this large paper fan as a memento of their stay (one of the Spanish officers called it "a souvenir of misfortune.") Mrs. Wise's daughter, Elinor Douglas Wise, was married in the Baltimore Cathedral in 1913, to Armand, Duc de Richelieu. She preserved the fan until her death and with it the photographs shown here as an example of the full documentation of a relic. The top photograph shows the duchesse as a young girl in 1899 with her baby sister and their nurse on board the U.S.S. *Enterprise,* the others the Spanish officers; the central figure in the lower left photograph is Alfonso XIII, last King of Spain, with some of the returned officers. *James F. Carr, New York.*

deal of entertaining. It is certainly "Hitler's silver"; the word *personal* is perhaps uncertain.

Certain places associated with Adolf Hitler have become places of pilgrimage or at least tourism. His wartime headquarters, the celebrated Wolfschanze (Wolf's Lair) at Rastenburg in East Prussia (now in northeastern Poland and called Ketrzyn), has many visitors today. The huge concrete bunker remains concealed deep in a forest. Around the principal bunker are similar shelters for his chief aides. During the Second World War the entire complex was surrounded by a mined death strip twelve miles long and 450 feet wide. Nevertheless, it was at Wolfschanze that the most serious attempt was made on the dictator's life. In 1944, Col. Count Claus von Stauffenberg tried to kill Hitler by planting a bomb under a conference table in the bunker. Although there was damage and some deaths when the bomb exploded, the dictator escaped. Stauffenberg and dozens of his fellow conspirators were captured and executed with the greatest cruelty. Now visitors come to view the scene of the attempt. Berchtesgaden, even more associated with Hitler in the public mind, is also visited.

The entire field of Nazi memorabilia is rife with misdescribed items and downright forgeries. Many phony items have been identified, and several books published to caution collectors. Typical pieces of Hitler memorabilia on the market are the various books and albums of photographs, each said to be unique and to have been prepared exclusively for Hitler. One of these, published in 1936, contains about two hundred tipped-in photographs by Heinrich Hoffman, who was Hitler's personal photographer (and a longtime friend). This is usually said by its owners to be worth at least $5,000. Some indication of its "uniqueness" may be surmised from the fact that one issue of a weekly antiques newspaper contained three different advertisements of copies for sale.

Relics of the other Nazi leaders are just as scarce as those of Hitler. A silver service of Heinrich Himmler's has been filtering onto the market for years. Again, all the pieces have been plated flatware. The handles are stamped "800" with the S.S. (Schutzstaffel, "home defense") runic symbol. The blades are marked "Rostfrei," which has no mystic meaning but merely indicates that the blades are stainless steel. Knives, forks, and spoons from the Himmler service sold in 1973 for only about $20 each.

Far more relics exist of Marshal Hermann Göring. He had a mania for personal possessions of all kinds. He especially liked artworks and jewels, and those who would court his very important favor rushed to present the marshal with splendid if garish examples. All sorts of organizations gave Göring jeweled weapons and batons (he always carried one from his collection). Mussolini gave him a splendid baton, as did various aircraft manufacturers in Germany and Italy. From 1933 on, Göring was Reich cabinet minister in charge of the air forces of Germany, and among his other innumerable offices and cumbersome titles, such as "Commissioner for the Execution of the Four Year Plan," he was especially fond of this distinction. He had been a World War I flying ace, commanding the Richthofen Squadron, and was famous throughout the world for his aerial exploits. The German Air Force gave him a gold baton with a long inscription describing him as "the creator of the winged armies." Several of these Göring batons have survived: the United States Army owns two that were seized at the end of the war, and there are examples in private collections. One bejeweled baton was sold by a Greek private collector at Sotheby's in 1973 for $5,700. Other Göring relics come on the market, usually sumptuous in materials and execution and decorated in the unmistakable Nazi 1930s taste. In 1973 a pair of his shoulder patches, a golden matchbox adorned with an eagle and swastika, and a gold pocketknife with six different functions engraved with his personal coat of arms sold for $2,950. A more homely relic, a pipe of white porcelain painted with a mountain scene, sold the same year for a much more modest price—$110.

Nazi gear even without associations with famous Nazis commands good prices. The most desirable is the early (prewar) equipment. Some typical prices have been:

- Daggers without sheaths: about $100
- Daggers with swastika-embossed sheaths: about $250
- Military blouses with Nazi emblems: about $50. (Full uniforms, difficult to get, are more.)
- Flags: about $250. (There are a surprising number of flags available; they were a Nazi speciality, as one can tell from any photo-

graph of a rally—a forest of flags is always visible.)

- Military boots: about $30. The alpine boots issued for the winter campaigns are about twice as much.

Manufacturers in operation today have not been slow to realize that there is a substantial demand for Nazi memorabilia, and reproductions have come on the market. Some are good, but most are given away by the superfluity of Nazi symbols used to decorate them. They are positively alive with eagles, swastikas, Iron Crosses, and other German motifs. Steins supposedly issued for Luftwaffe servicemen, U-boat sailors, and other Nazi servicemen and service organizations suddenly appeared on the market in the 1970s; these are, to say the least, suspect. They are stoneware and decorated with Nazi medals, campaign badges, even transfer-printed photographs of individual servicemen. Although the foot of each is cluttered with serial numbers, the names of localities, regiments, Iron Crosses, and so forth, there is no manufacturer's name. This omission is feebly explained by some collectors, who say that although the steins were supposedly issued during the high point of Hitler's success to honor his soldiers, the manufacturers were so ashamed of executing orders for the Third Reich that they refused to sign their work.

7

The Miraculous Mulberry Tree: Literary, Musical, and Artistic Relics

No undisputed relics of William Shakespeare are known to exist. Few enough facts are known about his life; objects that can be definitely connected with him are nonexistent, or at least unidentified. Through the centuries, however, numbers of supposititious relics have been shown at the Warwickshire village that has become famous as his hometown and of which he is the most famous former inhabitant. Visitors seeking Shakespearean associations and wanting to see the scenes of his life began to arrive at Startford-upon-Avon in the late seventeenth century.

"Bardolatry," extreme reverence for the playwright and his works, flowered with the famous Shakespeare Jubilee staged by the town's corporation and the celebrated actor David Garrick in 1764 on the two hundredth anniversary of Shakespeare's birth. The jubilee lasted for three days, 6–9 September. The beginning of the festivities was announced by a volley from thirty cannons. The program included parades, concerts, banquets, balls—there would have been fireworks but rain came down in torrents, raising the River Avon to flood level. Nevertheless, the jubilee put Stratford on the map, and since then the procession of pilgrims has never slackened.

Relics began to proliferate along with the increased interest in Shakespeare the man and his works. Shakespeare's direct descendants had come to an end with the death of Elizabeth Lady Barnard in 1670, but collateral descendants thrived in the village of Stratford and the surrounding suburbs. A Mrs. Hart, wife of a descendant of Joan Shakespeare Hart, William's sister, acted as custodian of the house known to be Shakespeare's birthplace. She showed (for a fee)—and even sold—hallowed personal possessions of the Bard said to have descended in her husband's family. These included the chair in which Shakespeare sat in the chimney corner after his retirement from the theatre. In 1785, the Hon. John Byng bought from Mrs. Hart first a large sliver of the chair and then the entire lower crossbar, despite a disturbing rumor that she had earlier sold an entire chair with the same story to a Polish princess.

By the beginning of the early nineteenth century the birthplace was kept by Mary Hornby, widow of another descendant of the Hart family. When Washington Irving visited her shrine, he was shown a much larger assortment of Shakespearean relics than earlier pilgrims had seen. As the fame of the shrine increased, the relics also seemed to be increasing. Irving was shown the matchlock with which Shakespeare had poached the deer of Sir Thomas Lucy, his tobacco box, the sword he wore playing *Hamlet*. That was 1815; four years later a visitor recorded seeing relics that spanned the whole lifetime of the poet: his christening bowl, baby chair, walking stick, the table at which he wrote, his reading glass, and still another chair, this one an "easy chair."

Over at the Anne Hathaway Cottage in nearby Shottery, rival collateral descendants

103

A typical casket carved from the celebrated tree planted by William Shakespeare. The date of this example is late eighteenth century. Note the portrait of the poet. *The Trustees & Guardians of Shakespeare's Birthplace, Stratford-upon-Avon*

were showing and dealing in other relics. The gullible Samuel Ireland (his son was the most famous forger of Shakespeare and his first believer was his father) bought from Anne Hathaway's Cottage an oak chair "in which the Bard sat with Anne on his knee" (the best the widow Hornby could show in that line was Mrs. Shakespeare's shoe).

Purchases made by visitors at Stratford-upon-Avon disseminated Shakespeare remains throughout England. Sir John Soane, for example, owned a sixteenth century German beer jug (still in Sir John Soane's Museum in London) that he persuaded himself was the drinking vessel referred to in *Hamlet*. Even the most enthralled visitors were skeptical of some of these relics, but little doubt was cast—at least for many years—on the most common and best-known mementos of Shakespeare: objects

carved from the celebrated Mulberry Tree of Stratford-upon-Avon.

The legend of this remarkable tree goes back no farther than 1740, more than a century after Shakespeare's death. The New Place, the house where the poet had spent his retirement, was by that time owned by one Sir Hugh Clopton, who was proud to be the owner although, in fact, the house had been completely rebuilt in the reign of Queen Anne. He boasted that the large mulberry tree in the New Place garden had been planted by Shakespeare with his own hands. Sir Hugh liked to show it to visitors, but his successor in the house was annoyed at having the curious—ever on the increase as Bardolatry spread—trampling through his house and garden, absorbing the true Shakespearean atmosphere. The new owner was a parson, the Reverend Francis

Gastrell, a name infamous in the history of Stratford-upon-Avon and ever foul upon the lips of Bardolaters. Increasingly impatient with sightseers, in 1753 he actually cut down the Mulberry Tree! Although a muttering mob surrounded the New Place, and the town fathers protested, Gastrell declared himself relieved that the tree was gone. (A few years later in another dispute with the town over real estate taxes, Mr. Gastrell became so irate that he tore down New Place altogether and shook the dust of Stratford from his shoes forever.)

In a nation of shopkeepers there will always be an entrepreneur, and when the Mulberry Tree toppled, an enterprising carpenter (also clockmaker) named Thomas Sharpe appeared and bought it from the Reverend Mr. Gastrell as so much lumber. Sharpe was an expert carver—or became one—and he began immediately to turn out small souvenir articles made from the wood—little boxes, goblets, punch ladles, toothpick cases, tobacco stoppers (tamps), canes. Some larger articles were produced, including a casket made to the order of the Stratford Corporation for presentation to David Garrick, embellished with Shakespearean emblems and showing Garrick in the role of Lear. Garrick himself bought several blocks of wood, from one of which he had a large armchair made. Eventually he owned so

A photograph of the dwelling in Shottery, just outside Stratford-upon-Avon, known as "Anne Hathaway's Cottage," made in 1894 before the cottage was restored. *James F. Carr, New York*

A goblet carved from the Shakespearean Mulberry Tree. Goblets were among Thomas Sharp's most popular items. One was used by David Garrick to drink toasts at the Great Shakespeare Jubilee of 1769. *The Trustees & Guardians of Shakespeare's Birthplace, Stratford-upon-Avon*

much Mulberry, the gift of admirers, that when his widow died in 1823, forty years after his own death, there were still five blocks of "the celebrated Mulberry Tree of Shakespeare" in her estate to be sold. At a Christie's auction they brought thirty-one guineas ($2,000 in today's money). The Garrick armchair made its final auction appearance in 1922, when it was bought by the great American Shakespearean collector Henry Folger, for a price of nearly $10,000.

Boxes, goblets, chairs—all the continued production of mementos from *one* mulberry tree? Thomas Sharpe was thirty-two when he bought the tree; for forty years he had been producing objects carved from it. He was disturbed by rumors, and on his deathbed, "being informed that hints were thrown out of his having expended all the original tree and purchased others, called in the mayor of Stratford and a justice of the peace and dictated the following affidavit, which is a model of the authentication of a relic and for that reason worth printing in full:

This is to certify, That I, Thos. Sharp, of the borough of Stratford-upon-Avon, in the county of Warwick, clock & watchmaker, was born in the Chapel-street, & baptiz'd Feby. 5th, 1724, that I was personally acquainted with Sir Hugh Clopton, Knight, Barrister at Law, & one of the Heralds at Arms; who was son of Sir John Clopton, Knight, that purchased a certain messuage or house near the Chapel, in Stratford, called the New Place, of the executors of Lady Elizabeth Barnard, and grand-daughter of Shakespear; and that I have often heard the said Sir Hugh Clopton solemnly declare, that the Mulberry-tree, which growed in his garden, was planted by Shakespear, and he took pride in shewing it to, and entertaining persons of distinction, whose curiosity excited them to visit the spot, known to be the last residence of the Immortal Bard: and, after the decease of the said Sir Hugh, in 1753 the premises were sold to the Reverend Jno. [Francis] Gastrel; who in 1756 cut down the said Mulberry-tree, and cleft it as fire-wood; when the greatest part of it was purchased by me, the said Thos. Sharp; who, out of a sincere veneration for the memory of its celebrated planter, employed one John Luckman to convey it to my own premises; where I have worked it into many curious toys and usefull articles from the same. And I do hereby declare, & take my solemn oath, upon the four Evangelists, in the presence of Almighty God, that I never had worked, sold, or substituted any other wood, than what came from, & was part of the said tree, as or for Mulberry-wood. Signed, and a true affidavit made by me. Thos. Sharp. Taken and sworn at and in the borough of Stratford-upon-Avon, this 14th day of October, 1799; before us, Richd. Allen, Mayor. Thos. Nott.

The high point of Mulberryism undoubtedly came with Garrick's Shakespeare Jubilee of 1764 (when plans were announced, some of the more rustic Stratfordians thought they were getting a "Jew Bill"). During the fete Garrick carried a wand made from the tree and at the great banquet he drank from a cup carved from it, reciting:

"Behold this fair goblet, 'Twas carv'd from the tree,
Which, O my sweet Shakespear, was planted by thee;
As a relic I kiss it, and bow at the shrine;
What comes from thy hand must be ever divine."

And so on for eight stanzas in which various other varieties of trees—the oak, myrtle, and birch, for example—were compared to the mulberry and found wanting. He then recited a panegyric on Shakespeare ending with a challenge (meant as rhetorical) to anyone present to refute it. A London comedian, Thomas King, who had been planted in the audience, rose to attack Shakespeare. The crowd, not recognizing he spoke in jest, became tumultuous and shouted, "Throw him out!" King was with difficulty rescued. During the confusion, some benches collapsed, and the whole jubilee building, put up for the occasion and weakened by days of rains during an English autumn, came near to collapsing. The aged Earl of Carlisle, one of many noblemen attending, was knocked cold by a falling door, and it was some time before order was restored.

The dearth of real Shakespearean relics, along with the lack of manuscripts from his hand and the general scarcity of biographical information, contributed to the many attempts beginning in the mid-nineteenth century and persisting into our own time to deny William Shakespeare of Stratford-upon-Avon any credit for writing the plays called by his name. The attempts began with Miss Delia Bacon, a well-connected but poor teacher from New Haven, Connecticut, who had probably turned her head by too much absorption in Shakespeare's writing. She almost literally worshipped the poet's work, although, oddly enough, she did

not think that it could be performed: "It is impossible to put Shakespeare on the stage in a way to satisfy one's expectations," she used to tell her girl students; "nothing can equal the imagination" (or was this really a Puritan prejudice against the stage? She came from a long line of Congregational ministers). Quitting teaching, she sailed to England to dedicate herself to proving that the plays we know as Shakespeare's were actually written by someone else.

Much of Delia Bacon's case against "The Old Player" as she disrespectfully referred to William Shakespeare of Stratford-upon-Avon rested on her deductions that he could only have had an elementary education and on his carelessness with his manuscripts and personal belongings. She developed the idea that the plays were produced by a sort of intellectual syndicate headed by Francis Bacon, Lord Verulam, with whom, incidentally, she did not claim any relationship. Many are the Baconian theories that have sprung from this original thought, and great the scorn heaped upon "The Stratford Poacher" or "The Old Pretender" by Baconians, who find all sorts of ciphers in the works and numerous hints planted for the knowing—after all, the most famous play is *Ham*let!

Sponsored by a number of important Americans, including Ralph Waldo Emerson, Delia Bacon visited Stratford and thought of disinterring Shakespeare from his grave in the Church of the Holy Trinity. She was not deterred by the famous verse on the grave said to have been put there at Shakespeare's order:

Good friend, for Jesus' sake forebeare
To dig the dust enclosed here
Blest be the man that spares these stones
And curst be he that moves my bones!

but decided that no useful purpose would be served by exhumation (or was she afraid of finding relics that would disprove her theory?). She did, however, spend a night in the church. Soon after this she went over the brink mentally, having in 1857 published *Philosophy of the Plays of Shakspere Unfolded,* in which she set forth her Baconian theories. She had to be rescued by Washington Irving, then American consul in Liverpool, who returned her to her family in the States for the remainder of her short life. Countless have been the books since her time agreeing with her Francis Bacon theory of authorship of the plays or putting forth other and even less likely candidates. W. S. Gilbert of operetta fame thought Shakespeare overrated, anyway, and said the dispute could be settled by digging up both Bacon and Shakespeare, setting their coffins side by side, and having Sir Herbert Beerbohm Tree, a Shakespearean actor Gilbert also disliked, recite *Hamlet* to them. The one who turned in his coffin would be the author of the plays.

The doubts of Baconians failed to deter collectors from purchasing Shakespeare souvenirs made of the "relic wood" of the mulberry tree. Early in this century a retired banker named W. C. Prescott, not satisfied with wood only from the mulberry tree, constructed an enormous wooden bookcase out of bits and pieces of that and other wood with Shakespeare associations: from Anne Hathaway's Cottage, from the grammar school at Stratford, from the thirteenth century roof of Westminster Abbey, from Windsor Castle, Kenilworth, Warwick Castle, and even Birnam Wood. The bookcase was specially fitted to hold a one-hundred-volume edition of Shakespeare that was "extra-illustrated" (i.e., had illustrations bound in) with no fewer than 13,000 engravings relating to Shakespeare and his works.

A collector interested in one of the mulberry wood items can probably find it today with a little search. Few of the larger caskets come on the market, although when they do, the prices are not high. Several have sold for $200 or less. The smaller boxes, such as snuffboxes, are more common and sell for about the same price; the goblets, generally for somewhat higher prices. Items made from the mulberry tree are not necessarily carved with their provenance, but they are usually easily identified by the decoration, which is full of references to Shakespeare and his plays. Often the mulberry tree and its fruit are represented. At auction, the mulberry wood pieces may be found offered in sales of "furniture and decorations" or in sales of literary property.

The total lack of authentic relics of the Bard has been an inspiration to the unscrupulous, and various belongings have been hawked as formerly the property of Shakespeare. According to one story, in the early years of this century, an enterprising employee of the Anderson auction galleries in New York found in a warehouse a bolt of chintz with a repeat pattern of a portrait of Shakespeare about every eighteen inches. Dazzled by the possibil-

ities of the bolt, the employee cut out one portrait, scuffed it up to give it the necessary appearance of age, framed it, and put it in an auction, where it was purchased by Henry Folger, Standard Oil millionaire and noted collector of Shakespeare, for the then substantial figure of $275. It is not known whether the same bolt has ever furnished any other "Shakespeare portraits."

Relics of other principal figures in English literature of the generation following Shakespeare's exist in some numbers. The Bunyan Meeting Museum at Bedford, England, with which John Bunyan was associated for more than thirty years (including seventeen as its minister) contains relics of the man important not only in English literature but in the history of religious freedom in the English-speaking world. Bunyan was by trade a tinker, and his brazier's anvil is in the museum. So are his violin, the chair used by him during his ministry, and an especially touching relic, the salt-glazed jug used for carrying ale to him while he was imprisoned at Bedford County Gaol from 1660 to 1672. It was during this long prison term—he was sentenced for preaching without a license—that he wrote *Grace Abounding to the Chief of Sinners* and eight other books. The door and doorway from the gaol are preserved, as is the door from Elstow Church, which is believed to be the inspiration of the wicket gate in *Pilgrim's Progress.*

Relic wood from Bunyan's pulpit was used like Shakespeare's mulberry tree (but with much better authority) to make small boxes and tea caddies.

The collecting of relics of Percy Bysshe Shelley and George Gordon Lord Byron has been much hampered by the impossible behavior of the friends, wives, lovers, heirs, guardians, and executors of those two celebrated poets. Now that both are incorporated into every respectable anthology of English verse, it is difficult to realize that they were shocking figures to most people in their time—it was not just because living abroad was cheaper that they set up housekeeping on the Continent. Both died there: Shelley was drowned in 1822 while sailing off Viareggio in Northern Italy, and Lord Byron died in 1824 of a fever at Missolonghi in Greece, where he had gone to assist in the war for Grecian independence from the Turks. Their fame and scandalous

Scotland has commemorated her favorite poet, Robert Burns, in many ways: preservations, museums, monuments. His birthplace at Alloway in Ayrshire is a museum. There is a Burns monument and museum at Kilmarnock. The cottage where "Souter Johnie," made famous in Burns's "Tam O'Shanter," lived, and the Bachelors' Club in Tarbolton, where Burns frolicked, are in the care of the National Trust for Scotland. Burns was popular from the first publication of his poems in 1786 (aged twenty-seven), and his fellow Scots in "the Burns country" preserved relics ranging from the stool on which the poet sat while correcting proof in Smellie's printing office in Edinburgh to the pistols he used as an exciseman (customs official). In fact, so much personal memorabilia of Burns is on display that Hugh McDiarmid, a modern Scottish poet, has written: "Burns cult, forsooth! It has denied his spirit to honour his name. It has denied his poetry to laud his amours. It has preserved his furniture and repelled his message." The Burns Museum at Alloway in Ayrshire is alongside the low-ceilinged thatch-roofed clay cottage where he was born; it holds many important manuscripts and relics of the poet. *Scottish Tourist Board, Edinburgh*

Alloway Church inspired one of Burns's most famous poems, "Tam O'Shanter," shown in the large open volume beneath a statue of Burns. *Scottish Tourist Board, Edinburgh*

Burns lived at Ellisland Farm in Dumfriesshire with Jean Armour, whom he finally married after she had twice borne him twins. Their dishes, glassware, and other relics are preserved there. *Scottish Tourist Board, Edinburgh*

reputations—Byron as profligate and Shelley as atheist—meant that after their deaths their circle of friends and relations would close ranks to create more respectable "images" for the two poets. Times were changing. Byron and Shelley were essentially eighteenth century figures; their survivors would be Victorians.

A curious person named Edward John Trelawny, of a well-to-do English family, was a friend—never so close as he claimed, but more than an acquaintance—of both poets, although only for a short time. Out of vanity and a desire to increase his own role in the poets' biographies, Trelawny did his best to muddle the records of the lives of Shelley and Byron, and he succeeded in clouding the history of the relics they left. He was undoubtedly one of the greatest liars of the nineteenth century.

In the first place, it was with Trelawny that the complicated story of Shelley's heart began. The poet and a friend, Edward Williams, were drowned together. Their bodies were washed ashore and the wives of the two men asked Trelawny, who was also living at Pisa (there was a little English expatriate colony there), to take charge of their burial. According to him, it was a government regulation to burn the bodies "as a precaution against the plague," rather than bury them. It has been shown that cremation was not, in fact, prescribed by the government or anybody else; it was merely Trelawny's way of making the event and his role more dramatic. Lord Byron was in attendance, apparently somewhat reluctantly; his relations with the deceased were not particularly happy. The bodies of Shelley and Williams were laid on funeral pyres on the beach, and with some difficulty set fire. It took a long time for the burning, which seems to have repelled Byron, as well it might. Trelawny gathered up Williams's ashes to be preserved by his widow Jane. Byron, who had a poor opinion of the widow Williams, said she would probably one day "forget what the urn contained and make tea in it." But the most famous anecdote connected with the cremation of Williams and Shelley on the beach at Viareggio is Trelawny's snatching of Shelley's heart from the flames. He burned his hand, of course, and showed the scars for the next sixty years. At least Trelawny called the recovered organ the heart; more likely it was the liver. When he returned to Pisa from the cremation he proudly presented the relic to Shelley's wife Mary, the author of *Frankenstein*. She was horrified when Trelawny offered the small, black, shriveled object to her, so Trelawny gave it to Leigh Hunt, another English writer also living impecuniously at Pisa, with his wife and six noisy children. Byron said, "What does Hunt want with the heart? He'll only put it in a glass case and make sonnets on it."

Later, Mary Shelley decided that in fact she did want her husband's heart. Hunt declined to give it up until Jane Williams made him surrender it to Mary. It had by then become so much dust. Mary Shelley did not die until 1851. Many were the stories about the heart during her lifetime: that she kept it in a silver case, in a cushion, or even carried it around with her in a fur muff! Her daughter-in-law, the wife of Shelley and Mary's only surviving child, Sir Percy Florence Shelley, had an affection for the memory—and reputation—of her late father-in-law (whom she never met) that reached the point of adoration. At her home, Boscombe Manor, near Bournemouth, she set up a Shelley shrine. She claimed to have found the heart after Mary's death in a folded leaf from the Pisa edition of *Adonais,* Shelley's famous poem on Keats, and it is known that she kept it in her Shelley shrine. But there has been

Lord Byron's English home was Newstead Abbey. His bachelor life there fascinated his contemporaries, who pictured it as rakish in the extreme. This is Byron's bedroom, furnished with many of his possessions in the then-current Regency style. *Museums and Libraries Committee, Nottingham Castle Museum*

much scholarly argument as to its later where-abouts. It may have been buried—finally—with Sir Percy in Saint Peter's Churchyard, Bournemouth.

Less grisly relics include the book Shelley is believed to have had with him on his fatal outing. This was long described as a volume from the Greek authors, "a Sophocles" or, alternatively, "an Aeschylus." These stories can be traced to Trelawny. He presented Sir Percy Florence Shelley with a brine-soaked copy of Sophocles that he said he had found on Shelley's corpse. It was given by the Shelley family to the Bodleian Library at Oxford, but in 1952 the literary scholar Leslie Marchand proved that the book was a fake, and it has been withdrawn from exhibition. In fact, the only book found on Shelley was Keats's *Lamia*.

Trelawny, again, was also involved with a famous sofa said to have been used by Shelley in his house at Pisa. Lord Byron bought it as a souvenir after Shelley's death and refused to give it to Mary Shelley because she was staying with the Leigh Hunts. Byron sent her another, and wrote with typical bluntness:

> I preferred retaining the purchased fur-niture, but always intended that you should have as good or better in its place. I have a particular dislike to anything of Shelley's being within the same walls with Mrs. Hunt's children. They are dirtier and more mischievous than Yahoos. What they can't destroy with their filth, they will with their fingers.

Years and years after this exchange—indeed, half a century—Trelawny suddenly said he was the possessor of that very sofa of Shelley's. He gave it with much pomp and sentiment to Wil-liam Rossetti, a passionate collector of literary souvenirs. Rossetti wrote gushingly in 1872 to thank him.

Trelawny also gave Rossetti a fragment of skull purporting to be Shelley's. Another bit that once belonged to Leigh Hunt is now in the Keats-Shelley Memorial House in Rome.

Shelley's ashes were buried at Rome, and in 1863 Alfred Austen, one of the best-forgotten poets laureate of England, planted violets on the grave. As Shelley's reputation grew, it be-came quite the custom for English tourists to pluck them to send to the folks at home. It is ironic that this pleasant custom honoring one of the greatest English poets was started by one

of the worst, a man who was capable of writ-ing, in his poem on the Boer War, the line:

> *They went across the veldt.*
> *As hard as they could pelt.*

Robert Browning owned one of these violets. He kept it so carefully that, when the Browning relics were sold after the death of his son in 1913, it was still intact and went to another collection.

Lord Byron lived only two years after Shel-ley's death. Byron was much the more famous of the two at the time of his death. His poems were best sellers and his scandalous love affairs, his desertion of his mathematician wife (the "Princess of Parallelograms," he called her, *not* lovingly), his campaign to assist the Greeks, and (not the least) his unusual habits of life kept public attention focused on him. He always traveled with a large entourage ("men, women, and donkeys," wrote Shelley in annoy-ance) and he kept the strangest pets—not merely cats, dogs, donkeys, and horses, al-though he had those, too. When he lived at Genoa he kept three geese that he originally bought to eat and then couldn't bring himself to have killed. He claimed to be testing a theory concerning their long lifespan, but actually the geese were kept as pets and used to roam about the grounds and even into the house itself. At his death they were still alive, and his executors had to find them a new home. Byron had a weight problem, and he dieted on cold potatoes with vinegar, crackers, and soda water. If he felt his waist thickening, he took Epsom salts and other purgatives that also made him more poetically pale.

At the time of Byron's death, he was sur-rounded by an entourage that included Count Pietro Gamba, the little brother of one of Byron's mistresses, Teresa Guiccioli, a Dr. Massingham (actually a young intern), a Greek orphan boy whom Byron had picked up as a page, and his valet "Tita" Falcieri. Most of these people later wrote accounts of Byron's last days that generally do not accord much with one another, and further complications arose after Trelawny appeared on the scene. His account not only does not agree with those of the other survivors, with most of whom he quarreled, but contains discrepancies in itself.

A portion of Byron's remains (probably the lungs and not, as was believed, the heart) was given to the town of Missolonghi. Although the poet had come to hate that "isthmus of Mud" and in fact had been killed by its "putrid fever," Missolonghi was, after the usual fashion of such places, anxious to show him honor after his death.

Byron's body was packed in "180 gallons of spirits" to preserve it for the trip home to England. It is not known whether this met with the approval of Colonel Charles Stanhope, whose duty it was to accompany the body; Colonel Stanhope was a strong temperance advocate. When the body arrived in London it was viewed by Byron's friends, and some determined souvenir hunters tried to purchase not only hair but small quantities of the preservative in which his body had traveled. Although the Dean of Westminster Abbey positively refused to allow the profligate poet to be buried in his church, a magnificent funeral was held, and the body buried at Newstead Abbey in Nottinghamshire, the poet's old home.

Doris Langley Moore, an expert on Byron and his posthumous reputation, has said that "Surely no great writer has ever been so unlucky as Byron in his choice of literary guardians!" The trustees committed one of the greatest literary crimes of the century by burning the manuscript of his unpublished memoirs and also did their best to censor the late poet and starch his reputation. The beneficiaries of these strenuous efforts, comparable to but not so successful as those to preserve Shelley's reputation, were Lady Byron, the last woman on earth that Lord Byron should have married, their only child Ada Lady Lovelace, an even more distinguished mathematician than her mother who has been credited with making the first computer program, and his half-sister (possibly also his mistress) Augusta Leigh, described by Byron's exasperated lawyer as "I think half-witted." Although memoirs, letters, and diaries of the late Lord Byron were destroyed, suppressed, or edited to the point of defacement, relics were preserved in great numbers. The destruction of many papers meant, however, that relics have often been undocumented.

For years after Byron's death Trelawny was busy building up a legend of his friendship with the deceased, although as a matter of record he had spent only a few weeks with him and they were seldom if ever alone. Typically, he told a long, involved story about a jacket he had lent to Byron so that he could make a good appearance while landing in Greece. Nothing was less

At Newstead Abbey is Lord Byron's helmet, specially designed for the Greek campaign during which he died. *Museums and Libraries Committee, Nottingham Castle Museum*

likely than this story. Byron, who was vain, had brought five trunks full of clothing and carefully planned what he would wear at his triumphant landing. After his death, his remaining clothes were given by Augusta Leigh, his principal heir, to Fletcher, his servant, and among these was apparently the jacket now on view in the museum at Newstead Abbey, which turned up years later among Fletcher's descendants in South Africa.

Very late in his life when everyone who could possibly refute his words was safely dead, Trelawny suddenly produced a whole slew of Byron relics about which he had been silent for forty-eight years, among them a sword that Byron had given him at Cephalonia and a cap of the poet's, both articles highly suspect on the point of provenance. He published his *Recollections of the Last Days of Shelley and Byron* in 1858, and his *Records of Shelley, Byron, and the Author* in 1878, when he was eighty-six.

A pipe believed to have been given to Trelawny by Lord Byron in the 1830s came into the possession long afterward of John Bright, the English radical politician, who was assured by Trelawny that it had been Byron's. When Bright's son some years later inquired for confirmation, old Trelawny, then in his eighties, reversed himself: "Our chief pleasures spring from our imagination. . . . Byron had nothing whatever to do with the pipe you mention. . . . In truth Byron never smoked either pipe or segar. . . ." Presumably this answer deprived the Bright family of their faith in this interesting relic, but the reply was simply an example of Trelawny's gratuitous malice, which was notorious, because Byron *did* smoke a pipe and left several among his possessions; so Bright's relic probably was genuine. The Bright family should have known it was most unlikely that Byron, who prided himself on having most of the vices of his time, did not smoke.

It is a rather surprising fact that whenever locks of Lord Byron's hair come up for sale at auction they bring substantial sums of money even when they are not accompanied by any manuscript. Byron's fame was so prodigious during his lifetime that it is unlikely anyone who received a lock of his hair ever threw it away, and so the auction market has had a thin but persistent supply. In 1970, Sotheby's sold a lock, for example, for the very good price of £320 ($775). A much more curious and sentimental relic was sold in the same rooms a year later. It was a gold and carnelian ring that was given to Lord Byron by John Edleston. Byron was sexually ambivalent, and while an undergraduate at Cambridge he became attached to Edleston, who was a chorister in the Trinity College Chapel. "His *voice* first attracted my attention, his *countenance* fixed it, and his *manners* attached me to him for ever," Byron wrote in one of his letters. He called Edleston "his carnelian," hence the symbol of the ring. Edleston came to a bad end: threatened with a morals charge, he was obliged to flee England and died young. It is now believed that he inspired some important passages in Byron's poetry, and Byron wore the ring on the little

finger of his left hand up until his death at Missolonghi. He bequeathed it to his valet Tita (Giovanni Battista) Falcieri, and it was a descendant of the valet who put it up for auction. It was bought by the namesake and descendant of Byron's publisher John Murray for £450 ($1,100).

George Byron, John Keats, and Percy Shelley maintain a sort of permanent lead among writers whose relics have been collected. Relics of all three, including locks of their hair, are kept in the chief shrine of English expatriate poets in Italy, the Keats-Shelley Memorial in Rome. Even amidst the disorder and tragedy of the Second World War there was concern for the preservation of the relics at the Keats-Shelley House. In December 1943, with the Allies approaching Rome and the German troops withdrawing, two boxes were packed with locks of hair, letters, and first editions and sent to the Abbey of Monte Cassino, where it was believed they would be safe among the treasures of that famous monastery. When shells began to fall on Monte Cassino too, the relics were evacuated back to Rome, where they were concealed until the end of the war.

Alexander Pope's poem on hair, *The Rape of the Lock,* contains the lines:

Fair tresses man's imperial race ensnare
And beauty draws us with a single hair

A single hair sometimes had to satisfy English literature's greatest collector of hair. Leigh Hunt, a poet of sorts and a radical journalist who served a two-year jail term for libeling the Prince Regent, assembled quite an array of the hair of famous persons, mostly his own contemporaries and friends, including Keats, Mary and Percy Shelley (he also briefly owned Shelley's heart, as noted above), Charles Lamb, S. T. Coleridge, Carlyle, and others of that ilk, that he kept on display in his study, where he delighted to show the various specimens to visitors. He wrote whole essays on the locks in his collection, their color, their fading, and graying, and the personal characteristics he deduced from studying them. Hunt had begun his collection with a strand of John Milton's hair that he received as a schoolboy. It had supposedly once belonged to Dr. Samuel Johnson (Hunt had some of Johnson's too, naturally). When the Brownings visited En-

gland for the first time after their runaway marriage, Hunt presented them with a few Miltonic hairs in honor of their poetic accomplishments.

Hunt's most sensational exhibit was a solitary strand of Lucrezia Borgia's tresses "stolen," he airily wrote, "by an acquaintance from an entire lock preserved in the Ambrosian Library in Milan." There is a hint that the thief was the ubiquitous Edward John Trelawny. That would have been entirely in character. Another essayist and poet, Walter Savage Landor, was so moved by the sight of this strand of Borgian hair that he apostrophized it in a poem beginning:

Borgia, thou once wert almost too august,
And high for adoration;—now thou'rt dust!
All that remains of thee these plaits infold—
Calm hair meand'ring with pellucid gold!

Everywhere the nineteenth century was, like our own time, a great era of relic collecting. To the people of the nineteenth century, history was not just a "record of crimes and misfortunes," as Voltaire said, but an intensely interesting and dramatic panorama that they saw as prologue to their own achievements. The age was rich, antiquarian, possessive, and sentimental, and relic collecting flourished. One of the century's most popular writers was Sir Walter Scott, although he lived only in its first third. A glance at Scott as a relic collector tells

much about the nineteenth century's attitudes toward the remains of the past.

If ever a man was lucky enough to build his dream house and live in it for years to his complete satisfaction, it was Sir Walter Scott. In 1812 he began to construct, on the banks of the River Tweed near the celebrated medieval ruins of Melrose Abbey, a little castle in the popular more or less "Gothic" taste. He called it Abbotsford, and he was still lord of the manor when he died there in 1832, the world's best-selling author.

Although Scott was not a "Victorian" in any chronological sense (he was born in the reign of King George III and died in that of William IV), his domestic taste, like that of Horace Walpole, was what the present age considers Victorian: he lived in an artistic and historical clutter that included many varieties of memorabilia. Abbotsford—Scott pronounced the name with the accent on the last syllable—was literally encrusted with relics. It actually incorporated historical souvenirs—stones, timbers, and architectural elements—in its very walls. When the Edinburgh Tolbooth, the old "Heart of Midlothian," meeting place of the Scottish parliament, later used as a jail, was being torn down, Scott begged a few carved stones from its walls to inlay into those of Abbotsford. The Tolbooth had been the setting of one of his most successful novels. Throughout the house were inscriptions, quotations, stained glass, arms, legends, heraldic devices, and historical remains. One

(*opposite page*) Jane Austen lived from 1809 on in the tiny Hampshire village of Chawton in a house which is still preserved with many relics. She usually wrote in this parlor, but with constant interruptions by her large and affectionate brood of nieces and nephews, to whom she used to relate the further histories of the characters she had created—whom the other Misses Bennett had married, for instance. *Jane Austen Memorial Trust, Chawton*

(*above*) The quilt hanging at right in Jane Austen's bedroom was made by Jane and her mother. Jane, who was a good needlewoman, was always asking her sister Cassandra to collect scraps ("peices," she wrote, as she wrote "neices") "for the Patchwork." When Jane died at Winchester at the age of forty-two, it was Cassandra who wrote her best memorial, "Never was human being more sincerely mourned by those who attended her remains than was this dear creature." *Jane Austen Memorial Trust, Chawton*

room contained panels with oak from the bed occupied by Mary Queen of Scots at Jedburgh.

Scott was also on the lookout for contemporary relics. When King George IV visited Edinburgh in 1822, the first Hanoverian monarch of Great Britain to see Scotland, which had cost so much bloodshed to subdue during the Jacobite risings, he drank a glass of whiskey with Scott (whose novels he greatly admired) while still on board ship in Edinburgh harbor. Scott asked for the glass as a souvenir and put it away in his capacious greatcoat pocket. Much to his chagrin, on the way home he sat on it.

The finished result at Abbotsford did not please all visitors equally. John Ruskin, that bad-tempered nineteenth century arbiter of taste, called it "perhaps the most incongruous pile that gentlemanly modernism ever designed." Few people considered the Abbotsford taste "modernism," but Ruskin seldom admired anything created later than the thirteenth century. Hugh Miller, the great Scottish geologist, thought Abbotsford "supremely melancholy."

Although the most peaceable and kindhearted of men, Scott had a lifelong affection for the military and its gear. He took particular pride in the armory of his house, a motley assortment of military impedimenta in which a suit of chain mail taken from the corpse of one of Tippoo Sahib's bodyguards on the battlefield of Seringapatam occupied a special place of honor. At Seringapatam (1791), the army of the British East India Company led by Lord Cornwallis (luckier in the Indian than in the American colonies) decisively defeated the Sultan of Mysore, who had challenged the expanding British power in India. Many relics of this encounter were and are preserved in Britain; Tippoo's mechanical tiger, which mauls the tin figure of a British soldier when it is wound up, is still on display in the Victoria and Albert Museum, London.

Scott owned a sword given by King Charles I of England to his ally the first Marquess of Montrose and the gun that belonged to "Rob Roy" (Robert Macgregor Campbell, a ferocious Highland cattle rustler whom Scott made the hero of one of his most successful novels). He also had Rob Roy's dirk, gun, and sporran, Bonnie Prince Charlie Stuart's hunting knives, and a torture instrument called "The Iron Crown of Wishart the Martyr" (Hugh Wishart was a Protestant martyr during the Scottish religious wars). Stags' horns and other souvenirs of the hunt ornamented the walls, along with every sort of ancient and modern weapon, pistols, swords, knives, and keys from various historic keeps and jails. There were numerous relics of the two battlefields that most interested Scott: Culloden, where the Scottish Jacobites were defeated in 1746, and Waterloo. He was able to add to his collection of militaria during a visit to the latter battlefield in 1815, when it was almost still smoking. Space was also found in the armory for "an Eskimo jacket" and "a South Seas fish-hook."

But his favorite "gabions" (as Scott, for some reason, termed his relics) were the memorabilia of Scottish history, of which he was a walking compendium. He had Mary Queen of Scots' seal, her mother-of-pearl crucifix, and a piece of one of her dresses. He had a whole collection of "quaiches." These are a characteristically Scottish form of cup, a small two-handled bowl made of wood with silver stripings, for drinking brandy (occasionally quaiches were solid silver). One had belonged to Bonnie Prince Charlie, one was made from a yew tree associated with Queen Mary, another from the tree under which Wellington had halted at Waterloo, still another from the oak tree known as "Sir William Wallace's" after the Scottish hero. Scott also had a cast of the skull of King Robert the Bruce made when

the king's coffin at Dunfermline Abbey was opened in 1819.

One of the relics Scott treasured most was "The William Wallace Chair," which was constructed from timbers of the house at Robroyston in which the noble Wallace, leader of the Scots against the English king, was betrayed in 1305, leading to his execution in London. A manuscript volume telling the story of the chair was contained in a drawer under the seat, and the back bore the following plate:

> This chair
> made of the only remaining wood
> of the
> House of Robroyston,
> in which the
> Matchless Sir William Wallace
> "was done to death by felon hand
> For guarding well his father's land"
> is most respectfully presented to
> Sir Walter Scott
> as a small token of gratitude
> by his devoted servant
> Joseph Train

Admirers sent many gifts for Abbotsford. Lord Byron sent a large sepulchral vase of silver filled with dead men's bones from the historic Piraeus in Greece, "suitably inscribed." Scott in return gave his fellow poet, of whom he was fond, a gold-mounted dagger taken (most appropriately) from a Turkish "corsair." A small folding box used as a writing desk "made from wood from the Spanish Armada" was accepted, as was Marie Antoinette's clock, but Scott rejected Joseph Addison's velvet house slippers because Addison was "a writer I do not admire."

Scott wrote a nine-volume *Life of Napoleon Buonaparte* (he belonged to the generation who loved to call Napoleon by his true name), and in the library at Abbotsford, which contained no less than 20,000 books, he had quite a collection of Napoleonic relics: the emperor's blotter and gold clasps in the bee form, found in his carriage after Waterloo, and his pen case and sealing wax recovered from the imperial writing table at the Elysée Palace in Paris after his flight in 1815. In the armory were a pair of the emperor's pistols, and of course Scott owned the inevitable lock of the imperial hair (he also had hair of the Bonnie Prince, Lord Nelson, and the Duke of Wellington).

Abbotsford was full of family portraits and

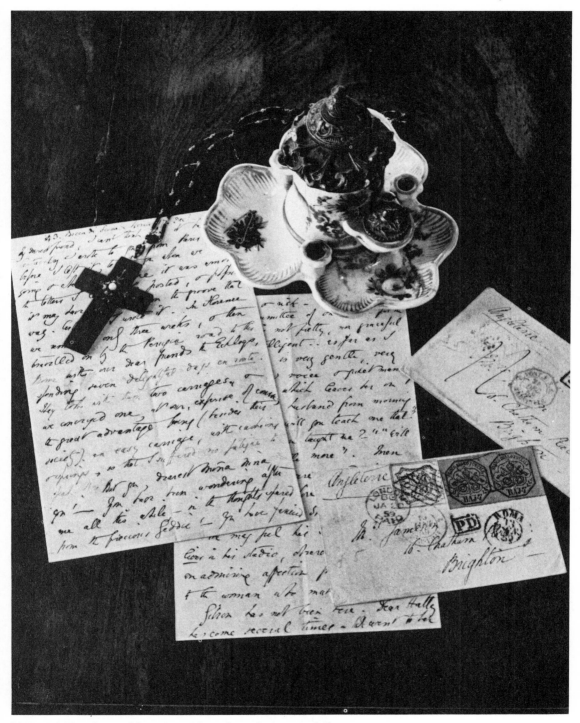

Memorabilia of most Victorian writers have been carefully preserved. Beside this letter written by Elizabeth Barrett Browning to a friend in 1859 are her Dresden china inkwell and onyx cross. *Armstrong Browning Library, Baylor University*

These relics of "EBB" are her fan, the lace gloves very characteristic of her time, a lace mantilla, and a cream pitcher from her tea service. *Armstrong Browning Library, Baylor University*

memorabilia, including the portrait of the author's great-grandfather, who had made a vow not to shave his beard until the Stuarts were restored to their throne in Scotland and naturally became known as "Beardie Walter" Scott. The house was also occupied by a succession of enormous mastiffs with which Scott had the most extraordinary rapport; when he was ill, their howls terrorized the whole neighborhood. The dogs were admired, somewhat uneasily, by most visitors. When Sir Edwin Landseer, the celebrated portraitist of animals, came to Abbotsford, "he painted," wrote Scott, "every dog in the house but me."

Late in life when his writing power had frankly given out, Scott conceived the idea of publishing a catalogue of his memorabilia and library under the contrived title *Reliquiae Trotcosiensis,* a "trotcosy" being a Scottish covering for head and shoulders. Written in his most painfully facetious style as the narrative of one Jonathan Oldbuck, it was—perhaps fortunately—never completed.

In 1826, when Scott was bankrupted by the financial failure of his publishers, he surrendered his Abbotsford collections, valued at ten thousand pounds, to his creditors, but in recognition of his honorable and strenuous attempt to pay off his enormous debts, they refused to take possession. All these relics have remained at Abbotsford, which is still in the possession of Scott's descendants.

The clock used by Robert Browning in his London home at DeVere Gardens. *Armstrong Browning Library, Baylor University*

The mutual esteem that so many of the great nineteenth century English writers seem to have felt for one another inspired them to preserve mementos. In their Casa Guidi apartment in Florence, Robert and Elizabeth Barrett Browning had a death mask of Keats and medallions of Tennyson and Carlyle.

A relic linking two important literary men, English and American, is "Grip," a stuffed raven that now makes the Free Library of Philadelphia his permanent home. Charles Dickens had an unusual devotion to pet birds. He owned several that spoke or sang, and he was tireless in writing to his friends about things the birds "said." Dickens was so attached to Grip, a talkative raven, that he wanted to make him a character in a novel. "I have been studying my bird," Dickens wrote to his illustrator George Cattermole, "and think I could make a very queer character of him." He gave the raven to Barnaby Rudge, in the novel of that name, as a companion. The new

Dickens book reached America in 1842, and was reviewed for *Graham's Magazine* by Edgar Allan Poe. He criticized Dickens's handling of the raven: "the raven . . . might have been made more than we now see it, a portion of the conception of the fantastic Barnaby. Its croakings might have been *prophetically* heard in the course of the drama." Poe himself used just that device in 1845 in his celebrated poem, "The Raven," with its prophetic "Nevermore."

Grip, having inspired two notable literary works, went to his reward on 12 March 1841, apparently to the relief of Dickens's family, who felt about the raven the way Sir Walter Scott's relatives felt about his mastiffs. In addition to chattering constantly, Grip had the habit of biting ankles at random. Grip's master, however, mourned him in characteristic fashion as he wrote to his friend, the painter Daniel Maclise:

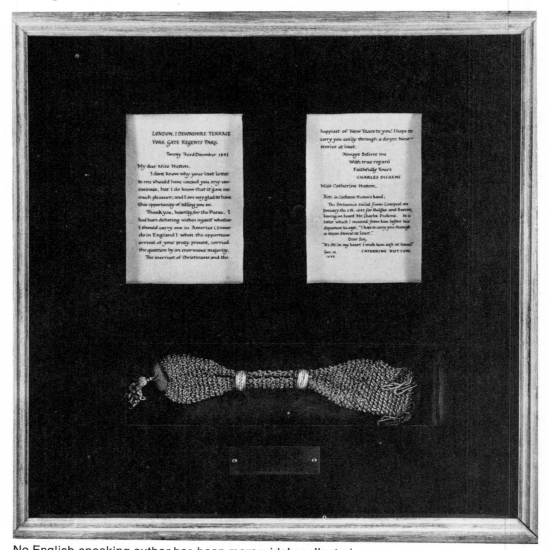

No English-speaking author has been more widely collected in every form than the beloved Charles Dickens—manuscripts, letters, first editions, and relics. The Free Library of Philadelphia has a notable collection of Dickensiana. This net purse was a gift from Catherine Hutton, a minor novelist of the time, to Dickens in 1841 as he was departing on his first tour of the United States, where he was received with an enthusiasm seldom accorded visitors in the whole of American history. The long provenance of this relic begins with the letter reproduced here and includes impressive documentation. It was once owned by the actor Charles Albert Fechter, famous for his interpretation of Hamlet as "a man of action," and is accompanied now by a letter of Fechter discussing it. *The Free Library of Philadelphia (Jacques Benoliel Collection)*

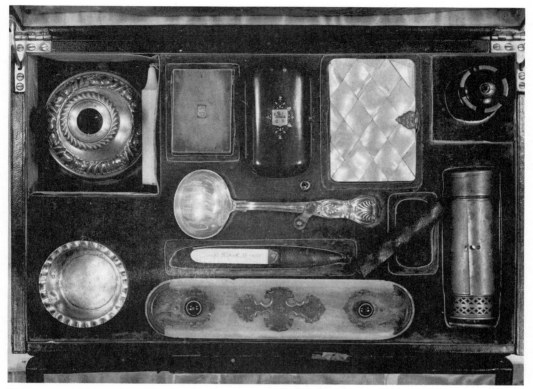

This group of important Charles Dickens relics includes many used on his desk: his pen tray (*at bottom*), letter opener, candlestick, and so on. The mother-of-pearl box is his card case. The letter opener is engraved "From M.S.H. to C.D. 1837"; it was a gift from his sister-in-law Mary Scott Hogarth on his birthday in 1837. *The Free Library of Philadelphia (Elkins Collection)*

You will be greatly shocked and grieved to hear that the Raven is no more. He expired today at a few minutes after twelve o'clock at noon . . . on the clock striking twelve he appeared slightly agitated, but he soon recovered, walked twice or thrice along the coach-house, stopped to bark, staggered, exclaimed *Halloa old girl!* (his favorite expression) and died.

Dickens had the bird stuffed and placed in a glass case in his library: Grip was still in a place of honor when Dickens died at his home, Gad's Hill, in 1870. At the auction of the late novelist's belongings, Grip sold for the amazing sum of 120 guineas ($5,000 today), then passed through the collections of several other Dickensians until, in 1970, he was bequeathed to the Free Library of Philadelphia by his last owner.

Dickens was especially fond of "Dick," a canary that escaped innumerable perils from what his owner described as "two particularly tigerish and fearful cats" during a singularly dangerous existence. Dick died in 1866, and Dickens buried the canary in the garden at Gad's Hill Place, London, and put up a painted metal tombstone inscribed:

This is the Grave of Dick. The Best of Birds. Born at Broadstairs Mids 1857. Died at Gads Hill Place 14 October 1866

That tombstone is now in the Free Library of Philadelphia. The year it arrived, a Philadel-

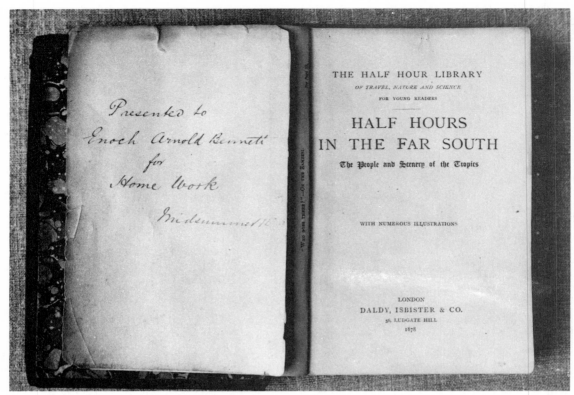

Naturally the relics of authors often take the form of books. This book belonged to Arnold Bennett, author of *The Old Wives' Tale.* Preserved in his early home in the city of Stoke-on-Trent, with which he is forever associated, the volume is inscribed on the outside: "Burslem Endowed School Prize 1880." It was given to Bennett at the age of thirteen for assiduity in doing his homework. The Stoke-on-Trent Museums also have his family Bible, fountain pen, wallet, watch, walking stick, Gladstone bag, and opera coat. *City Museums Stoke-on-Trent*

phia newspaper hailed its acquisition as "the least consequential event of the year."

America's literary past may be centuries shorter than England's, but it is not difficult to locate relics of this country's writers. As for shrines, every writer from Washington Irving to Sinclair Lewis seems to have his hallowed spot "open to the public." It is hard to imagine that James Whitcomb Riley has any readers today, but he has his shrines. He was one of those homespun American poets who thought dropping letters out of words the height of verbal accuracy. Writing "git" for "get," "an" for "and," and "o'er" for "over" were trying

demonstrations of his folksiness. In his complete works there must be thousands of apostrophes substitued for letters. Riley's former homes at Greenfield and Indianapolis, Indiana, are kept as shrines. At Greenfield, "Birthplace of the Hoosier Poet," visitors can see the Riley family dining room "where they et on Sundays," the "cubby hole where the feather duster hangs," and "the kitchen, the room in which the poet was born [sic]." Among the Riley memorabilia are his pince-nez, pen and inkwell, and his academic cap and gown. Incidentally, the motto of Hancock County, where Greenfield is situated, is "where we re-live the life of Riley."

There are dozens of similar homesteads in the United States. Herman Melville was a New Yorker, born in 1819, on Pearl Street, then as now in the heart of the business district, and died on East Twenty-sixth Street, a quiet residential area in 1891. But he had family connections in Pittsfield, Massachusetts, and after 1850 spent summers at his house there, Arrowhead, meeting Nathaniel Hawthorne, who was living in Stockbridge, and other New England writers. Important relics of Melville are kept in the Berkshire Athenaeum, Pittsfield (see illustration).

Also in New England are the remains, extremely carefully preserved, of a curious enterprise called Fruitlands, near Harvard, Massachusetts. In 1844, Bronson Alcott, the Transcendentalist, led a group of high-minded relatives and friends in what would now be called a commune but then was called a "Consociate family" at Fruitlands. Its objective was to establish a peaceable kingdom, self-sustaining and with ideal conditions for healthful and lofty contemplation. Everything the "Consociates" needed was to be produced on the spot. They would eat nothing that "exploited" a living creature; hence, no fish or meat, no butter, eggs, milk, or cheese could be con-

sumed. Naturally, the participants had to wear linen since leather and wool deprived animals of their covering. (The use of cotton was out because it was cultivated by slaves in the South.) They planned to grow "aspiring" vegetables—i.e., those that grew upward—rather than such things as potatoes that grew in the earth. It is hardly necessary to add that these sincere cranks lasted only a few months at Fruitlands and had to be rescued during a hard winter by some of their meat-fed neighbors.

Probably the most famous member of the colony was Bronson Alcott's spinster daughter, Louisa May, author of *Little Women.* Like so many nineteenth century women writers, she was the support—and slave—of an affectionate but selfish father; the Brontës, Mary Russell Mitford, and Maria Edgeworth, to name but a few, were similarly afflicted. As Samuel Butler, who was an authority on the subject, wrote in *The Way of All Flesh,* "in the nineteenth century the relations between parents and children were still far from satisfactory." Some interesting relics of Louisa May Alcott remain at Fruitlands, including the water jug used when she nursed soldiers during the Civil War.

A desk of Henry David Thoreau's is at

John Greenleaf Whittier spent nearly all his eighty-five years within a very small New England circumference. This is the garden room of his house in Amesbury, Massachusetts, with many relics of the poet. *Whittier Home, Amesbury*

Relics of Herman Melville are preserved in the Berkshire Athenaeum at Pittsfield, Massachusetts. The objects are typical of the personal belongings of notable people that are attractive to relic collectors. They include three of his canes, a cup and saucer with the Melville monogram, the key to Arrowhead, his Berkshire house, his badge as a U.S. Customs Inspector, in which position he worked on the New York docks for nineteen years, a tomahawk pipe, pens (on desk tray), and a metal matchbox with compass inset. The circular object farthest right is a once-popular board game called "Fox and Geese." *The Berkshire Athenaeum, Pittsfield*

Fruitlands; he was a friend, although not a member, of the colony. During his lifetime, and for years later, Thoreau was known to his neighbors in Concord, Massachusetts, who mostly did not admire him, as "the man who set fire to the woods," and boys used to yell "burnt woods" at him when he passed along the street. Thoreau had set alight the timber surrounding the town while on one of his naturalist tramps. The ensuing conflagration also burned some buildings. Thoreau coolly remarked:

I have set fire to the forest, but I have done no wrong therein, and now it is as if the lightning had done it. These flames are but consuming their natural food. It has never troubled me from that day to this more than if the lightning had done it.

He had the face to tell neighbors who had had their property destroyed that they should "bear their loss like men."

Many of the furnishings of Thoreau's own house, which he built for $28.12½ at Walden

Pond, are at the Concord Antiquarian Society —his desk, rocker, the bed he caned himself, and, ironically, a fire bucket. Thoreau used to list himself in his Harvard class anniversary record as "surveyor," and his surveying chain still exists; but he is more famous as a pencil maker. His father started the family business, the first in this country to use graphite in pencils. The pencils came in bundles with a printed wrapper and were graduated from 1 to 4 in proportion to their hardness. Thoreau pencils were a quality product; they cost twenty-five cents each, very expensive at a time when the ordinary price was fifty cents a dozen. Thoreau and his sister Sophia made them in the family house.

Thoreau pencils are fairly frequently on the market today. They usually sell for $25 to $50 per pencil; small wooden boxes of them are occasionally to be found for sale at about $100. They are unmistakable, having printed on their sides: J. Thoreau & Son, Concord, Mass. Bundles with the original wrapper are of course extremely rare.

Although it now seems out of character, Thoreau was a man of his time, and not above

Walt Whitman lived in Camden, New Jersey, from 1873 to his death in 1892, selling copies of his books by mail and shipping them himself. Here he issued five new editions of *Leaves of Grass,* and here he received devoted believers in his notions and assorted cranks. This is his bedroom with the bed made for him by his father, and beneath it Whitman's bathtub. *New Jersey Bureau of Parks, Trenton*

collecting mementos himself. When he made his famous trip to Fire Island, New York, to search for the bodies of his friend Margaret Fuller Ossoli, her husband, and child, who had been drowned in a shipwreck, and located Ossoli's body, he ripped a button off the coat as a relic.

The principal house associated with Mark Twain, whose restlessness and many residences were proverbial, is at Hartford, Connecticut. He built it in 1874, and it is full of curious conceits reflecting his charm and imagination. The structure itself is reminiscent of a Mississippi paddle boat. The fireplace in the dining room is unique: it has a window above the mantelpiece so that Twain could sit before the fire and "see the flames devour the snow flakes." Twain wrote his most important books in the house, including both *Tom Sawyer* and *Huckleberry Finn.*

Literary shrines are subject to the same kind of painstaking reconstruction employed at the shrines of political notables. "Jack London

(*above*) After renting the house at 330 Mickle Street, Camden, for a number of years, Whitman bought it with the assistance of friends for $1,750 in 1884. This is the living room with Whitman's furniture. *New Jersey Bureau of Parks, Trenton*

(*opposite page, top*) In the 1870s Mark Twain built his family home at Hartford, Connecticut, in the area known as "Nook Farm," where his neighbors included Harriet Beecher Stowe. Many features of the exterior of the house are reminiscent of the Mississippi River steamboats of Twain's youth. The house was an elaborate and expensive undertaking; Louis Comfort Tiffany had a hand in its decoration. In the billiard room Twain not only played his favorite game but wrote some of his most noted works. *Mark Twain Memorial, Hartford*

(*opposite page, bottom*) In the basement of the Twain house sits the massive "Paige Typesetter," an invention to improve printing, on which Twain is said to have lost $300,000. The room also contains, among other relics, his Russian sleigh and his bicycle. *Mark Twain Memorial, Hartford*

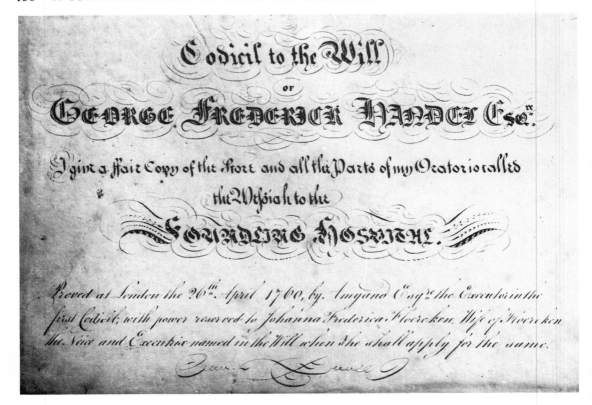

(*opposite page, top*) George Frederick Handel, a lifelong bachelor, was interested in the Foundling Hospital in Brunswick Square, London, which had been established by Captain Thomas Coram in 1739. He organized a concert for the hospital's benefit in 1749 (at which the *Fire Works Musick* was played), gave an organ for the chapel, and from 1750 on he conducted an annual performance of the *Messiah* there. The composer's will left to the hospital a most important gift: "a fair copy of the score and all the parts of my oratorio called the Messiah," which is still preserved there. This is the codicil to Handel's will making the gift. *Thomas Coram Foundation for Children, London*

(*above*) Franz Schubert was born in this house at Nussdorfer Strasse 54 in Vienna in 1797. In the house are many relics of his short life of thirty-one years. *Austrian Information Service, New York.*

(*opposite page, bottom*) Bonn was Beethoven's birthplace. The house in which he was born is carefully preserved and, as may be seen, contains many relics of the composer, including his stringed instruments. *German Information Center, New York*

One of the most famous shrines in the world is Bayreuth in southern Germany, mecca of the Richard Wagner cult. In addition to the opera house, Wagner built there a house that he called Wahnfried, a word that he—characteristically— made up and that means something like "peace from illusion." The villa is still in the Wagner family's possession; Cosima Wagner lived there until her death in 1930. Both Richard and Cosima are buried in the garden. The bronze bust in front is that of King Ludwig II of Bavaria, Wagner's patron, a contribution from the king after broad hints from the composer about the empty space in front of the villa. The house is crammed with Wagner relics. *German Information Office, New York*

Thousands of tourists annually visit this house in Salzburg where Wolfgang Amadeus Mozart was born in 1756. Among its relics are his first small violin, a clavier on which he played, and a watch given to him by the Empress Maria Theresa when he played for her at the age of six. *Austrian Tourist Office, New York*

Square" in Oakland, California, has the Yukon cabin in which London spent the winter of 1897/98, which was brought down from the Canadian wilds and rebuilt. The same tendency is shown in the older literary shrines on the Continent. After a visit to George Sand's country home, Nohant, where the dining table was set for dinner circa 1840 and "everything is as it was," the American writer Robert Craft summed up this style as "waxworks." At Nohant are the quill pen that Sand used in writing her dozens of novels, Delacoix's umbrella, and Chopin's white gloves, and, as Craft pointed out, a George Sand inn, restaurant, parking lot, and bookshop, and "Rosa Bonheur cows" grazing.

Nevertheless, there are in the twentieth century fewer literary shrines than historical,

and fewer literary relics reach the salesroom. Some of the things sold at auction are relics of recent authors and bring surprisingly high prices. In 1972, a leather briefcase belonging to the late F. Scott Fitzgerald, with a silver label giving his name and address and containing a few of his school medals and a silver locket of his wife Zelda, sold for $1,000.

After historical and literary relics and shrines, those of musicians and artists come in a very poor third. As the illustrations here show, most of the relics of the greatest composers are in museums. Artists seem to leave few possessions for relic collectors; their works are their relics. Typical of what does remain is the collection bequeathed to the Musée du

Albrecht Dürer lived and died—in 1528—in this half-timbered house in Nuremberg. During the Second World War it was badly damaged by bombs, but like so many Central European landmarks was reconstructed after the war with immense scholarly care. The interior gives a remarkably vivid impression of life in Germany at the turn of the sixteenth century. *German Information Office, New York*

Like his contemporary Handel, the painter William Hogarth was interested in the Foundling Hospital established by Captain Coram, of whom he painted a famous portrait. This is Hogarth's punch bowl, now in the collections of the hospital. His London house (in Hogarth's Lane, Chiswick) also has many relics of the painter of London life. *Thomas Coram Foundation, London*

(*opposite page*) Johann Wolfgang von Goethe was born (1749) in the house of his prosperous family in Frankfurt, which is now kept as a Goethe Museum. In 1944 the house was greatly damaged by Allied bombers, and it had to be reconstructed after World War II. The Goethe relics were not damaged; they had been evacuated to a safe storage spot and were put back in place after the war. The silhouettes and paintings shown are those of Goethe's relatives; elsewhere in the house hangs the famous portrait by J. H. W. Tischbein of the young Goethe in Italy in 1787. The Goethe House is similar to literary shrines in many parts of Germany. *German Information Center, New York*

Louvre by Dr. Paul Gachet, friend and patron of Vincent Van Gogh and Paul Cézanne. He gave the museum Van Gogh's palette, the bamboo pens he used for drawing, and the white hat that he wore while painting in the sun. At the Orangerie Museum is a gray Japanese vase belonging to Dr. Gachet, undistinguished as porcelain but celebrated in the history of modern painting because it is shown by Cézanne in his *Bouquet of Yellow Dahlias* and by Van Gogh in his *Roses and Anemones*.

One of the twentieth century's greatest private collectors of relics was the late Austrian novelist and playwright Stefan Zweig, who well expressed in his memoirs the lure of owning memorabilia of famous men of the arts. Zweig said he revered "every earthly manifestation of genius." He acquired the furniture that had been in Beethoven's room at the time of his death, including his desk and "the little money box out of which when in bed he drew the necessary change for the maid with a trembling hand already touched by death." One room in the Zweig house was devoted to what he referred to as "my cult." He wrote of Goethe's pen that it was carefully preserved under glass "to avoid the temptation of taking it into my own unworthy hands."

8
Relics of Stage, Screen, and Sports

Relics of the entertainment world—legitimate stage, music, screen, and sports—are plentiful, often attractive, and generally of modest price. It is small wonder, then, that they are perhaps the most widely collected relics today. Those available for collecting are overwhelmingly from the nineteenth and twentieth centuries. Although a few historic European theatres and opera houses preserve various relics of great performers of the eighteenth century, and there are a few ancient trophies and sports equipment in museum collections, material of earlier date than the mid-nineteenth century is not likely to come into the reach of the average collector. The motion pictures of course are almost entirely a twentieth century phenomenon. This chapter will deal first with relics of the legitimate stage including opera, ballet, and music, then with the motion pictures, and finally with sports relics.

No shortage exists today of theatrical relics; both the beginner and the advanced collector have opportunities for general collecting and for specialization within the field. Important theatrical relics by the hundreds can be studied in museums and libraries, and in New York City alone a score or more antique shops specialize in selling theatrical memorabilia. There are probably nearly as many in London. These figures do not include the bookshops, even more numerous, specializing in printed works on the stage, playbills, prints, manuscripts, librettos, and scores that have the occasional theatrical relic.

Auctions have played a great role in the redistribution of relics of the performing arts. For generations there have been public sales of the possessions of theatre personalities: David Garrick's personal belongings were sold at auction in the 1840s, long after his death. A red hat said to have belonged to Cardinal Wolsey was in the collection of Horace Walpole at Strawberry Hill. When the contents of the house reached auction in 1842, the famous actor Charles Kean bought the hat over strong competition for the remarkable sum of £21 (about $1,000) and later wore it in some of his stage roles.

In more recent times there have been auctions of the personal possessions, libraries, stage costumes and properties, and jewelry of Joseph Jefferson, Clyde Fitch, Julia Marlowe, Lillian Russell, and Enrico Caruso. At the Caruso dispersal the estate apparently sold everything the tenor possessed, even his shirts. His wigs and costumes brought very low prices; the complete costume he wore in *Pagliacci* sold for only $25. Lillian Russell's sale was replete with gilded and bejeweled items, including a gold birdcage and a pair of the singer's golden shoes. The possessions of Sophie Tucker, Tyrone Power, Alfred Lunt and Lynn Fontanne, John Barrymore, and innumerable other contemporary actors and actresses have come under the hammer.

Sports relics include trophies. Every sport has awards, badges, medals, and cups. This handsome sterling silver cup with silver oars was made about 1900 by the Gorham Company for the National Association of Amateur Oarsmen. *James F. Carr, New York*

There has never been in the United States, however, another auction to compare with the sale of the theatrical library, art, and memorabilia of Augustin Daly, a New York playwright and producer who died in 1899. That sale, in 1900, lasted for days—it consisted of more than six thousand lots! Those were the days of the giants in collecting. Daly was much interested in the history of the English-speaking theatre and had a passion for theatrical memo-

rabilia, which he bought for his collection at very high prices. Two typical lots at the Daly sale were the bond, scales, and knife used in the role of Shylock by both Edmund Kean and his son Charles (sold for $115) and the dressing table with drawer and sliding mirror for making up that was used by David Garrick in his theatre dressing room ($550).

Auctions of theatrical memorabilia are becoming more rather than less frequent. The successful—and enormous—sales of the properties of the great motion picture studios in the late nineteen sixties and early seventies undoubtedly indicate that more such auctions will be held for collectors in this field. The collector should be particularly alert to the unusual number of charity and fund-raising events; they are an important source of theatrical relics. The Actors' Fund and other charities often hold sales of memorabilia donated by members of the profession to raise funds. Organizations like the Festival of the Two Worlds at Spoleto, Italy, have sponsored sales, and first-rate relics have been offered. In the last few years the New York Public Library's Lincoln Center for the Performing Arts Research Center has sold duplicates and unwanted objects, such as stage models, plaster busts of famous theatrical figures, locks of hair (Edwin Booth's and Franz Liszt's in 1973), at bazaars and auctions for the benefit of the Dance Collection at the library.

Benefit sales offer such a variety of objects that it is almost impossible to enumerate even categories. Many donated objects carry notes or descriptions by the donor, which of course are, in effect, certificates of authenticity that make an object much more attractive to the collector. But many of the objects appeal to the eye anyway, as—for obvious reasons—the donors generally select gifts that look good on display.

A typical sale of theatrical memorabilia was a benefit held for the Actors' Fund in 1973 in New York. Among the interesting items were:

• A silver-headed walking stick initialed A.L., for Archie Leach, the real name of the actor Cary Grant. It was accompanied by a note from Mr. Grant stating that he carried the stick "in the vainful style of the period, throughout the opening scenes of a musical comedy (on Broadway) entitled *Boom-Boom.* Seriously!" *Boom-Boom,* which opened 28 January 1929, had a run of 72

An example of a relic of sports success is this handsome loving cup presented to Will Rogers. Called "The Ranelagh Cup," it was given to him by the English Ranelagh Club in 1907 as an award for his polo playing and was one of Rogers's favorite trophies. The Will Rogers Memorial in his birthplace at Claremore, Oklahoma, holds many relics of this famous American stage personality, including his collection of saddles from all over the world and many of the ropes with which he performed his famous exploits in trick and fancy roping. *Will Rogers Memorial Commission, Claremore, Oklahoma*

performances. The stick was sold for $325 to the musical comedy star Debbie Reynolds (many show business people were active bidders at the sale).

- A sword used by Douglas Fairbanks in his dashing roles in the silent movies. This sold for $200.
- The wood tiller from the boat used by Humphrey Bogart and Katharine Hepburn in *The African Queen,* along with a note reading: "To the bidder for the tiller my

thanks—Katharine Hepburn. This was given to me by John Huston on the completion of *The African Queen,* and it was the short tiller we used at times during the making of the picture." It brought $750.

- The top item of the sale, a shawl belonging to Eleonora Duse, modeled during the exhibition by Gloria Swanson. The Theatre Collection of the Museum of the City of New York purchased the shawl for $2,000.

At another 1973 "celebrity auction" to benefit the University of Montana, collectors could bid on items like:

- Glass beads worn by Elizabeth Taylor in *Cleopatra*
- Frank Sinatra's monogrammed cigarette case
- One of Pancho Gonzales's tennis racquets (a sports relic).

The main categories of memorabilia of the theatre, opera, and ballet are costumes, properties, and relics of theatre buildings and attendance. Printed and pictorial material, superabundant in this field, cannot ordinarily be considered in the nature of relics.

Costumes from twentieth century theatrical productions are those usually found by collectors; anything earlier than 1900 is rare. Identification of the role and even of the performer is not always difficult. Many famous people of the stage have been painted dressed as they were in their best-known roles, and since the invention of photography, literally thousands have been caught by the camera. Costumes on the market are usually offered with either written documentation or a photograph showing their authenticity.

Some nineteenth century costumes do survive. The Theatre Collection of the Museum of the City of New York has the outfit worn by Joseph Jefferson in 1895 in his celebrated role as Rip Van Winkle, the one worn by Fanny Davenport in *Divorce* (1871), even Edwin Booth's Hamlet costume from his famous production of 1870. Theatrical museums in Europe have a few costumes that are even older.

In addition to complete costumes, fragments of costumes identified as to their illustrious provenance have entered the market many times. The elaborate gowns of late nineteenth and early twentieth century actresses especially have lent themselves to preservation, entire or

in fragments. Bits and pieces of Sarah Bernhardt's costumes have circulated, and larger pieces of the dresses of famous actresses have been used in picturesque ways—to bind books, for example.

On the legitimate stage today costumes are less associated with individual actors and actresses and may have been worn by many performers, thereby losing their special identity. When a show closes, they are usually sold back to the theatrical costuming firm that made them. Some contemporary costumes do, however, get on the market for collectors. In 1973, shops in London were selling costumes used in the famous productions of the Royal Shakespeare Company, identified as to roles and players. Prices ranged from about $100 to $300. More of course is charged for especially luxurious apparel such as fur coats.

About 1910, a costume art developed that today attracts collectors willing to spend often-considerable sums to obtain examples of it. The costumes are those designed for Sergei Diaghilev's Ballets Russes by artists like Pablo Picasso, Georges Braque, Alexandre Benois, Leon Bakst, Natalia Gontcharova, and others. They are widely regarded not only as historically important costumes but as masterpieces of twentieth century design. Sotheby's held the first auction of some of these relics in 1967. Among the lots were:

- The costume worn by Vaslav Nijinsky in the ballet *Le Dieu Bleu,* designed by Bakst (1912). The costume was annotated: "The part of the Dieu Bleu was danced only by Nijinsky and this costume is unique." Sold for $2,500.
- The costumes worn by Nemtchinova as an acrobat in *Parade,* designed by Pablo Picasso (1917). Sold for $560.

That historic auction has been followed in London and New York by costumes from the collections of many famous ballet figures. Examples from sales of the early 1970s show that

there are opportunities for the more modest collector even in this important area:

- The dancer Barnova's costume as the Spinning-Top in the ballet *Jeux d'Enfants,* designed by Joan Miró (1932), sold for $2,200.
- Costumes designed by Nicolas Roerich for the celebrated *Le Sacre du Printemps* (1913), sold for about $200 each.
- Costumes by Mikhail Larionov for the ballet *Chout* sold for under $100 each.

The artistic designers for the Ballets Russes and other companies also created frontcloths, set designs (in pencil, watercolor, India ink, gouache, and other media), backdrops, and curtains for the companies' productions. These flat objects are sold as paintings and drawings, often for very large sums. Their prices reflect their value as twentieth century art, not as relics.

In ballets there are not many properties, but on the legitimate stage and in opera, they abound. Seldom have performers failed to preserve some property from a favorite role. They have not often been permitted by the management to carry off furniture from the set because it can be used again; so most properties for sale are hand-held objects, of which the following are typical:

- Stage jewelry and trinkets, especially common in operatic roles
- Eating and drinking equipment
- Weapons, including swords (again, very common in opera collections), knives, daggers, and pistols. So many murder mysteries used to be presented on Broadway that there is an abundance of supposedly lethal objects on the market.
- Fans (which seem to have been employed by actresses in every nineteenth century play)
- Canes, riding crops, umbrellas
- Smoking equipment such as lighters, snuffboxes, and cigarette cases
- Conductors' batons
- Objects that were an integral part of a specialized performance, such as the magnifying glass used by William Gillette in his celebrated role as Sherlock Holmes or the ropes used by Will Rogers in his fancy roping act, a number of which have been preserved.

(*opposite page*) Historic costumes are relics of the theatre when they are identifiable as to performer and role. John Barrymore wore this suit of armor as Richard III in his 1920 production (27 performances). *Museum of the City of New York*

When the great Danish heldentenor Lauritz Melchior died in 1973, he willed back to the Metropolitan Opera House three relics of his triumphs there: the Nothung sword he carried in *Die Walküre, Siegfried,* and *Götterdämmerung* (forged by a Long Island smith and presented to Melchior by Mayor Fiorello La Guardia on the tenor's hundredth *Siegfried*) and the ring and horn used in that role.

Properties often have fascinating histories that are the delight of the collector. An English Shakespearean actor named George Frederick Cooke scored a series of triumphs on the American stage on a visit in the early 1800s, despite the fact that he refused to act unless each performance began with the playing of "God Save the King." He died in Boston in 1812. A few years later he was reburied in the churchyard of Saint Paul's Church in New York, where Edmund Kean, who considered Cooke the greatest actor after David Garrick in the history of the English-speaking stage, had a monument erected to him, which is still there. During the removal of the body, for some elusive reason the head was taken off and the skull preserved by a physician. Once when Edwin Booth was playing Hamlet many years later, he needed a skull for the "Alas, poor Yorick" speech; the Cooke skull was volunteered by the physician without his telling Booth whose it was. After the performance, in returning the skull a tooth fell out. Booth then learned to his horror (for he was extremely superstitious) whose skull he had used. Nevertheless, he accepted—perhaps also out of superstition—the tooth, which he had made into a stickpin he frequently wore and which is now the property of the Players' Club in New York.

The more recent Yorick skull for sale to collectors of theatrical memorabilia was a plastic one used by the Royal Shakespeare Company, offered at $75.

What may be called "relics of attendance" are tickets and objects deriving from an actual theatre or opera house building. Usually priced today at under $50, they include:

- Box tickets for nineteenth century theatres. These were usually made not of paper but of wood or metals. Some for the Covent Garden Opera House, for example, are tablets of octagonal shape, engraved with the name of the boxholder, his number, and so forth, and embellished with tags of purple ribbons. Keys to boxes have also been preserved.
- Replicas of actual tickets made in metal or other permanent material. These are usually commemorative. A gold replica was made of the opening night ticket of *Merry Malones* (1927) starring George M. Cohan. Paper tickets, usually for opening night, have also been framed and are often preserved with a program of the event.
- Bricks from the structure of famous theatres. These have often been sold at benefits for a new theatre. The same is true of theatre and opera curtains.

Theatre folk are great givers of congratulatory and commemorative items to one another. Silver has been engraved, glassware etched, and even jewels pressed into service to mark an occasion in the theatre. This habit remains quite widespread, and many such gifts are still being presented. Some are extraordinarily elaborate. Cole Porter's wife used to have a new cigarette case, inscribed in honor of the occasion, made for him on the opening of each of his musical comedies. The cases were sold at auction in 1967. A typically flamboyant case made by the jeweler Verdura for the show *Red, Hot, and Blue,* which opened on 29 October 1936 and starred Ethel Merman, Jimmy Durante, and Bob Hope, was paved with diamonds, rubies, and sapphires, the jewels referring to the title (sold for $4,000).

Audiences were occasionally given souvenirs in the generous days of the late 1800s. These small gifts usually marked special days in the New York run of a show. The very long run on

(*opposite page*) Lavish presentation items are characteristic of opening nights and anniversaries in the theatre. When George Gershwin's "American folk opera" *Porgy and Bess* opened in 1935, the response of both critics and audiences was lukewarm. One critic described the work as "a curious blend of Broadway and what Gershwin believed to be serious music." The musical ran only 124 performances; not until its 1942 revival was it considered a success. On opening night 139 friends of Gershwin gave him this silver tray with their engraved signatures and presentation inscription. *Museum of City of New York*

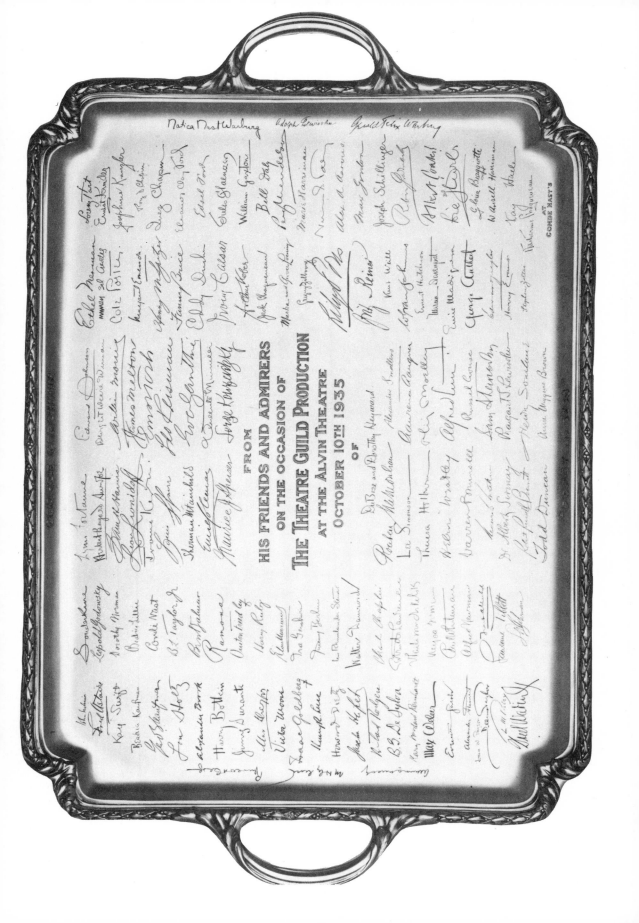

FROM
HIS FRIENDS AND ADMIRERS
ON THE OCCASION OF
THE THEATRE GUILD PRODUCTION
AT THE ALVIN THEATRE
OCTOBER 10TH 1935
OF

A selection of souvenirs of theatrical anniversaries (*left to right*): (1) urn marking the hundredth performance in 1895 of *His Father's Wife* by the William H. Crane Co.; (2) pottery clock marking the hundredth performance of Edward Rice's *The Girl from Paris* (1897), with anniversary inscription on the dial; (3) umbrella marking hundredth performance of *Caslett in the Rain* (1907); (4) box with cat's head marking the hundred fiftieth performance of *Charley's Aunt* in 1894; (5) statuette of James O'Neill (father of the playwright Eugene) in fiftieth performance of *Count of Monte Cristo* (1900); (6, *foreground*) portrait of Lillian Russell in *Le Cigale,* hundredth performance (1892); on the back of the portrait is a printed program of the occasion. *Museum of the City of New York*

Broadway is, with only a few exceptions, a phenomenon of the mid-twentieth century. Up to the nineteen thirties, for a play to run one hundred or even fifty performances was worthy of note. It is not known exactly when the custom began of the management giving souvenirs to audiences to celebrate these anniversaries.

In 1876, Augustin Daly put on Wednesday matinees "for suburban ladies" and gave them photographs of the stars, programs of the plays printed on silk, and sometimes silver tickets. Later, silver spoons were given on Wednesday and Friday matinees "to every lady holding a ticket." Most theatrical souvenirs, however, are dated mementos of a special anniversary in a play's run such as the hundredth performance, and most of those known are dated in the 1890s.

No catalogue or list of these charming souvenirs has been located, and collecting them is a neglected area of specialization. Prices are difficult to estimate, but most should be under $50. Identification is no problem, since they are always marked with the name and date of the occasion.

To give an idea of what exists, the following souvenirs are typical of those seen in instituional collections:

- A white metal cat, souvenir of the hundredth performance, 28 December 1893, of *Charley's Aunt*. This was the premier American run of this celebrated English comedy.
- A bronze inkwell, souvenir of the 150th performance of the same play, 7 February 1894
- Glove buttoner, souvenir of the fiftieth performance of *Little Christopher Columbus* by Edward Rice at the Garden Theatre, 18 November 1894. Manufactured by Gorham & Co.
- Silver paper knife, souvenir of the 150th performance of *The Highwayman*, 21 March 1898
- Gilt stamp box, souvenir of the hundredth performance of Charles Frohman's *On and Off*, 9 January 1899

Gift-giving by management to audiences had vanished by the turn of the century, although there have been a few revivals of this pleasant custom. More often, souvenirs have been issued to commemorate a landmark performance and *sold* to the audience. When *Life with Father* reached its sixth year on Broadway a pack of playing cards depicting the play was issued as a souvenir, and a souvenir china plate was issued on 14 June 1947, when the play reached the record-breaking total of 3,183 performances.

Less glamorous relics of attendance are actual fragments of theatres preserved as remembrances. Stefan Zweig relates that when the historic Burgtheater in Vienna, in which Mozart's *Marriage of Figaro* was first given, was torn down in the late nineteenth century, the curtain had hardly fallen when the audience, for whom the theatre was a sort of temple, leaped upon the stage to bring home at least a splinter as a relic of the boards on

which beloved artists had trod. "For decades after, in dozens of bourgeois homes, these insignificant splinters could be seen preserved in costly caskets as fragments of the Holy Cross are kept in church." When the old Metropolitan Opera House in New York was torn down in 1967, the management went one better and brought in revenue by cutting up the celebrated gold curtain and selling pieces to sentimental opera lovers.

Collecting relics of motion picture actors and actresses has been a worldwide hobby for nearly the whole of this century, but until very recently was regarded by most adults as a juvenile enterprise. The earliest stars of the screen had fans, and their successors in today's films have their followers, too. The golden years, however, were the nineteen twenties and thirties; fans have not adored their favorites since with quite the fervor common in those days. The brief career of Rudolph Valentino was certainly the high-water mark of the cult of the movie star. The most frenzied fans of the present generation are devotees of popular musicians, not motion picture personalities, and they too are forming collections. As the motion picture industry has declined—attendance has fallen drastically and consistently since World War II—the collecting of movie memorabilia has become much more sophisticated. There are now many adult collectors and even organizations interested in the preservation of movie relics. Plans are afoot for a museum in Los Angeles devoted to the history of the industry and well equipped with relics. The adult collectors are usually more selective than their earlier and younger counterparts: sheer accumulation is becoming less important.

The dedicated and, by inference, unselective fan still exists, however, although his numbers are much depleted. One single-minded Southern California fan calls himself "king of the movie collectors." With years of diligence he has assembled what is referred to as "nothing less than the world's largest collection of memorabilia ever gathered on a single star." The star is Jeanne Crain, and the collection consists of 85,000 movie stills, over 100,000 news clippings, hundreds of fan magazines, four of her original paintings, lobby cards, tapes of television, radio, and movie appearances, her drinking cup, letters, programs, dress labels, and an English tea label carrying her picture. Yet the object of this stupendous archive has never been a particularly well-known actress! One wonders what the collector would have accumulated had he directed his attention to Bette Davis.

And a California schoolteacher recently decided to collect the cast-off shoes of "celebrities" (mostly entertainment figures) because he wanted his students "to think in whose shoes they would walk in the future." Among the celebrities who responded with shoes were Leonard Bernstein and the singer Pat Boone, who sent a pair of the white bucks that were his trademark as a hero to teen-age girls. (A non-show-business celebrity was Sir Edmund Hillary, who promised to send the pair of hiking boots worn when he made his famous ascent of Mount Everest.)

The great movie studios of the thirties and forties were in severe financial straits by the 1960s, and a great selling-off of their physical assets began. These included hundreds of feature films "in the cans" that were sold or leased to television, and real estate favorably situated in Southern California. The sales brought in huge sums, but a series of disastrously expensive musicals and other lavish films failed to attract the public, and new financial problems arose in Hollywood. The studios looked around for other assets to put on the market. The management of Metro-Goldwyn-Mayer Studios was the first to think of selling their enormous warehouses full of properties. The first MGM auction sale was held in May 1970. The publicity it generated was enormous. The sale coincided with a national interest in the recent past referred to loosely as "nostalgia," and prices were realized that clearly proclaimed a new epoch of collecting motion picture relics. Among the most successful lots were:

- $30 for a pair of black lace panties worn by Gina Lollabrigida
- $300 for a hat worn by Greta Garbo
- $300 for the hat Charles Laughton wore as Captain Bligh in *Mutiny on the Bounty*
- $1,250 for the trenchcoat worn by Clark Gable in *Comrade X* (1939)
- $15,000 for the ruby red slippers worn by Judy Garland in *The Wizard of Oz,* then the world record for movie memorabilia. The original cost of the slippers in 1939, when the movie was made, was $14.

This first MGM sale brought in a total of over $2,000,000. There were so many prop-

erties that a long series of sales ensued, followed by a tour of still other artifacts under the title "Movieland Glamorama," which crisscrossed the country. Many working models of vehicles and ships were sold in the later sales. Mechanical marvels, reduced in size but still large enough to make impressive exhibit items, the models sold extremely well. Many were bought by amusement parks, restaurants, trolley museums, and other commercial enterprises, to use as admission-attracting exhibitions. The Texas millionaire Lamar Hunt paid $15,000 for the model of the steamboat *Cotton Blossom,* made for the movie *Showboat,* which he planned to display in a projected "Mississippi River Museum," in Saint Louis.

Entrepreneurs found the MGM sales a veritable stockpile: one imaginative fellow snapped up all the many MGM neon signs and announced that he was opening a "neon museum" in Los Angeles. The old-time movie-fan collector was little in evidence during this part of the sales.

The MGM sales brought to public attention the wealth of properties and wardrobe the great studios possessed, and provided collectors with opportunities to buy entire new categories of "filmic" relics that had previously come on the market only in dribs and drabs or never been available at all because the studios never released them. These categories included:

- Set properties such as furniture (some of it antiques of good quality), glassware, silver, draperies, rugs, porcelain, paintings
- Vehicles, including wagons, carts, coaches, sleighs, prairie schooners, police wagons, gypsy wagons, horse trolleys, city buses, chariots, and hearses
- Fire-fighting equipment
- Advertising posters
- Studio art, including watercolor, India ink, and gouache sketches for various productions
- Models, many of them in working condition, of ships, tanks, and planes, and all sorts of vehicles.

The MGM sales were followed in 1971 by two sales (together containing over two thousand lots) of movie memorabilia from Twentieth Century Fox Studios. These were held by the Los Angeles branch of Sotheby Parke Bernet of London and New York; and most of the objects offered for sale were described as objects are in a fine arts sale. The catalogues contained a list of nearly two hundred feature films made by the company between 1928 and 1970, with the names of stars and directors and cross-indexed to the property included in the sale; each lot was also identified as to which picture or pictures it had appeared in. The properties were from such famous screen features as *All About Eve, In Old Chicago, Forever Amber, Laura, The King and I, The Robe,* and *The Razor's Edge.* Many pieces, of course, had been used by the studio again and again. A seven-piece suite of walnut furniture, more or less in the German Renaissance style and inlaid with pewter, had appeared in a strange medley of films: *Romance of the Rio Grande, Dragonwyck, Suez, Blood and Sand,* and *Professional Soldier.* The prices of the various pieces ranged between $150 for the dressing table to $950 for the huge bed, which was accompanied by a photograph of Tyrone Power lying languorously in it in *Blood and Sand* while receiving a dinner tray from a beaming Linda Darnell. Some of the props had seen long service. A full-size old-fashioned omnibus, made to be horse-drawn and marked "Fifth Avenue," appeared in Noël Coward's *Cavalcade* in 1933, and returned with Barbra Streisand in *Hello, Dolly!* in 1969. It sold for $3,400.

Many objects had a movieland story. An English wing chair had been used by Orson Welles in *Jane Eyre.* The script called for him to be hidden while seated; since the actor was oversized, an oversized chair had to be constructed to conceal him. This relic sold for $250. Among the furnishings, however, were hundreds of lots of good antique furniture used in movies that were sold for their value as antiques and not primarily as relics.

Oil portraits of actors and actresses have figured in a great many movie plots as they have on the stage. The collector will find these relatively common in the market. The older portraits often sell for less than those of actors and actresses still before the public. There were many lots of portraits in the 20th Century-Fox sale; and their prices are a fair indication of this general trend:

- Portrait of Francis X. Bushman as Messala in *Ben-Hur,* $100
- Portrait of Carmen Miranda used in *Greenwich Village,* $110

- Portrait of Ronald Colman as *The Late George Apley,* $190
- Portrait of Maureen O'Hara, $200
- Family-style portrait of Olivia de Havilland, Bette Davis, and Victor Buono, used in *Hush, Hush, Sweet Charlotte,* $330
- Portrait of Bette Davis as Margo Channing in the film *All About Eve,* painted in 1952, sold for $800 (the highest price for a portrait).

The true spirit of relic collecting showed itself in the sales of items that were actually used in some way by the stars or that formed an integral part of the plot of the motion picture. Among such items were:

- The Scotch bottle that tempted Humphrey Bogart as an alcoholic priest in *The Left Hand of God* (1955) sold for $115.
- A *gros point* carpetbag used by Julie Andrews in *The Sound of Music* (1965) sold for $650.
- "The Sarah Siddons Award," a seated figure in gilded composition of the celebrated actress, which played a major role in the film *All About Eve.* Perhaps the most interesting of all these relics, as it was actually featured in its film, this nine and one-half-inch statuette sold for $550.

There is a very active commerce outside the auction rooms in the relics, souvenirs, and mementos of various individual screen stars. The "Jeanne Crain collector" mentioned above exemplifies the fan dedicated to a single star, and over several generations of moviegoers there have been numerous collectors devoted to outstanding stars, such as Mary Pickford, Douglas Fairbanks, Shirley Temple, Judy Garland, James Dean, Bette Davis, Marilyn Monroe, and, above all, Rudolph Valentino.

The public's affair with Shirley Temple began in 1931 with her appearance in one-reelers called *Baby Burlesques,* at the age of three years. She was a star at five; at six she got a special Academy Award, at seven she was the number one box office attraction in America, and at eight it was claimed she was the most photographed person in the world, which might well have been true. All manner of commemorative items were issued to honor the child star during her mid-1930s career, among them Shirley Temple mirrors, figurines, mugs, pitchers, salt and pepper shakers, and—sur-

The teddy bear that was Shirley Temple's in her movie
Captain January (1936), sold at auction in 1971 for $450.
Sotheby Parke Bernet, Los Angeles

prisingly for a child star—cigarette boxes. These items are popular with collectors today and sell for between $10 and $20. The Shirley Temple dolls are much more expensive, up to $100. Miss Temple herself, who has survived into a prosperous and politically minded middle age, has controlled the manufacture of new memorabilia (dolls, dresses, books, hats) made since 1958, when she was acting as hostess on television's *Shirley Temple's Storybook*. Collectors of course prefer the original items of the 1930s.

The commemorative wares are not relics, but at the 20th Century-Fox auction there were some real relics of Miss Temple, used in one of her most famous pictures, *Captain January* (1936), which also starred Guy Kibbee. In that film the eight-year-old Shirley Temple had a nursery full of oversize toys. These included wooden blocks, twenty inches square, carved with animals and the letters of the alphabet. At the auction they sold for the moderate figure of $100 a pair. A pair of life-size wooden soldiers brought $240, and an enormous teddy bear on wheels, twenty-six inches high and twenty-one inches long, sold for a substantial $450. The

20th Century-Fox Company's records for 1936 show the purchase of "one fuzzy bear, large toy, brown, on wheels, as is, $3.00." The toy had to be "as is," since the plot called for an already-played-with teddy.

The all-time favorite of fans and movie collectors, hands down, is Rudolph Valentino. Since his death in 1926, no star has held quite his place in the heart of fans, and certainly none has been the object of the adoration that Valentino received even years after his death. He was born in Castellaneta, Italy, in 1895, and christened Rodolpho Alfonzo Rafaelo Pierre Filibert Guglielmi di Valentina d'Antonguolla. He was twenty-six in 1921, when he burst upon the feminine consciousness of the world in the screen version of Blasco Ibáñez's antiwar novel *The Four Horsemen*. Before taking up acting, Valentino had had a variety of occupations, the most respectable of which were dishwashing, dancing, and picking up litter in Central Park for the New York City Parks Department. His success as a screen actor was fabulous, especially in *The Sheik* (1922), the film that ruined the pronunciation of the Arab word for years ("sheek" instead of "shake") but drew millions of women into the movie houses. Detested by most men, by critics, and by newspapers—the *Chicago Tribune* called him "the pink powder puff"—nothing could injure him with his fans. His acting consisted of protruding his enormous eyes until an alarming amount of the white showed, flaring the nostrils of his Roman nose, and baring his teeth. The New York *World* said "the whole gamut of feeling was expressed by blinking." But then the films were silent, and little more was required. His public life—his fans allowed him no private one—was depressing and ridiculous. He was once arrested for bigamy, and was notoriously bossed by his second wife, an actress who had changed her name, perhaps understandably, from Winifred Shaughnessy to Natacha Rambova. A believer in astral influences, he wrote a volume of poetry called *Daydreams* that gave critics a further cause for hilarity. Nevertheless, he could go nowhere without receiving attentions from his female fans that amounted to physical assaults. So many objects were stolen from his dressing rooms by relic hunters that guards had to be posted wherever he was working.

Valentino died on a visit to New York City on 23 August 1926. Rioting broke out in front of the Frank E. Campbell Funeral Home, then on Broadway near where Lincoln Center now stands, when thousands of women attempted to view the body. Those that were admitted stole flowers, tassels and fringes from the coffin, and even decorative greenery as souvenirs. The "floral tributes" were impressive: the actress Pola Negri sent a pall composed of 4,000 blood-red roses, eleven feet long and six feet wide, with her name written in the center in white buds.

The funeral was not held until a week later. It was said 100,000 fans jammed the streets around Campbell's. Crowd figures are notoriously overblown, but to judge from contemporary newspaper photographs, they may in this case have been accurate. Humanity, apparently exclusively feminine, filled Broadway from Forty-ninth Street, where the service was held at Saint Malachy's Church, to the sixties while squads of mounted policemen, the only males visible, tried to keep the women from rushing the funeral cars. After the funeral the body had to be smuggled out of the building and onto a train for California, where fresh scenes of grief took place when it arrived.

All sorts of mourning publications were issued, and a song hastily produced in commemoration was entitled "There's a New Star in Heaven Tonight."

Valentino loved to shop, and at his death his houses at Whitley Heights in Los Angeles and the famous "Falcon Lair" he had built in Hollywood were full of clothes (the year he died he had already bought fifty suits and owned a thousand pairs of sox), Turkish and Arabic furniture, guns, armor, books, and paintings. His estate was in dire financial state, and an auction of more than two thousand lots of his possessions was held in December 1926, only four months after his death. Prices were disappointing: the total realized for all these possessions was less than $100,000. Every effort had been made by his desperate executors, including publication of an elaborate catalogue and much advance publicity. Other encouragements were exercised, as became known much later. Irving Shulman, in his biography of Valentino, quotes an executor as saying:

Of course, I resorted to some tricks. For instance, Rudy had lots of books, but he had only autographed a few of them, and he didn't have a book mark. I had a mark [i.e. bookplate] designed, stuck it inside the covers, which were worth about two bits apiece, and at the sale they fetched $3.00 apiece, and nobody knew the difference.

Valentino's art, mainly portrayals of himself, brought especially disappointing prices. The portrait of Valentino as a Persian warlord by the then well-known Spanish painter Beltrán y Masses sold for but $400, and even the same painter's portrait of the star in one of his most famous roles as an Argentine gaucho brought only $1,550. A sculpture of his hand by the highly regarded sculptor Prince Paul Troubetskoy sold for a mere $150.

During the years after Valentino's death, his two houses were virtually destroyed by souvenir hunters who became mere looters in their quest for relics. Gardeners and caretakers used to sell fans minor items from Falcon Lair, such as sheets of the Valentino notepaper, vials of his perfume, and—most ingeniously of all—individual feathers from his pillows, framed.

The fans, although surely a dwindling group by now, still love Valentino. Forty-seven years

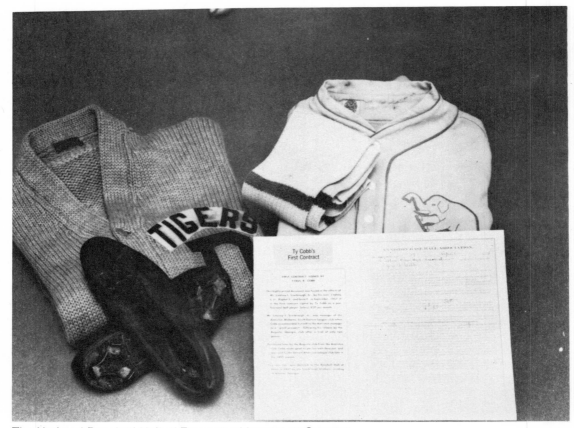

The National Baseball Hall of Fame and Museum at Coopers-town, New York, where, according to tradition, the game began with Abner Doubleday over a century ago, has a large collection of relics of famous players, including Doubleday's own ball. These are some of the baseball belongings that Ty Cobb, "The Georgia Peach," generally rated the greatest player in the game's history, gave to the Hall of Fame: his Detroit sweater, his Philadelphia uniform, and contract. The Baseball Hall of Fame, one of the earliest sports museums in the country, opened in 1939. *National Baseball Hall of Fame and Museum, Cooperstown, N.Y.*

after his death advertisements appear constantly in the antiques press seeking relics and commemorative items. Prices are very high in proportion to those asked for memorabilia of other stars. Valentino posters cost $100 or more, six or eight times the cost of the average movie poster. Glass ashtrays and candy boxes carrying his portrait are at least that expensive. Dolls were made during his career showing him

in his famous roles. They are very difficult to find, and it is hard to estimate prices.

In the early 1970s a cult arose around the late actress Marilyn Monroe (real name Norma Jean Baker, born 1926, died a suicide in 1962). It is far from rivaling Valentino's, but a large number of books about her have appeared, albums of songs sung in her wavering voice have been released, and an entire line

(*above*) Elegant sports like polo are commemorated with elegant trophies, such as this C. Hartman Kuhn Polo Challenge Cup dated 1891. It was won that year from the Philadelphia Country Club by the Westchester Country Club. *James F. Carr, New York*

(*right*) Babe Ruth's glove, preserved at Cooperstown. *National Baseball Hall of Fame and Museum, Cooperstown, N.Y.*

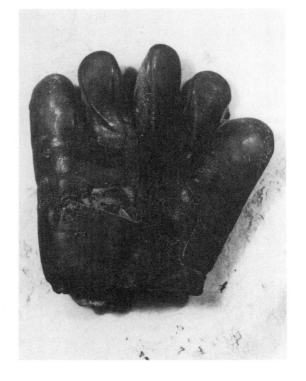

of products issued to memorialize her. A famous calendar for which she had posed nude in 1952 was reissued twenty years later. By 1973, a company called "Marilyn Monroe Products" was selling jigsaw puzzles ($5.00), playing cards ($2.00), and other items decorated with photographs of the late star. In the same year some real relics of Miss Monroe reached the salesrooms. The prices realized were not high. Her school certificates, citizenship reports, graduation programs, athletic awards, sweater patches, report cards, and other relics of her foster homes and school

Tiffany & Co., New York, made this magnificent sterling silver cup for presentation to Robert Livingston Gerry of the New York Yacht Club. *James F. Carr, New York*

years brought only $3,585 for the entire thirty-one items. The highest price was $350 for her contract to play the role of Angela in the motion picture *The Asphalt Jungle,* directed by John Huston (1950), which started her real career in the movies.

Relics of famous sports figures and events are devotedly collected by the same youthful fans who collect baseball cards and the auto-graphs of players. There are a few museums, most notably the National Baseball Hall of Fame, that preserve personal relics of sports-men. These are generally either equipment or trophies. A few relics of sport are very valu-able. Such are the "Championship belts" awarded to boxing champions. These exist in gold (value $1,000 and more) and in baser metals. A solid gold championship belt won in 1918 by the Briton Dick Smith sold in 1966 for $1,200. Smith was the first light-heavy-weight champion of Britain.

Sports trophies, awards, medals, and badges are in long supply. They seldom cost more than $25 and many times, less. By their very nature, these items are fully inscribed with the name of the winner, date, and occasion, and are therefore ideal for the relic collector.

Some unusual items that are both relics and commemorative have been produced for famous sports events by alert manufacturers. In 1973, a plaque was prepared containing "uncashed winning parimutuel tickets" on the racehorse Secretariat from the Kentucky Derby, the Preakness, and the Belmont Stakes—the "Triple Crown of Racing." This was offered in an edition of 152 at a price of $350 each, presumably because Secretariat was so heavily favored in these races that it became more worthwhile to keep the tickets as relics than to cash them.

Relics of the scenes of famous sports events come on the market when such sites are torn down or renovated. When Yankee Stadium was closed for renovation in October 1973 at the end of the season, home plate was saved and presented to Mrs. George Herman "Babe" Ruth. First base was given to Mrs. Henry Louis "Lou" Gehrig. There was a burst of vandalism on the part of fans: people brought screwdrivers and removed the box seat numbers as souvenirs of the place that had witnessed baseball's greatest days. As demolition proceeded, the management of Yankee Stadium set up a shop to dispose of the relics by regular merchandising. A pin-stripe uniform with Joe DiMaggio's famous number 5 was located in one of the supply rooms, and offered at $500. There were paintings of assorted Yankee teams and individual heroes priced at $150 to $350. These were big favorites with Japanese buyers, and a large number were bought for exhibition in an Osaka department store. A ticket drum cost $50, a seat cost $10, and finally, if the fan could afford nothing else, he could purchase a brick from "The House that Ruth Built" for one dollar.

9
Relics of Transportation

Mankind has been fascinated with the wheel for a long time, but serious collecting of wheeled vehicles does not have a long history. Earlier generations preserved some of their coaches, carriages, and (occasionally) wagons for their craftsmanship or historical associations, but it is only in very recent years that a commerce has developed in antique conveyances—that museums displaying such vehicles have been opened and that dealers and auction houses have set up in the business of buying and selling them. In this country there are only a few transportation museums—rail, automotive, trolley, or carriage—that are more than twenty years old, but their number is being augmented very rapidly. By 1973, more than fifty museums in the United States were devoted solely to antiques of transportation, in addition to the hundreds of other museums that counted a vehicle collection among their holdings. Vehicle collecting is now a growing field. This chapter will be concerned only with vehicles of unquestioned value as relics of a well-known person, place, or, in some cases, company.

Horse-drawn vehicles do not approach antique automobiles in price on the current market, but they have a romance about them that is attracting a new band of enthusiasts in the United States. There is now a Carriage Association of America that had two hundred members in 1963 and two thousand members just ten years later. These members buy old horse-drawn vehicles that almost invariably need reconditioning or, as it is called by devotees, "restoration." A restored four-in-hand coach can cost as much as $5,000, not to speak of the horses to draw it, which can cost over $1,000 apiece. Most carriage collectors are interested in restoring and actually driving their vehicles; the provenance and probable historical association are not particularly important to them.

There were singular opportunities at the movie studio sales of 1970–72 for collectors to acquire horse-drawn vehicles, both standard and unusual, and there will be others as businesses clear out their warehouses. Many vehicles in the sales were described as being in "fair" or "poor" condition but "worthy of restoration." No doubt the exigencies of motion picture plots had often caused these vehicles to be wrecked deliberately or at least damaged. Prices for vehicles in good condition and "roadable," as the term is, ran about as follows (the vehicles were original except when otherwise noted):

- Farm wagons: $150 to $250
- Phaetons: $750 to $1,000
- Sleighs: $100 to $200
- Prison wagons: $350 to $450
- Railway baggage carts: $25
- Crane-neck coaches (reproductions): $500
- Surreys and buggies: $500 to $850
- Egyptian chariots (reproductions, of course): $350.

155

(*above*) Rudolph Valentino loved luxurious cars and driving them as fast as possible. He had so many collisions and near-collisions and received such bad publicity that his studio chiefs forbade him to drive at all except under certain stated safety conditions. This Avions Voisin Victoria Phaeton was built for him in France in 1923. At the sale of his possessions after his death in 1926, the luxurious automobile sold with two others and a Ford truck for a total of only $4,600. When it appeared again at sale in 1972, however, the selling price was $22,000. *Sotheby Parke Bernet, Los Angeles*

(*opposite page*) In 1969, Sotheby & Co., London, sold this 1936 Buick D. A. 90 Limited Limousine, which had belonged to Edward Duke of Windsor. Delivered to the former king at St. James's Palace, London, in 1936, it was taken by him and his wife, Wallis Warfield Simpson, to their exile in the south of France. It had a recorded mileage of 40,000 miles and was sold with the original logbook, beginning with this note of ownership: "H. M. The King, St. James's Palace, S. W. 1." *Sotheby & Co., London*

All these had a history of movie appearances and the movies were in each case named; many had appeared in a number of films.

Among the more unusual items were:

- State chariot made by Hooper & Co., London, circa 1840, used in the films *Lillian Russell, High Time,* and *Hello, Dolly!* Sold for $7,000.
- Child's hearse used in *Broken Lance* and *The Comancheros.* Sold for $2,000.
- Concord coach (i.e., "a stagecoach," so famous in American folklore), used in the film *The Silver Whip.* Sold for $8,000.
- Combination pumper and hose wagon made for the New York City Fire Department's Metropolitan Fire Brigade in 1876 and used in *Hangover Square* and *Hello, Dolly!* Sold for $4,500.
- Police wagon (i.e., "Black Maria") used in *Can-Can.* Sold for $3,500.

These figures are quite substantial for horse-drawn vehicles but would be insignificant for automobiles of comparable association. By and large, collecting historic motorcars is a rich man's hobby.

The twentieth century is the automobile age, but only in the last decade there has developed a true market for "antique automobiles," as opposed to the extensive everyday market for "used cars." In recent years, old and especially historic automobiles have become a major collecting interest, and the traffic, so to speak, in them a very large one, with extremely high prices paid for important vehicles that are relics of famous persons.

Collectors consider any car built before the end of 1904 as "Veteran." These are the cars eligible for today's famous London to Brighton run. Cars built between approximately 1905 and 1919 are called "Edwardian," and "Vintage" cars are those roughly dating from 1919 to 1930. "Classics" are distinctively designed cars dated between 1925 and 1942. The principal names associated with the production of "classics" are Rolls-Royce, Cadillac, Duesenberg, LaSalle, Bentley, and Mercedes-Benz.

A landmark event in the history of automobile collecting was the first "Veteran and Vintage" car auction held by Sotheby's auction house at the London exhibition hall Earl's Court in November 1965. At that sale a 1911 Rolls-Royce 40–50 horsepower "Silver Ghost Ceremonial Phaeton" specially built for an Indian maharajah brought a record price of $27,440. This price was widely regarded as heralding a new era in automotive collecting. Since then, auctions of notable motors have been held frequently. The prices have usually advanced. The highest prices of all have been realized by cars of aesthetic quality and appeal as relics. By 1971, a "57 SC Atlantique" electron coupe built by Jean Bugatti in 1936 for Lord Rothschild was sold in Los Angeles for $59,000, then the world auction record for a historic car.

The relic value of cars appears to be growing rapidly; certainly any association with the famous is emphasized by sellers. At a big Labor Day sale in 1972, a 1933 Duesenberg once driven by the elusive movie star Greta Garbo sold for $90,000, and in the same year a very showy 1923 Avions Voisin Victoria Phaeton with tonneau windshield that had formerly been Rudolph Valentino's sold for $22,000. There was a $15,000 asking price for a 1935 six-cylinder seven-seater Cadillac once owned by Marlene Dietrich. It was nineteen feet long and said to get only ten miles to the gallon of gas.

Automobiles belonging to Adolf Hitler or said to have been his property fascinate collectors and have been in the news for years. Since Hitler did not know how to drive, any car he had was chauffeured (he liked to be driven fast), and he rode in vehicles of stately proportion made to order for his public occasions. Although during the Second World War Hitler made few public appearances and went more or less into a strange seclusion, in his early political days he made innumerable public appearances in street parades. Since he generally flew from one engagement to another— the slogan was "Hitler over Germany"—and joined the parade when he landed, it is obvious

that many cars were used by the dictator. Small wonder, then, that there is excited controversy over just which motor can properly be called "Hitler's car."

An automobile referred to as "Hitler's personal parade car," but admittedly used by him for only two months, made a sensation at its sale in 1973. It is a specially built 1940 model 770K Mercedes-Benz touring car with a retractable top, bulletproof doors, and windshield glass two inches thick, as well as armor plating. Despite its weight of 10,000 pounds, its 230 horsepower made it capable of traveling 135 miles per hour—although it is reputed to get only about three miles to the gallon, at best. It was given by Hitler to Marshal Mannerheim of Finland, who stored it in Sweden. Following Mannerheim's death in 1951, the car was seized for back taxes, and after various vicissitudes it came to the United States, where it was once displayed at Rockefeller Center. About 1959, it was sold for around $40,000. When it came up for sale in a Scottsdale, Arizona, auction in early 1973, however, an amusement park operator bought it for $153,000, a record price for an automobile at auction. Later the same year, the car changed hands again, selling this time for no less than $176,000, again to an exhibitor who planned to charge admission to see it.

An almost identical Mercedes-Benz said to have been used by Hitler, but not even so often, sold at Scottsdale for $93,000. Its new owner also announced his intention of displaying the acquisition for public viewing for a fee. Unfortunately, a Finnish expert on historic cars had in the meantime studied the car's serial numbers, and he declared that it had never been Hitler's.

A 1934 Ford, the so-called "deluxe model" but probably costing less than $1,000 when new, had a gruesome history attached to it when it was sold in 1973, but one that, owing to the American fascination with criminal activity, caused it to bring the incredible price of $175,000, a new world record at the time. The Ford was the one in which the murderous Bonnie Parker and Clyde Barrow met their well-merited end, killed by law officers, 23 May 1934. This event took place at Arcadia, Louisiana, where lawmen ambushed the pair and brought their vicious careers to an end. The car, new at the time, was punctured by "several hundred" bullets. A film exists that was taken at the time by highway patrolmen. It

This silver trophy engraved with well-executed scenes of railroad construction in the Rockies was presented to David H. Moffat (1839–1911), whose name is associated with many western roads, notably the Denver, Northwestern & Pacific, and the construction of the six-mile Moffat Tunnel at Long's Peak, Colorado. Many similar pieces survive from the great days of railroad building in the second half of the nineteenth century. *James F. Carr, New York*

shows the car, the thugs, and their traveling armory, which included a submachine gun, rifle, shotgun, and handcuffs. The car has been displayed at innumerable state fairs and carnivals, earning over a million dollars in entrance fees, according to its owners. The buyer at the 1973 sale planned to keep the car on exhibition at a Nevada gambling casino, charging $2.50 admission to view it.

Apparently a criminal connection has to be the real thing to make an automobile attractive to collectors. An attempt to sell a 1948 Lincoln Continental, also full of bullet holes, used in the movie *The Godfather*, for $30,000 failed.

Equipment for historic motorcars is referred to as automobiliana; it is mainly used in their restoration. Individual parts can be extremely expensive, $100 for a pair of headlights or the same price for a rare hubcap. A professional automobile restorer often charges $15 to $20 an hour for his services in installing such items and otherwise putting a collector's automobile in working order. It would be difficult to name many pieces of equipment that are truly relics, but a few such do exist. In 1973, three New Mexico state license plates, dated 1928, 1929, and 1930, stamped number "1" and known to have been issued to the then governor of the state, sold at an auction for the amazing total of $275.

Mementos of historic sailing vessels available for collecting today are mostly limited to pieces of relic wood and objects made from it. The famous wooden figureheads are collected as objects of high folk art and not as relics. They have been so keenly sought by maritime museums that the market is sparsely supplied today. Relic wood usually is a piece from the mast of a famous ship such as the U.S.S. *Constitution*. On several occasions in the past, bits and pieces of historic ships have been cut up and sold as souvenirs to raise funds.

Ships' mechanical equipment such as barometers, binnacles, compasses, chronometers, and so forth is collected but as finely made devices not as relics, since such items seldom have any specific association with famous naval figures or specific ships.

Although most American-flag passenger ships have gone out of service in the last decade, so far there have not been sales of their equipment like those of trains. The silver and china of the great American trains are being actively collected, but so far that of the great vessels has not attracted a following.

American collectors are taking up souvenirs of railroading. The hobby has long been a favorite in Great Britain. Today, in the United States, interest is bounding ahead, but as some of the prices mentioned here will show, railroadiana can be a field for the modest collector.

Exactly as did the motion picture studios, the more ailing railroads began in the early seventies to clear out their storage rooms and raise what money they could by selling equipment that was no longer in use and not likely ever to be used again. The Penn Central Railroad held several auction sales in the awesome great hall of their 30th Street Station in Philadelphia. This clearing out of the attics of one of the largest and oldest American enterprises resulted in the offering of enormous quantities of office furniture, dining car equipment such as silverware and glassware, manuscripts, drawings, models, and miscellanea—in all, thousands of items. Three thousand people jammed the concourse, hundreds of them bidders, for the first sale held in 1971, which realized $150,000. The premier Penn Central sale has been followed by others; it takes a long time to dispose of the accumulation of a business organized in 1846 (Pennsylvania Railroad) and 1853 (New York Central). Collectors had a field day, but prices were not particularly high. Some of the more interesting items of a relic nature sold in these sales were:

• The handsomely embossed brass doorknob from the Broad Street Station in Philadelphia: $90
• The oak case clock from the Pennsylvania Station in Newark: $535
• The walnut desk used by the railroad magnate E. H. Harriman: $510.

Collectors naturally seek out objects that have on them—embossed, printed, or engraved —not only the name of the line but also the particular train. Demand is greatest for items marked with the names of the great trains of the past that were household words: "The Twentieth Century Limited," "The Super Chief," "The Broadway Limited," and many others. The equipment used on these trains was distinctive and luxurious. Their heyday was perhaps the 1930s, and much of the equip-

Plate made for the Baltimore and Ohio Railroad, to mark the centenary (1827–1927) of this oldest railroad in the United States. Several firms made up samples, in the hope of getting the order. This plate was made by Shenango China. The central reserve shows Harpers Ferry, West Virginia. Around the rim locomotives formerly used by the railroad are depicted. *Philip W. Stein*

Shown here is the border motif featuring an early (1831) locomotive, on typical china made by the Buffalo Pottery for the New York Central Lines. *Philip W. Stein*

ment, especially that used in dining cars, is Art Deco in style, and consequently especially popular with collectors today. In 1973, the Penn Central held a sale of silver used on deluxe trains. The number of pieces offered was 1,527, and the sale grossed about $10,000, so for the most part prices were not high for individual items. Of course much of the silver had been in service for many years and bore marks of long wear. Some typical prices for the better single items were:

- Large silver pitcher: $250 (the high price of the sale)
- Carafes: $10 to $15 (many examples were sold)
- Crumb trays used in dining cars: $17.50 each
- A champagne bucket marked "Pullman": $45
- A menu holder from the Broadway Limited: $65.

An unkind reporter calculated that the $10,000 realized at this sale for the Penn Central was equivalent to what the railroad was *losing* on its operations every twenty-five minutes and twelve seconds that it operated.

Only a few collectors have sufficient money or space to go in for rolling stock, and it is difficult to imagine any relic more difficult to add to one's railroad collection, but there are sales of historic railroad coaches. At a typical recent auction of railroad coaches a commuter car built about the time of the First World War sold for $8,500, two passenger coaches built in the 1930s for the Erie Railroad sold for $4,500 and $5,000, and a 1914 Pennsylvania Railroad business car built for the president of the line and used by him for traveling sold for $2,800. To these figures must be added, as in the case of historic automobiles, high charges for restoration.

10
Practical Relic Collecting

Sources for the relic collector. Shops dealing in antiques, rare book shops, autograph dealers, and auction houses are the most likely places to buy relics of famous people, places, and events. There are, so far as is known, no dealers who make relics and memorabilia their sole stock, but nearly every antique shop occasionally has a lock of hair, a piece of historic wood, or some object valued for its association. Traditionally, dealers in rare books and manuscripts have handled many such objects because relics have often accompanied Bibles or other volumes handed down in a family, or autograph letters. The relics market, too, has often rested on book collectors' wanting a relic of a favorite author to place beside his works in print or manuscript. Or even be incorporated in them: collectors of the recent past used to have bound in the covers of a rare edition a portrait and a lock of hair or similar small relic of the collected author. The most likely place to find a lock of George Washington's hair or Abraham Lincoln's is usually the shop of one of the booksellers dealing in Americana. Nearly any shop with theatrical interests will be able to come up with mementos of famous plays or players. Galleries of sporting art often have a sports relic. The collector must remember, of course, when buying an item valued solely as a relic—a lock of hair is the prime example—that the reputation of the relic is only as good as the reputation of the shop selling it—unless there is accompanying documentation.

Auction houses delight in selling relics, all auction houses from the largest and most international to the country auction. The reason is simply that relics, regardless of their sale price, produce publicity and public interest. They seldom fail to attract attention in the press and from auction audiences, often—since many relics do not sell for large sums—more attention than money. A nearly certain way for an auction house to get columns of press attention is to offer a relic of Lord Byron or Napoleon I or Marie Antoinette or Adolf Hitler; the newspapers will pick up the story for sure. In the course of an auction season, dozens of relics in many fields will pass through both major and minor auction houses. These will be sold in specialized sales of furniture, decorative objects, automobiles, militaria, ballet, jewelry, books, autographs—in fact, in virtually every department of a large auction house and in nearly every sale of a small one. It takes a keen eye to spot them, as sales of only relics or memorabilia are very rarely held, and objects of interest may be lurking in a variety of sales. Objects carved from the famous Shakespeare Mulberry Tree may be in a furniture sale (because they are wood), a sale of decorative arts (because they are objects of art), or of books (because they are Shakespeare). That statement holds true for the large auction houses; the situation is worse for the collector at the smaller houses—there, relics will be in a jumble along with all sorts of miscellany. Of course, it is fun to seek them out.

In one respect, buying relics from an auction house is no different from buying them at a shop: their history is only as good as the reputation of the auction house. The catalogue of the auction house can be a great bolster to the authenticity of the relic if the reputation of the house is good. The world's two major auction houses, Sotheby's and Christie's, both headquartered in London, have for a number of years published annual reviews of their sales in which many relics are illustrated and described. By no means are all those shown very expensive items, and even the modest collector will do well to familiarize himself with these publications. The Sotheby volume was called first *The Ivory Hammer,* but is currently entitled *Art at Auction.* The Christie volume is called *Christie's Review of the Year.* Both are available in bookstores in the United States.

As auctions are a prime source for relics now, so have they always been. A high proportion of all relics have been through the salesroom more than once. Auction catalogues can therefore be an excellent source for provenance. References to sales held in the United States can be verified in two remarkably complete works of reference published by the New York Public Library: Harold Lancour's *American Art Auction Catalogues, 1785–1942* (New York, 1944) and George L. McKay's *American Book Auction Catalogues, 1713–1934* (New York, 1937, reprinted by Gale Research Co., Detroit, 1967).

Advertisements to sell relics priced in the range of the average collector appear occasionally in the deluxe art magazines, but many more are run in the pages of such antique publications as *Collector's Weekly, Hobbies, The Antique Trader,* and *Spinning Wheel.* A considerable number of advertisements to buy relics, especially in the fields of entertainment, militaria, and sports, also appear in these magazines. Editorially, these periodicals carry a great many stories about relics, relic collectors, and collections that are very informative. As mentioned, newspapers like relic stories and run a surprising number of news and feature stories. In this book many anecdotes have been drawn from the pages of New York dailies (the *News, Post,* and *Times*), the London *Times,* and the *International Herald Tribune* of Paris. Some of the best anecdotes and stories of eccentric collections are to be found in feature stories in the *Wall Street Journal.*

Charity sales, either public or restricted to members of an organization, have already been mentioned in connection with theatrical memorabilia as a source for the relic buyer to add to his collection. Sales to benefit museums, libraries, and performing groups are increasingly popular, and these sales are usually full of relics because their managers rely heavily on well-known people for the contribution of lots that will thrill the audience because of a contact with a celebrity and loosen the purse strings. A high proportion of items sold on such occasions are unmistakably personal or inscribed. At some auctions items of local interest, such as wood or bricks from an important local building—a fort, for example—will be sold. Funds have often been raised by selling relic wood. A famous beech tree on Boone Creek in Washington County, Tennessee, on the bark of which was carved the words "D. Boone cilled a bar 1760," died in the winter of 1917/18. Twenty years later the lumber was still available, and the John Sevier Chapter of the Daughters of the American Revolution purchased the tree and had small wooden gavels made, to be sold to raise money for D.A.R. projects.

Provenance. Some relics incorporate their provenance into their very selves. At Ashland, Henry Clay's home near Lexington, Kentucky, is a silk quilt embroidered with the legend that it was made in 1844 for Henry Clay "by the Ladies of Philadelphia." That is a good example of the self-explanatory relic.

If a relic does not have that kind of inscription its authenticity depends on written documentation. Sentiment and tradition are not enough. Verbal histories are not necessarily less reliable than written—both become muddled over the years—but written provenance always takes precedence over verbal with the relic collector. Naturally, the best provenance is that written by the first owner of an object: each step away from the first is a weaker one. In other words, a letter of note from a celebrated general saying "I wore this sword at such and such a battle" is regarded as much more reliable than an affidavit by the general's grandson recording "My father told me his father wore this sword at such and such a time."

Written provenance accompanies many items. From the seventeenth century on, but especially in the Victorian age, documentation—sometimes quite lengthy, sometimes only

An example of a relic of local interest is this tile from the New York State Capitol in Albany, made by the famous firm of Minton & Co. of Stoke-on-Trent, England. A monument to bureaucratic ineptitude and political corruption, the capitol was under construction for thirty-two years, 1867–99. *Philip W. Stein*

a scrap of paper, tag, or label—has recorded the history of various relics. In the nineteenth century, a great period of relic collecting, connoisseurs liked to write detailed descriptions of their collections with anecdotes, provenance, and often speculations—mostly, alas, unwarranted. It was a romantic age and thousands of these "provenances" are still more romance than fact. In the 1840s the catalogues of auction sales, at least in London, began to be more elaborate and a body of printed descriptions and notes on provenance came into existence, knowledge of which is indispensable to dealers and collectors of relics today. At the same time, auctioneers and dealers began to dilate on illustrious prior ownership, and the tradition commenced of not only constantly referring to earlier owners but of either marking the object

itself or placing with it a card or label to indicate its provenance, especially when the object had little else to set it apart from others of its kind.

When the executors of Queen Victoria sold part of her immense wine cellar, described as "the overstock of wine purchased before 1890" (of sherry alone, there were five thousand dozen bottles!), they carefully noted in the sale catalogue that "each bottle will bear the royal label indicating from which cellar the wine comes." When President Franklin Roosevelt's stamp collection was sold after his death, each stamp was mounted on a card with a printed message to the effect that it had been part of the presidential collection, which helped raise prices considerably for an essentially mediocre collection. The same method was followed

Silver fire horn, seventeen inches long, engraved with three fire-fighting scenes and the following inscription: "Presented by the Hook and Ladder and Chemical Engine Company No. 1 of Princeton, N.J., to Foreman Wm. B. Applegate, Jan. 6th. 1909." Fire companies, often voluntary, and police were responsible for many presentation items. *James F. Carr, New York*

when the personal property of Mrs. Eleanor Roosevelt was sold at a New York art dealer's after her death.

Occasionally a relic is buttressed by several kinds of provenance. Seldom can any historical jewel's provenance have been better than that of the "Mancini pearls," a pair of huge pearl earrings surrounded by diamonds, sold at auction in Switzerland in 1970. Maria Mancini, first owner of the earrings, was the niece of the seventeenth century French prime minister Cardinal Mazarin and was renowned in her time (and to readers of Alexandre Dumas) as the first love of the adolescent King Louis XIV. Forced by her uncle to give up the king, Maria later married the Roman nobleman Prince Colonna. The "Mancini pearls" were not only offered for sale by a descendant and mentioned in various printed books: there is at the Colonna palace in Rome a portrait of Maria Mancini painted from life wearing these very earrings, easily recognizable in the painting. Such a complete provenance may have contributed to the high price they brought at auction—320,000 Swiss francs (then $75,000).

Initials, inscriptions, heraldic devices, and other obvious marks of ownership are of course good and usually irrefutable provenance, but collectors still show a preference for written provenance, if at all possible in the original owner's hand. The documentation that accompanies a relic may be a letter in which the relic is described or mentioned, the catalogue of a sale in which the relic has appeared, an affidavit of authenticity by a previous owner or an authority, a citation to a reference in a published book or periodical.

The makers of contemporary commemorative items well understand the production of a provenance for their objects. When the Sheffield, England, manufacturer Wostenholm, who had long been the producer of the famous "Bowie" knives, ceased to make them, the firm issued a group of "classic" Bowie knives, fifteen inches long, marked with the manufacturer's name, and with the blade etched as follows: "One of One Hundred of the Last Bowie Knives made by George Wostenholm & Son Prior to Our Merger with Joseph Rodgers & Sons, Sheffield, November 1971." Each knife, in a red leatherette box embossed with gold and lined with silk, was available for $150.

The City of New York gives eminent visitors and citizens of achievement a brass key about six inches long in a velvet-lined box, which is carefully marked with a metal plaque stating "Facsimile of key made in 1812 for the door of City Hall, New York."

Any provenance should be carefully preserved by the collector, although he need not go so far as the widow of the English Victorian painter Holman Hunt, who tagged nearly everything in her house, even items in everyday use, with "historical documentation." A tea guest might be served with a cup whose label read: "Mr. Robert Browning drank from this cup while Mr. Hunt's guest." Whatever form provenance takes, it should be preserved carefully—more than one copy of each letter or document is a good precaution. Provenance is important in many fields of collecting, but in none more than relic collecting, where the very identity of a lock of hair, daguerreotype, or piece of wood may easily be lost forever.

The price of a relic, like that of all unique objects, can be determined only by the willing buyer. Hundreds of real prices have been cited in this book; it may be seen that any absolute statements about what a relic *ought* to cost are unrealistic. In a field in which sentiment plays a large role, the buyer has to decide for himself how strong his sentiment is when it comes to laying out money to add items to his collection. Purchase records should be very carefully kept, since relics are so difficult to appraise. Records of prices paid are indispensable in getting insurance or in settling an estate. Most relics can be covered under a fine arts insurance policy, but the premium rate is very high. It is surprising but true that in recent years a great many relics, including locks of hair, have been stolen. Relics of Robert Burns and Lord Tennyson have been stolen in Britain, and in the United States there have been all sorts of losses, including Benjamin Franklin's sword and a lock of General Philip Schuyler's hair.

The care of a relic collection is important because a high percentage of relics are physically fragile. Ideally, small relics are kept in the sort of display cases made of morocco and lined with velvet shown in some of the illustrations in this book. Such equipment is very expensive to have made today, however, and out of reach of the average collector. The type of plain glass or lucite box used by collectors of fine porcelain to preserve their treasures and yet display them is often usable for relics of china or fragile substance or textiles that suffer from prolonged exposure to dust. These boxes are sold by the firms that supply china stands, plate racks, and other display equipment to antique shops. Many attractive relics like fans and lace are framed by collectors. Great care must be taken that they are not hung in direct sunlight, which fades them. When a small relic is placed under glass or in a leather or metal box, it should of course be properly tagged with a card identifying it and giving its history. All these comments apply only to those relics that can be kept in a private house. Collecting automobiles with famous earlier owners generally means building one's own museum.

Some collectors have created their own relics by buying wood from a famous tree or building and carving it or using it to make canes, boxes, or other small objects. Such objects should always be identified either by carving their history on them or by inserting a metal plaque with that information. Flowers from notable occasions of today can be pressed, as they so often were in Victorian times. It is not necessary or desirable to place them between the leaves of a heavy book in the traditional manner. Drying flowers make bad stains on a book. Flower presses are sold (they can be had for under $10 at some gift shops) in which the flowers are put between layers of corrugated cardboard and special drying paper and held in place with adjustable screws. Once dried, they can be placed in albums and properly labeled.

BIBLIOGRAPHY

Allen, Gay W. *Melville and His World*. New York: The Viking Press, Inc., 1971.

Allingham, Emily G. *A Romance of the Rostrum*. London: Witherby, 1924.

Armstrong, Margaret N. *Trelawny; a Man's Life*. New York: The Macmillan Company, 1940.

Blunden, Edmund. *Leigh Hunt and His Circle*. New York: Harper & Brothers, 1930.

Buck, Peter H. *Arts and Crafts of Hawaii*. Honolulu: Bishop Museum Press, 1957.

Burdick, Loraine. "The Sheik Is Still a Star" (Rudolph Valentino). *American Collector,* December 1973.

Crockett, William S. *Abbotsford*. London: Black, 1905.

Daiches, David. *Robert Burns and His World*. New York: The Viking Press, 1971.

———. *Sir Walter Scott and His World*. New York: Viking Press, 1971.

Daly, Joseph F. *The Life of Augustin Daly*. New York, 1917.

Deelman, Christian. *The Great Shakespeare Jubilee*. New York: The Viking Press, 1964.

Dickens, Charles. Letters. 3 vols. London: Chapman & Hall, 1880–82.

Flanner, Janet. *Paris Journal, 1944–65*. New York: The Viking Press, Inc., 1971.

Flores, Maria. *The Woman with the Whip: Eva Perón*. Garden City: Doubleday & Company, Inc., 1952.

Fraser, Antonia. *Mary, Queen of Scots*. New York: Delacorte Press, 1969.

Gibb, William. *The Royal House of Stuart*. London: The Macmillan Company, 1890.

Griffith, Richard and Arthur Mayer. *The Movies*. New York: Bonanza Books, 1957.

Hadley, Caroline. "Wells Fargo Buckles: the English Connection." *American Collector,* November 1973.

Halliday, Frank C. *The Cult of Shakespeare*. New York: Thomas Yoseloff, Publisher, 1960.

Haslip, Joan. *The Crown of Mexico. Maximilian and His Empress Carlota*. New York: Holt, Rinehart & Winston, Inc., 1971.

Herold, J. Christopher. *Horizon Book of the Age of Napoleon*. New York: Harper & Row, Publishers, 1963.

Hibbert, Christopher. *Charles I*. New York: Harper & Row, Publishers, 1968.

Hopkins, Vivian C. *Prodigal Puritan. A Life of Delia Bacon*. Cambridge, Mass.: Harvard University Press, 1959.

Howe, Thomas C. *Salt Mines and Castles*. Indianapolis: The Bobbs, Merrill Co., Inc., 1946.

Irving, Washington. *Journals and Notebooks*. Vol. I, 1803–06. Milwaukee: University of Wisconsin Press, 1969.

Jarves, James J. *History of the Hawaiian or Sandwich Islands*. Boston: Tappan & Dennet, 1843.

Johnson, Edgar. *Sir Walter Scott*. 2 vols. New York: The Macmillan Company, 1970.

Ketton-Cremer, R. W. *Horace Walpole*. Ithaca: Cornell University Press, 1964.

Laski, Marghanita. *Jane Austen and Her World*. New York: The Viking Press, 1969.

Lockhart, John Gibson. *Memoirs of the Life of Sir Walter Scott*. 5 vols. Boston, 1902.

McLeave, Hugh. *The Last Pharaoh. Farouk of Egypt*. New York: McCall Books, Saturday Review Press, 1970.

Marchand, Leslie A. *Byron, a Biography*. 3 vols. New York: Alfred A. Knopf, Inc., 1957.

Marie Louise, Princess. *My Memories of Six Reigns*. New York: E. P. Dutton & Co., Inc., 1957.

Masson, Frédéric. *Napoleon at Home,* trans. by James E. Matthew. 2 vols. London: Grevel, 1894.

Meltzer, Milton and Walter Harding. *A Thoreau Profile*. New York: Thomas Y. Crowell Company, 1962.

Mitford, Nancy. *Madame de Pompadour*. New York: Random House, Inc., 1968.

Moore, Doris Langley. *The Late Lord Bryon*. Philadelphia: J. B. Lippincott Company, 1964.

Norman, Sylva. *Flight of the Skylark. The Development of Shelley's Reputation*. Norman: University of Oklahoma Press, 1954.

Nye, Russel B. *The Unembarrassed Muse. The Popular Arts in America*. New York: The Dial Press, 1970.

Pearson, Hesketh. *Dizzy. The Life and Personality of Benjamin Disraeli*. New York: Harper & Brothers, 1951.

————. *Gilbert. His Life and Strife*. New York: Harper & Brothers, 1957.

————. *Sir Walter Scott*. New York: Harper & Brothers, 1954.

Ponsonby, Arthur. *English Diaries*. London: Metheun, 1923.

Pope-Hennessy, James. *Queen Mary, 1867–1953*. New York: Alfred A. Knopf, Inc., 1962.

Redford, George. *Art Sales*. 2 vols. London: Privately Printed, 1889.

Reed, John F. "Final Dispositions of Washington's 'Estate,' " *Manuscripts*, XXIV, No. 3, pp. 182–85.

Round, J. Horace. *Studies in Peerage and Family History*. New York: Longmans, Green & Company, 1901.

Sandburg, Carl. *Lincoln Collector. The Story of Oliver R. Barrett's Great Private Collection*. New York: Harcourt, Brace & Co., 1950.

Shulman, Irving. *Valentino*. New York: Trident Press, 1967.

Smith, Warren H., ed. *Horace Walpole, Writer, Politician, and Connoisseur*. New Haven: Yale University Press, 1967.

Swain, Margaret. *The Needlework of Mary Queen of Scots*. New York: Van Nostrand Reinhold Company, 1973.

Thacher, John Boyd. *Christopher Columbus. His Life, His Works, and His Remains*. 3 vols. New York: G. P. Putnam's Sons, 1903/4.

Towner, Wesley. *The Elegant Auctioneers*. New York: Hill & Wang, 1970.

Turner, Justin G. and Linda L. Turner. *Mary Todd Lincoln*. New York: Alfred A. Knopf, Inc., 1972.

Vaughan, Herbert M. *The Last Stuart Queen: Louise, Countess of Albany*. New York: Brentano's, 1911.

————. *The Last of the Royal Stuarts: Henry Stuart, Cardinal Duke of York*. New York: E. P. Dutton & Co., Inc., 1906.

Wadsworth, Frank W. *The Poacher from Stratford*. Berkeley: University of California Press, 1958.

Waller, J. G. "Some Account of Relics." *Living Age* 39 (1853), pp. 559–63.

Wecter, Dixon. *The Hero in America*. New York: Charles Scribner's Sons, 1941.

Wedgwood, C. V. *A Coffin for King Charles*. New York: The Macmillan Company, 1964.

Wheler, R. B. *History and Antiquities of Stratford-upon-Avon*. Stratford, n.d.

Williams, Neville. *The Royal Residences of Great Britain*. New York: The Macmillan Company, 1960.

Williamson, Hugh Ross. *The Day They Killed the King*. New York: The Macmillan Company, 1957.

Winwar, Frances. *The Immortal Lovers: Elizabeth Barrett and Robert Browning*. New York: Harper & Brothers, 1950.

Zweig, Stefan. *The World of Yesterday: an Autobiography*. New York: The Viking Press, 1943.

Index

LOOK WHAT TAILS CAN DO

LOOK What ANIMALS Can Do

LOOK WHAT TAILS CAN DO

LOOK What ANIMALS Can Do

BY D. M. SOUZA

Lerner Publications Company · Minneapolis

photo on page 2: **The tails of kangaroos help them balance when sitting, hopping, or even fighting.**

Lerner Publications Company
A division of Lerner Publishing Group
241 First Avenue North
Minneapolis, MN 55401 U.S.A.

Website address: www.lernerbooks.com

Library of Congress Cataloging-in-Publication Data

Souza, D. M. (Dorothy M.)
    Look what tails can do / by D. M. Souza.
        p.   cm. — (Look what animals can do)
    Includes bibliographical references and index.
    ISBN-13: 978-0-7613-9458-7 (lib. bdg. : alk. paper)
    ISBN-10: 0-7613-9458-3 (lib. bdg. : alk. paper)
    1. Tail—Juvenile literature. I. Title. II. Series: Souza, D. M. (Dorothy M.) Look what animals can do.
    QL950.6.S68 2007
    573.9'98—dc22   2005032480

Manufactured in the United States of America
1 2 3 4 5 6 – DP – 12 11 10 09 08 07

TABLE OF CONTENTS

LOOK AROUND.
TAILS ARE EVERYWHERE.

Some tails are long and skinny. Others are short and bushy. There are flat tails, curly tails, striped tails, and dotted ones. There are scaly tails, prickly tails, feathery tails, and hairy ones.

Ring-tailed lemurs hold their long striped tails high when they move around.

No matter what they look like, tails are important body parts for many animals. Think of a monkey trying to move from branch to branch without its tail. How would a fish swim without its tail? And how would a cow, horse, or giraffe shoo away flies and insects without its tail?

Most of the time, tails help animals keep their balance as they run or climb. But tails do other things too. Let's take a look at a few amazing tails and what they do for the animals that have them.

Armadillo lizards put their tails in their mouths to protect their soft bellies from enemies.

9

ALL-PURPOSE TAIL

A gray squirrel uses its tail in many ways. On rainy days, the animal curls its tail over its head like an umbrella. On cold nights, it wraps its tail around itself like a blanket.

During fights, the animal flicks its tail back and forth to distract its enemy. Sometimes during a fight, it holds its tail up like a shield to soften blows. But when the squirrel is searching for food, its tail becomes a lifesaver.

A young girl fills a bird feeder with sunflower seeds. A squirrel watches from a treetop. As soon as the girl leaves, the squirrel races down the tree.

The squirrel sits high in a tree getting ready to make its move.

Halfway down, the animal leaps into the air. It swings its tail from side to side, steering toward the feeder. Kerplunk! Its tail helps the squirrel make a perfect landing.

The squirrel jumps onto a clothesline with a mouthful of seeds. It races across the wire with its tail swinging from side to side. It uses its tail for balance the way an acrobat uses outstretched arms. When the squirrel reaches a post, it leaps back onto the tree. It makes another perfect landing. Where would the gray squirrel be without its tail?

The squirrel's tail is perfect for helping it keep its balance.

BUSY TAIL

A beaver swims across a moonlit pond. It has a small branch in its mouth. Nearby, another beaver paddles along. It is pulling a large limb through the water.

The beavers are busy every night. Before winter they must store food for themselves and their **kits**. They must repair their **lodge** and add more sticks, grass, and mud. They will also build a dam to raise the water level in the pond. Then their food supply will not freeze in the deep water.

Beavers are strong swimmers because of their paddle-shaped tails.

The beavers' tails help in many ways. They are flat, wide, and covered with scales, like those of a fish. When beavers swim forward, their tails flop up and down. When they want to change directions, their tails swing to one side or the other.

While a beaver is standing on land cutting a tree, its wide tail serves as a stool. When the animal is walking on its hind legs, the tail keeps it balanced.

If a **predator** suddenly appears, the tail sounds an alarm. One beaver slaps its tail against the water with a mighty splash. The sound is as loud as a pistol shot. All the beavers in the area know it's time to swim to safety. Yes, the beaver's tail does many things on land and in the water.

Beavers don't just use their tails for swimming. Their tails are very useful on land too.

ONE OF A KIND

This skinny tail is long and hairless. You might think it belongs to a rat. But it can do something the rat's tail cannot. It can grab onto objects. The tail belongs to an opossum. It's called a **prehensile** tail.

When an opossum is climbing a tree, its tail acts like an extra paw. The tail grabs one branch until the opossum's paws can grab onto another. If the animal is collecting fruit, the tail curls around a branch. The opossum can then reach for fruit with both of its front paws.

Opossums' tails wrap tightly around tree limbs. Their tails' grip gives them extra support while climbing.

The opossum's tail also plays a role during nest building. The female rakes together leaves and grass for her nest. Then she grabs the pile with her tail and carries it away.

Young opossums often ride on their mother's back. They hold on by curling their tails around her fur. If they don't weigh too much, the young can also hang from branches by their tails. It must be fun having a prehensile tail.

Young opossums travel on their mother's back and hold on with their tails.

POISONOUS TAIL

Darkness covers the desert. A yellowish brown scorpion crawls out from under a log. It has been hiding from the hot rays of the sun. Now, in the cool of evening, it is ready for a meal.

The scorpion stands on its eight legs. It cannot see too well, but it feels movements. It raises two large **pincers** near the front of its body. Its long tail armed with a stinger curves over its back.

A cockroach zigzags across the sand. It does not see the scorpion. It comes close to where the creature is standing.

The dark stinger at the end of the scorpion's tail holds deadly poison.

23

In a second, the large pincers reach out and grab hold of the insect. The cockroach struggles but cannot escape. Quickly the scorpion's tail strikes. It fills the insect's body with deadly poison.

In minutes the cockroach is lifeless. Slowly, the scorpion tears it apart. After it finishes its meal, it rests.

Scorpions may wait for weeks or even months between meals. They do not need much food. But when they do get hungry, their poison-filled tails are always ready to strike.

Scorpions capture and kill insects with their large pincers and deadly tails.

TALKING TAILS

If you have a pet dog, you probably know that its tail often sends messages. A wagging tail lets you know that your dog is glad to see you. A drooping tail gives you a clue that your dog is not feeling well. A tail between its legs may signal that the dog is frightened.

Wolves are related to dogs and live together in **packs**, or groups. They travel and hunt together. Members of the pack communicate with their tails.

Wolves are social animals. They live most of their lives with other wolves.

Wolves warn one another of danger by pointing their tails straight out. Pups let others know they want to play by wagging their tails.

The **alpha**, or head wolf, shows it is top wolf by holding its tail high. The **omega** shows it is the lowest-ranking wolf by lowering its tail. Like a pet dog's tail, wolves' tails say many things without ever making a sound.

You can tell by how they hold their tails that one wolf is weaker than the other.

A WRIGGLING TAIL

A skink, a lizard with shiny skin, warms itself in the morning sun. It flicks out its tongue, trying to pick up the scent of food. An insect, earthworm, or spider would make a tasty meal.

Suddenly a cricket lands nearby. The skink jerks forward. But the cricket is too quick. It hops away and disappears deeper in the forest.

A cat has been watching the action. It crouches low and creeps closer. The skink flicks out its tongue again, but it's too late. Slam! One of the cat's paws comes down on top of the skink's shiny blue tail.

This skink has five light-colored stripes on its body. They run from the lizard's neck to the tip of its tail.

The cat looks at its catch. The bright blue tail is wriggling wildly on the ground. But there is no skink. The animal has gotten away.

Many lizards escape predators by leaving their tails behind. Their tails can break off in several places without harming the animals. In a short time, a new tail grows back. But until it does, the lizard must be careful. If it gets caught again, it has no wriggling tail to leave behind.

Skinks' tails break off so they can escape a predator.

A DANGEROUS TAIL

Did you know that porcupines have hidden weapons in their tails? These weapons are called **quills**. They are stiff, hollow hairs that are sharp and pointed like needles.

Quills are hidden in the animal's fur. More than 30,000 are on the porcupine's head, back, and tail. Most of the time, the quills lie flat. But if the animal is frightened, its quills and long hairs stand up. They make the porcupine look like a giant pincushion.

Porcupines have sharp quills on their heads, backs, and tails. Their quills usually lie flat.

If a porcupine meets a predator, the porcupine clicks its teeth together. If the predator does not leave, the porcupine puts its nose between its feet. Next, it turns its back end toward the enemy. Swat! The tail strikes, and several quills may get stuck in the animal's face.

Once a quill enters the skin, it is hard to remove. Quills that land in some animals' eyes can blind them. Quills in their mouths can make it hard for them to eat. Most animals try to stay away from the porcupine's dangerous tail.

Porcupines stick their quills straight out when they feel threatened.

MORE TAILS

Wolves and dogs are not the only animals with tails that send messages. White-tailed deer have short tan or brown tails. When danger is near, one deer will flip its tail up. White fur underneath flashes and sends a warning to others, "Run for your life."

White-tailed deer show the white fur underneath their tails to warn that danger is near.

A rattlesnake's buzzing tail tells predators, "Stay away." A skunk's tail raised over its head says, "Leave if you don't want to get sprayed."

Male peacocks and turkeys use their tails to win mates. These birds spread their feathers like fans. Then they **strut** around, waiting for females to notice them.

Male peacocks use their huge colorful tails to impress females.

Some animals use their tails to catch meals. Alligators often wait along riverbanks for creatures they can eat. When a meal arrives, the gators swing their powerful tails. One blow can throw an animal into the water. There the gator easily makes a catch.

Alligators use their strong tails for swimming and catching meals.

Manatees have large paddle-shaped tails. The tails move up and down when the giants are swimming. But when they are resting, the heavy tails act as anchors. They keep the manatees near the bottom of the water.

Manatees' tails keep them at the seafloor so they can rest.

Ring-tailed lemurs sometimes fight with their tails. They have "stink fights" with one another. Each lemur rubs its long tail across scent spots on its body. Then it spreads the smell by waving its tail over the head of the other lemur. The lemur with a "stink" that lasts the longest wins the fight.

A ring-tailed lemur stands up with its long tail flying high.

Birds from Central America called quetzals have long tail feathers. The male's feathers are almost three times as long as its body. The quetzal flies high and then swoops down. Its brilliant tail floats across the sky like a colorful scarf. Now that's a tail to top all tails.

Quetzals' colorful tail feathers flow behind them while they fly.

43

GLOSSARY

alpha: the top wolf, or leader, in a pack

kits: the young of beavers or foxes

lodge: home of a family of beavers

omega: the lowest-ranking wolf in a pack

packs: groups of animals such as wolves

pincers: a pair of claws used for grabbing

predator: an animal that hunts other animals for food

prehensile: able to curl around or grab onto objects

quills: stiff, pointed, hollow hairs on the tail, head, and back of a porcupine

strut: to walk proudly

FURTHER READING

BOOKS

Jenkins, Steve. *Slap, Squeak, & Scatter: How Animals Communicate*. Boston: Houghton Mifflin, 2001.

Jenkins, Steve, and Robin Page. *What Do You Do with a Tail Like This?* Boston: Houghton Mifflin, 2003.

Miles, Elizabeth. *Tails*. Chicago: Heinemann Library, 2003.

Pipe, Jim. *Paws, Tails, and Whiskers*. Danbury, CT: Franklin Watts, 2004.

Schwartz, David. *Animal Tails*. Milwaukee: Gareth Stevens Publishing, 1999.

Warrick, Karen Clemens. *If I Had a Tail*. Flagstaff, AZ: Rising Moon Books, 2001.

WEBSITES

About Porcupines
http://www.nativetech.org/quill/porcupin.html
If you've ever wondered what a porcupine quill looks like, this
Native American site shows a close-up of one. It also has fun
facts about porcupines.

Animal Tails—Northwest Trek
http://www.nwtrek.org/page.php?id=233
At this Northwest Trek Wildlife Park site, you can play a game
matching tails with their animal owners.

The Beaver
http://www.saskschools.ca/~gregory/animals/bvr.html
This Canadian school site is filled with photos and facts about
beavers and their amazing tails.

Opossum Society
http://www.opossumsocietyus.org/opossum_photo_page.htm
The Opossum Society has many photos of these creatures with
prehensile tails, as well as facts about them.

INDEX

Page numbers in *italics* refer to illustrations.

PHOTO ACKNOWLEDGMENTS

Images reproduced with permission from:
© Martin Harvey/Peter Arnold, Inc., p. 2; © Nigel J. Dennis/Photo Researchers, Inc., p. 6; © Rod Patterson; Gallo Images/CORBIS, p. 9; © Gary W. Carter/CORBIS, p. 11; © J. Paling/OSF/Animals Animals, p. 13; © Erwin & Peggy Bauer/Animals Animals, p. 14; © Lynda Richardson/Peter Arnold, Inc., p. 17; © Steve Maslowski/Visuals Unlimited, p. 19; © Phyllis Greenberg/Animals Animals, p. 20; © Roger De La Harpe/Animals Animals, p. 23; © Charles Melton/Visuals Unlimited, p. 24; © Art Wolfe, p. 26; © Tom & Pat Leeson/Photo Researchers, Inc., p. 29; © Scott W. Smith/Animals Animals, p. 31; © W. Cheng/OSF/Animals Animals, p. 33; © Tim Davis/Photo Researchers, Inc., p. 34; © Joe McDonald/Animals Animals, p. 37; © Stephen J. Krasemann/Photo Researchers, Inc., p. 38; © William Weber/Visuals Unlimited, p. 39; © George McCarthy/CORBIS, p. 40; © Brandon Cole/Visuals Unlimited, p. 41; © Frank Krahmer/zefa/CORBIS, p. 42; © Gregory G. Dimijian, M.D./Photo Researchers, Inc., p. 43.

Front cover: Steve Maslowski/Photo Researchers, Inc.